A Field Guide to 101 of the MOST
Odd, Extreme, and Outrageous
American Subcultures

**KATE STEVENS**

**Dedication**

For all freaks with a sense of humor

Published by
Adams Media, a division of F+W Media, Inc.
57 Littlefield Street, Avon, MA 02322. U.S.A.
*www.adamsmedia.com*

ISBN 10: 1-4405-0646-9
ISBN 13: 978-1-4405-0646-8
eISBN 10: 1-4405-1006-7
eISBN 13: 978-1-4405-1006-9

Printed in the United States of America.

10  9  8  7  6  5  4  3  2  1

**Library of Congress Cataloging-in-Publication Data**
is available from the publisher.

*This book is available at quantity discounts for bulk purchases.*
*For information, please call 1-800-289-0963.*

# CONTENTS

Introduction . . . . . . . . . . . . . . . . . . . . . . . . . . . . . . . . . . . . . . . . . . . . . vii

## COLLECTIBLES
Comic Collectors . . . . . . . . . . . . . . . . . . . . . . . . . . . . . . . . . . . . . . . . . 2
Collectible Card Gamers . . . . . . . . . . . . . . . . . . . . . . . . . . . . . . . . . . . 5
Model Railroaders . . . . . . . . . . . . . . . . . . . . . . . . . . . . . . . . . . . . . . . . 8
Numismatists . . . . . . . . . . . . . . . . . . . . . . . . . . . . . . . . . . . . . . . . . . . . 11
Stamp Lovers . . . . . . . . . . . . . . . . . . . . . . . . . . . . . . . . . . . . . . . . . . . . 14

## FASHION
Trekkies . . . . . . . . . . . . . . . . . . . . . . . . . . . . . . . . . . . . . . . . . . . . . . . . 18
Preppies . . . . . . . . . . . . . . . . . . . . . . . . . . . . . . . . . . . . . . . . . . . . . . . . 21
Elves . . . . . . . . . . . . . . . . . . . . . . . . . . . . . . . . . . . . . . . . . . . . . . . . . . . 24
501st Legionnaires . . . . . . . . . . . . . . . . . . . . . . . . . . . . . . . . . . . . . . . 27
Cosplayers . . . . . . . . . . . . . . . . . . . . . . . . . . . . . . . . . . . . . . . . . . . . . . 30
Steampunkers . . . . . . . . . . . . . . . . . . . . . . . . . . . . . . . . . . . . . . . . . . . 33
Rennies . . . . . . . . . . . . . . . . . . . . . . . . . . . . . . . . . . . . . . . . . . . . . . . . 36
Civil War Re-enactors . . . . . . . . . . . . . . . . . . . . . . . . . . . . . . . . . . . . 38

## ART
Local Thespians . . . . . . . . . . . . . . . . . . . . . . . . . . . . . . . . . . . . . . . . . 42
Slam Poets . . . . . . . . . . . . . . . . . . . . . . . . . . . . . . . . . . . . . . . . . . . . . . 45
Suzukis . . . . . . . . . . . . . . . . . . . . . . . . . . . . . . . . . . . . . . . . . . . . . . . . . 47
Tattoo Artists . . . . . . . . . . . . . . . . . . . . . . . . . . . . . . . . . . . . . . . . . . . . 49
Happening Artists . . . . . . . . . . . . . . . . . . . . . . . . . . . . . . . . . . . . . . . . 51
B-Boys . . . . . . . . . . . . . . . . . . . . . . . . . . . . . . . . . . . . . . . . . . . . . . . . . . 53
Yarn Bombers . . . . . . . . . . . . . . . . . . . . . . . . . . . . . . . . . . . . . . . . . . . . 55

## FOOD AND DRINK

Vegans . . . . . . . . . . . . . . . . . . . . . . . . . . . . . . . . . . . . . . . . . . . . . . 59
Oenophiles. . . . . . . . . . . . . . . . . . . . . . . . . . . . . . . . . . . . . . . . . . . 61
Locavores . . . . . . . . . . . . . . . . . . . . . . . . . . . . . . . . . . . . . . . . . . . . 63
Macrobioticists . . . . . . . . . . . . . . . . . . . . . . . . . . . . . . . . . . . . . . . . 65
Homebrewers . . . . . . . . . . . . . . . . . . . . . . . . . . . . . . . . . . . . . . . . . 67
Raw Food Nuts . . . . . . . . . . . . . . . . . . . . . . . . . . . . . . . . . . . . . . . . 69

## LIFESTYLES

Bohemians . . . . . . . . . . . . . . . . . . . . . . . . . . . . . . . . . . . . . . . . . . . 72
Nudists. . . . . . . . . . . . . . . . . . . . . . . . . . . . . . . . . . . . . . . . . . . . . . 74
Homeschoolers . . . . . . . . . . . . . . . . . . . . . . . . . . . . . . . . . . . . . . . . 76
Hoarders. . . . . . . . . . . . . . . . . . . . . . . . . . . . . . . . . . . . . . . . . . . . . 78
Trustafarians. . . . . . . . . . . . . . . . . . . . . . . . . . . . . . . . . . . . . . . . . . 80
Urban Homesteaders. . . . . . . . . . . . . . . . . . . . . . . . . . . . . . . . . . . . 82
Survivalists. . . . . . . . . . . . . . . . . . . . . . . . . . . . . . . . . . . . . . . . . . . 84
Houseboaters. . . . . . . . . . . . . . . . . . . . . . . . . . . . . . . . . . . . . . . . . . 86
Bilderbergers . . . . . . . . . . . . . . . . . . . . . . . . . . . . . . . . . . . . . . . . . 89
Dumpster Divers . . . . . . . . . . . . . . . . . . . . . . . . . . . . . . . . . . . . . . . 91

## MUSIC

"Ring"-Nuts . . . . . . . . . . . . . . . . . . . . . . . . . . . . . . . . . . . . . . . . . . 94
KISS Army . . . . . . . . . . . . . . . . . . . . . . . . . . . . . . . . . . . . . . . . . . . 96
Punk Rockers . . . . . . . . . . . . . . . . . . . . . . . . . . . . . . . . . . . . . . . . . 98
Audiophiles . . . . . . . . . . . . . . . . . . . . . . . . . . . . . . . . . . . . . . . . . . 100
Goths . . . . . . . . . . . . . . . . . . . . . . . . . . . . . . . . . . . . . . . . . . . . . . . 102
Rockabillies . . . . . . . . . . . . . . . . . . . . . . . . . . . . . . . . . . . . . . . . . . 104
Grungers. . . . . . . . . . . . . . . . . . . . . . . . . . . . . . . . . . . . . . . . . . . . . 106
Rivetheads . . . . . . . . . . . . . . . . . . . . . . . . . . . . . . . . . . . . . . . . . . . 108
New Romantics . . . . . . . . . . . . . . . . . . . . . . . . . . . . . . . . . . . . . . . . 110
Beatlemaniacs . . . . . . . . . . . . . . . . . . . . . . . . . . . . . . . . . . . . . . . . . 112
Dance Partiers . . . . . . . . . . . . . . . . . . . . . . . . . . . . . . . . . . . . . . . . . 114
Deadheads. . . . . . . . . . . . . . . . . . . . . . . . . . . . . . . . . . . . . . . . . . . . 117
Phish Heads . . . . . . . . . . . . . . . . . . . . . . . . . . . . . . . . . . . . . . . . . . 120
Rappers . . . . . . . . . . . . . . . . . . . . . . . . . . . . . . . . . . . . . . . . . . . . . 122

## SPORTS AND GAMES

Jan Ken Pon Players . . . . . . . . . . . . . . . . . . . . . . . . . . . . . . . . . . . . . . . . 125
MMORPGers . . . . . . . . . . . . . . . . . . . . . . . . . . . . . . . . . . . . . . . . . . . . . 127
Dungeon Masters . . . . . . . . . . . . . . . . . . . . . . . . . . . . . . . . . . . . . . . . . 129
Jugglers . . . . . . . . . . . . . . . . . . . . . . . . . . . . . . . . . . . . . . . . . . . . . . . . . 131
Bodybuilders . . . . . . . . . . . . . . . . . . . . . . . . . . . . . . . . . . . . . . . . . . . . . 133
Yoginis . . . . . . . . . . . . . . . . . . . . . . . . . . . . . . . . . . . . . . . . . . . . . . . . . . 135
Skaters . . . . . . . . . . . . . . . . . . . . . . . . . . . . . . . . . . . . . . . . . . . . . . . . . . 137
Spelunkers . . . . . . . . . . . . . . . . . . . . . . . . . . . . . . . . . . . . . . . . . . . . . . 139
Rodeoers . . . . . . . . . . . . . . . . . . . . . . . . . . . . . . . . . . . . . . . . . . . . . . . . 141
Thru-Hikers . . . . . . . . . . . . . . . . . . . . . . . . . . . . . . . . . . . . . . . . . . . . . 143
NASCAR Fans . . . . . . . . . . . . . . . . . . . . . . . . . . . . . . . . . . . . . . . . . . . . 145
Marathoners . . . . . . . . . . . . . . . . . . . . . . . . . . . . . . . . . . . . . . . . . . . . . 147

## PASTIMES AND CAREERS

Grammaticasters . . . . . . . . . . . . . . . . . . . . . . . . . . . . . . . . . . . . . . . . . . 150
Tavern Trivia Players . . . . . . . . . . . . . . . . . . . . . . . . . . . . . . . . . . . . . . . 152
Ghost Hunters . . . . . . . . . . . . . . . . . . . . . . . . . . . . . . . . . . . . . . . . . . . . 154
Birders . . . . . . . . . . . . . . . . . . . . . . . . . . . . . . . . . . . . . . . . . . . . . . . . . . 157
Scrabblers . . . . . . . . . . . . . . . . . . . . . . . . . . . . . . . . . . . . . . . . . . . . . . . 159
Fisch Heads . . . . . . . . . . . . . . . . . . . . . . . . . . . . . . . . . . . . . . . . . . . . . . 161
Clowns . . . . . . . . . . . . . . . . . . . . . . . . . . . . . . . . . . . . . . . . . . . . . . . . . . 163
Disney Cast Members . . . . . . . . . . . . . . . . . . . . . . . . . . . . . . . . . . . . . . 165
Conspiracy Theorists . . . . . . . . . . . . . . . . . . . . . . . . . . . . . . . . . . . . . . . 167
Cryptozoologists . . . . . . . . . . . . . . . . . . . . . . . . . . . . . . . . . . . . . . . . . . 169

## POLITICS

Tea Partiers . . . . . . . . . . . . . . . . . . . . . . . . . . . . . . . . . . . . . . . . . . . . . . 172
Utopians . . . . . . . . . . . . . . . . . . . . . . . . . . . . . . . . . . . . . . . . . . . . . . . . . 174
Libertarians . . . . . . . . . . . . . . . . . . . . . . . . . . . . . . . . . . . . . . . . . . . . . . 176
Tree Huggers . . . . . . . . . . . . . . . . . . . . . . . . . . . . . . . . . . . . . . . . . . . . . 179
ACT UP Members . . . . . . . . . . . . . . . . . . . . . . . . . . . . . . . . . . . . . . . . . 181
Conscientious Objectors . . . . . . . . . . . . . . . . . . . . . . . . . . . . . . . . . . . . 183
Tax Protesters . . . . . . . . . . . . . . . . . . . . . . . . . . . . . . . . . . . . . . . . . . . . 185

## SEX

Furries. . . . . . . . . . . . . . . . . . . . . . . . . . . . . . . . . . . . . . . . . . . . . . . . . 188
Swingers. . . . . . . . . . . . . . . . . . . . . . . . . . . . . . . . . . . . . . . . . . . . . . . 190
Polyamorists. . . . . . . . . . . . . . . . . . . . . . . . . . . . . . . . . . . . . . . . . . . . 192
Sadomasochists . . . . . . . . . . . . . . . . . . . . . . . . . . . . . . . . . . . . . . . . . 194
Cartoon Porndogs . . . . . . . . . . . . . . . . . . . . . . . . . . . . . . . . . . . . . . . 196
Adipophiles . . . . . . . . . . . . . . . . . . . . . . . . . . . . . . . . . . . . . . . . . . . . 198
Bears. . . . . . . . . . . . . . . . . . . . . . . . . . . . . . . . . . . . . . . . . . . . . . . . . . 200

## SOCIETY

Gawkers. . . . . . . . . . . . . . . . . . . . . . . . . . . . . . . . . . . . . . . . . . . . . . . 203
Slummers. . . . . . . . . . . . . . . . . . . . . . . . . . . . . . . . . . . . . . . . . . . . . . 205
Shriners . . . . . . . . . . . . . . . . . . . . . . . . . . . . . . . . . . . . . . . . . . . . . . . 207
Townies . . . . . . . . . . . . . . . . . . . . . . . . . . . . . . . . . . . . . . . . . . . . . . . 210
Hipsters . . . . . . . . . . . . . . . . . . . . . . . . . . . . . . . . . . . . . . . . . . . . . . . 212
Beauty Queens. . . . . . . . . . . . . . . . . . . . . . . . . . . . . . . . . . . . . . . . . . 214
Hot Rodders. . . . . . . . . . . . . . . . . . . . . . . . . . . . . . . . . . . . . . . . . . . . 216
MENSA Members . . . . . . . . . . . . . . . . . . . . . . . . . . . . . . . . . . . . . . . 218
Bennies. . . . . . . . . . . . . . . . . . . . . . . . . . . . . . . . . . . . . . . . . . . . . . . . 220
Greeks . . . . . . . . . . . . . . . . . . . . . . . . . . . . . . . . . . . . . . . . . . . . . . . . 222
HOGs. . . . . . . . . . . . . . . . . . . . . . . . . . . . . . . . . . . . . . . . . . . . . . . . . 225
Junior Leaguers . . . . . . . . . . . . . . . . . . . . . . . . . . . . . . . . . . . . . . . . 228
Genealogists. . . . . . . . . . . . . . . . . . . . . . . . . . . . . . . . . . . . . . . . . . . 231

## TECHNOLOGY

Hackers . . . . . . . . . . . . . . . . . . . . . . . . . . . . . . . . . . . . . . . . . . . . . . . 235
HTPCers. . . . . . . . . . . . . . . . . . . . . . . . . . . . . . . . . . . . . . . . . . . . . . . 238
Early Adopters . . . . . . . . . . . . . . . . . . . . . . . . . . . . . . . . . . . . . . . . . . 240

# INTRODUCTION

The word "freak"—like the word "America"—means different things to different folks.

In the carny circuit, the freak is the bearded lady; in the 1960s, the freak was the bearded hippie. "Freaking out" has meant, alternately, overdosing on drugs, flying into a rage, or becoming overly enthused. Lately, you can say "freakin'" on television as a substitute for the F word, and to describe one's self as a "freak" for a hobby or passion or obsession carries no opprobrium whatsoever.

Avowed Christians may refer to themselves as "Jesus Freaks" with no more than a shrug and a smile, and even Rick James meant the term "Superfreak" as a compliment to that girl he won't take home to Mother. Sixties icons Crosby, Stills, and Nash sang of lettin' one's "freak flag fly"—that is, celebrating personal eccentricity and nonconformity—and according to a late-'70s disco band, all that needed to be said about the dance "Le Freak" was C'est chic. And in 1999, the cult TV show *Freaks and Geeks* introduced us to freaks James Franco and Seth Rogen, and those guys are doin' pretty well today.

What all these designations of the word "freak" have in common is that they refer to something that deviates from the norm, and while in America's classrooms we celebrate diversity, in America's public spaces and private lives, we celebrate deviance. Deviance is a reminder to ourselves and to others that we are unique, our own person, and dedicated to not entirely fitting in.

So we who are about to freak, salute you. Be yourself, know thyself, tune in, turn on, and freak out!

# COLLECTIBLES

- Comic Collectors
- Collectible Card Gamers
- Model Railroaders
- Numismatists
- Stamp Lovers

# COMIC COLLECTORS

**ALSO KNOWN AS:**
*Comic Book Guys (or Gals, if there are any)*

**JUST DON'T CALL THEM:**
*Nerds, Losers, Fools and Their Money*

**CORE BELIEF:**
*This is art, too.*

> *"[Sigh]. Let me show you something. This—this is a Snagglepuss,*
> *drawn by Hic Heisler. It is worth . . . something. This—this is an arm,*
> *drawn by nobody. It is worth . . . nothing."*
>
> —Comic Book Guy, *The Simpsons*
> ("Lady Bouvier's Lover," Season 5, Episode 21)

## WHO THEY ARE:

Collectors of comic books and/or the the original artwork on which cartoons, comic strips, comic books, or animation are based.

With the rise in the late 1980s of the graphic novel (spearheaded by the Batman saga *The Dark Knight Returns*), comic books rose in popularity as an investment: the subsequent buying craze inspired the industry to flood the market with rare and special editions, and inevitably, the bubble burst. Comic art and rare comic books can still command big bucks, but the economic recession and a cooled market has calmed the comic hysteria of the 1990s.

To be sure, not all Comic Book Art Collectors make their purchases according to aesthetics: the collector may make selections based on nostalgia or resale value.

Classic superhero comic books fetch the largest auction numbers: e.g., the legendary copy of *Action Comics #1* featuring the premiere of Superman sold at auction in 2010 for $1.5 million (that's one of about 100 copies believed to be in existence). Resale value for other original art depends on the artist, the character portrayed, and what the character is doing: action always trumps stasis, and nostalgic fondness helps value: so a cell of all seven dwarves cavorting in Disney's *Snow White* has more value than an original art page of D-list characters like Marvel Comics' Ms. Marvel or She-Hulk.

## HOW TO RECOGNIZE:

Desk at home or work decorated with action hero figurines; *Comic Book Price Guide* always close at hand; subscribes to comic industry magazine *Wizard*; keeps lighting dim, room temperature at 67, and humidity levels at 45 percent for ideal storage conditions.

## TO BE FOUND:

Looking up elderly comic book artists online and in the phone book; trawling comic-cons; surfing eBay; stretching midsection fabric of Fantastic Four T-shirt.

## HEROES:

Artists Stan Lee, Jack Kirby, Frank Miller, Will Eisner; also celebrities such as Nicolas Cage, Ben Affleck, and Samuel Jackson, who have copped to being comic-collecting freaks.

## THEIR IDEA OF FUN:

Being in the company of collectors to trade, trash talk, gossip, and geek out.

## MOST DISTINCTIVE TRAIT:

The absence of other stereotypical male "toys" in the house (widescreen TV, motorcycle, super grill) because the money has gone elsewhere.

### Art with Attitude

In the 2000 movie *Unbreakable*, the owner of a comic art gallery berates a customer for wanting to buy high-end original comic art for his toddler. Comic Collectors can be as prickly as their fine art counterparts at the suggestion that one should buy art strictly as an investment, to be sold when the market is hot. Both groups of art collectors will tell you the same: Start collecting what you love, regardless of cost or resale value.

## BIGGEST CONTROVERSY:

"Slabbing": that is, submitting your comic book to a professional service that will permanently encase it in protective plastic and rate its value. While this process preserves the comic, it also makes it unreadable and unenjoyable, and there is some concern that the rating scale . . . well, overrates.

## BIGGEST MISCONCEPTION ABOUT:

That their love of comic art excludes an appreciation for any other type of visual art.

## WHAT YOU MAY HAVE IN COMMON:

Love of figurative art that expresses and defines character and tells a story; a hatred of elitist attitudes in art appreciation; a love of Roy Lichtenstein, who used comic book imagery in his pop art paintings.

## BUZZWORDS:

"PET film bags" are archival protective bags in which rare comics are stored: the comics are reinforced by "boards," or thin sheets of cardboard.

## SIGN OF FAN:

Owns one or two original drawings or cells, framed in rec room or den.

## SIGN OF GEEK:

Finds comic book and art pieces at live auctions instead of online.

## SIGN OF SUPERFREAK:

When presented with the choice of purchasing their ultimate find of original art and sending a child to college, they reply, "I'm thinking, I'm thinking!"

# COLLECTIBLE CARD GAMERS

**ALSO KNOWN AS:**
Card Gamers, CCGers

**JUST DON'T CALL THEM:**
Fanboys, Geeks, Nerds

**CORE BELIEF:**
"Old Maid" is for kids; Poker is for weird grown-ups; you can't always be online playing video games.

*"Lucky at cards, unlucky at love."*

—Proverb, Anonymous

## WHO THEY ARE:

People (usually tween or young adolescent males) who play a relatively new form of card game called Collectible Card Games, the most well-known of which is Magic: The Gathering (MTG).

Take the appeal of collecting trading cards (baseball cards, Wacky Packages), add the strategy of a card game (Poker, Gin Rummy), toss in a point system and competitive play out of *Dungeons & Dragons*, and you've got Collectible Card Gaming.

Kids who are into magic, wizards, and role-playing games almost certainly have a deck of *Magic: The Gathering* in the house. (MTG is published by Wizards of the Coast, whose parent company is Hasbro.) But MTG isn't the only CCG present in the mainstream.

*Pokémon* and *Yu-Gi-Oh!*, once seemingly simple sets of cards, turned into television, movie, and merchandising jackpots. Beloved television series like *Star Trek* and *Babylon 5* both have CCGs, as do *Doctor Who* and *G.I. Joe*. And not all collectible card games are fantasy or sci-fi based: one of the earliest games of this breed was *The Base Ball Card Game* first released in 1904.

CCG cards look like trading cards from whatever realm players battle for: they depict characters (from mythical creatures to human warriors to alien masterminds) and assign them point values, abilities and powers, and strategies for play. Like baseball cards, there are rare cards that have increased value and power in the game. Unlike in traditional card games, players may choose their own cards: wielding powers and using strategy is key to success here. There's no betting, no poker chips, and the rules are more imaginatively sophisticated than for Crazy Eights.

New cards, new decks, and different editions come out over time, making play more interesting with more possible outcomes. The medieval-Japan-themed *Legend of the Five Rings*, for example, releases new editions that each advances the overarching plot; one year players battle to become the emperor, but with the next release they battle to unseat the new ruler. So unlike poker, where the rules and objectives remain constant, CCGs are like a video game played with cards. And indeed, some CCGs have online components and boards for enhanced play.

## HOW TO RECOGNIZE:
They're the kids with the tall stack of dark cards with beasts and colorful creatures and characters on them.

## TO BE FOUND:
Among brainier, perhaps less socially adept kids, mostly boys.

## HEROES:
MTG creator Richard Garfield; winners of the Magic World Championship, held annually since 1994: e.g., André Coimbra of Portugal (2009), Antti Malin of Finland (2008), Uri Peleg of Israel (2007).

## THEIR IDEA OF FUN:
Remembering the names of all these different characters and creatures and places, to the extent that players sound like walking Tolkien encyclopedias.

## MOST DISTINCTIVE TRAIT:
An active imagination.

## BIGGEST CONTROVERSY:
As the CCG subculture is global, questions of taste and appropriateness often arise. Not all countries and cultures around the world approve of the occasionally demonic or violent imagery found in CCGs, and some parents would rather buy their kid one deck of playing cards through which they could learn hundreds of games as opposed to funding an endless stream of collectible cards in order to play one game.

## BIGGEST MISCONCEPTION ABOUT:
That their card game is any dorkier or more representative of a waste of time than Bridge, Pinochle, Gin, or Texas Hold 'Em.

## WHAT YOU MAY HAVE IN COMMON:

Discretionary income, indulgent parents, willingness to debate who would win in a fight between Gandalf and Professor Dumbledore.

## BUZZWORDS:

"Starter" sets or decks are for the initiate and contain, respectively, cards for two newbies to play with and a complete set for more advanced play; "booster packs" add to your growing card collection and arsenal; "card sleeves" (or, more casually, "card condoms") are plastic protectors that guard the physical integrity of the cards from wear and tear and make it easier to shuffle.

## SIGN OF FAN:

Occasional player, demurs to "not being that into it" for fear of sounding like a dork.

## SIGN OF GEEK:

Makes Halloween costume based on favorite CCG character, regrets having to explain who he is at every door.

## SIGN OF SUPERFREAK:

Pleads with parents to schedule family vacation time and place around CCG tournaments; cards useless in shouting match.

# MODEL RAILROADERS

**ALSO KNOWN AS:**
*Railroad Modellers, Home Conductors, Railroad Hobbyists, Toy Train Collectors*

**JUST DON'T CALL THEM:**
*Boys with Toys*

**CORE BELIEF:**
*No technology of transport can equal the nobility and romance of the train.*

*"The introduction of so powerful an agent as steam to a carriage on wheels will make a great change in the situation of man."*
—Thomas Jefferson (1743–1826)

## WHO THEY ARE:

Men (characteristically) whose fondness for toy train sets extends to the construction of large environments with electric trains and all manner of buildings and props.

As with any subculture, there are degrees of involvement, investment of time, financial expense, attention to detail, and obsession.

The Model Railroader is running on twin engines: nostalgia for childhood and romance of the rails, the latter of which is more pronounced and widespread in the U.K. and European countries, where railroads are still a major form of transportation.

Your entry-level Model Railroader is an adult male who has rigged the upper perimeter of his den or office with a functioning toy railroad set. Taking a step further would be setting up a large flat environment, known as a "layout," in the basement or attic. More money and more space allows the mere hobbyist to dedicate an entire room to a sophisticated layout with weather sound effects, or one that replicates in the most minute detail an actual place, such as the King's Cross Rail Station in London. (See? It's even got a model "Platform 9 3/4" like in Harry Potter!)

Once past the threshold of historical and mechanical accuracy, the fun of proportionate scaling can begin: e.g., debates over whether or not trains, tracks, buildings, and props have been scaled down to historically and authentically correct proportions.

Model Railroaders tend to be men somehow affiliated with the railway industry or with products often transported by rail (e.g., coal), or, more commonly and quite simply, they are grown-ups for whom the sound of that whistle beckons memories of boyhood.

## HOW TO RECOGNIZE:
Overalls, red kerchief, and blue pin-stripe cap are a giveaway.

## TO BE FOUND:
In attics or basements; in toy stores; ordering components online from specialty manufacturers.

## HEROES:
Famous Model Railroaders in movies and TV include: Cary Grant (*People Will Talk*, 1951), the Reverend Lovejoy (*The Simpsons*), Dudley Moore (*Arthur*, 1981), Tom Cruise (*Risky Business*, 1983). Real-life Model Railroaders include Tom Brokaw and Eric Clapton.

## THEIR IDEA OF FUN:
Watching it go.

## MOST DISTINCTIVE TRAIT:
An eye for detail.

## BIGGEST CONTROVERSY:
Debates over authenticity and whether or not one "scratch builds" things like fauna or houses (i.e., makes them by hand) or just buys them pre-made.

## BIGGEST MISCONCEPTION ABOUT:
That they're infantile. Collecting old baseball cards or Rolling Stones memorabilia is one thing, but the amount of time, energy, and expense that can go into running a toy train gives outsiders not only pause but also cause for concern over the Model Railroader's maturity level.

### All Aboard! (No, Really!)
A model railroad or train is any railroad or train that has been scaled down from the real thing, which means that the scaled-down version need not be a toy engine that fits in your hand. If your backyard and expense budget permits, you could purchase a model engine and railroad that your friends and family could use. It could be tiny like in children's amusement parks, or it could be adult-sized, like in zoos. They run on gasoline or diesel fuel, and while you'll be popular with your little nephews and nieces, the wife and your accountant may need more convincing.

## WHAT YOU MAY HAVE IN COMMON:

Nostalgia for toys that don't involve avatars, blowing stuff up.

## BUZZWORDS:

A model train's "scale" has a numerical value to describe its size proportionate to its real-life counterpart, and "gauge" refers to the distance between rails on a track.

## SIGN OF FAN:

Keeps trains from youth on desk.

## SIGN OF GEEK:

Subscribes to *Model Railroader* magazine.

## SIGN OF SUPERFREAK:

Card-carrying member of the NMRA: National Model Railroader Association, founded in Wisconsin in 1935.

# NUMISMATISTS

**ALSO KNOWN AS:**
*Coin Collectors*

**JUST DON'T CALL THEM:**
*Scrooges, Nickel and Dimers, Change Chumps*

**CORE BELIEF:**
*Money talks, and it speaks volumes.*

> *"All passes. Art alone / enduring stays to us; /*
> *The bust outlasts the throne— / the coin, Tiberius."*
>
> —Henry Austin Dobson (1840–1921)

## WHO THEY ARE:

Coin collecting is an accessible hobby whose rewards are more than monetary.

It usually starts with the kid collecting pennies, to see how many he can amass. Next, he'll take a trip to the local Coin and Stamp Store, to get a glimpse of horizons ahead: he'll start collecting the new state quarters, a mint set from the year of his birth, or an untouched two-dollar bill. If the lad sticks with it, he may graduate to combining his collecting with investing in silver or gold, and finally, if he's got the bug (and the bucks), he'll graduate to collecting coins of the realm, ancient specimens, and pieces so beautiful that you couldn't think of spending (or selling) them.

Coin collecting encompasses the history of money, finance, and trade; it involves the art of engraving and design; and when you hold in your hand a coin from ancient Rome and contemplate that this same coin could have crossed the palm of a Caesar, you know the thrill that coin collecting can give to the human imagination.

King Louis XIV of France reportedly visited his royal coin collection every day, saying that he could "always find something new to learn" by studying it.

## HOW TO RECOGNIZE:

Examining the change a cashier hands them for silver dimes and quarters.

## TO BE FOUND:

Amateurs may be found at your local coin store, if you have one; the more hardcore may be found at the annual New York International Numismatic Convention, which features auctions and more than 100 specialists from around the world.

## HERO:

Dr. George Heath, founder of the American Numismatics Association, which celebrates its twentieth year in 2011.

### Sorry, George!

The guy on the quarter, aka George Washington, opposed the idea of putting presidential portraits on coinage, because he thought it smacked too much of the king's noble visage on currency. The first Washington quarter was minted in 1932 to commemorate the bicentennial of the founding father's birth. When the coin proved immensely popular, the U.S. Mint made the Washington quarter permanent, in 1934.

## THEIR IDEA OF FUN:

Attending coin shows, joining coin clubs, reading *Coin World* magazine.

## MOST DISTINCTIVE TRAITS:

Eye for detail, interest in history, often romantic or patriotic attachment to their collection.

## BIGGEST CONTROVERSY:

Anything involving money excites controversy, big and small: from numismatists upset that Presidential "gold" coins minted in 2007 do not feature "In God We Trust" prominently enough, to collectors of non-U.S. currency (aka "global numismatists") taking issue with federal restrictions on the importation of certain foreign currencies.

## BIGGEST MISCONCEPTION ABOUT:

That collecting money is a sign of greed or a materialistic frame of mind.

## WHAT YOU MAY HAVE IN COMMON:

Interest in economics or the art of engraving.

## BUZZWORDS:

The lexicon of numismatic terms is huge, but some examples: "denticles" are the ridges along the edge of coins; the two sides of a coin are its "face" and "obverse"; and a "loupe" is a magnifying glass used in examining coins.

### SIGN OF FAN:

Purchases annual mint collection in hopes that one day, his sons might thank him for it, maybe.

### SIGN OF GEEK:

Tries to get younger nephews interested in numismatics, insists they call it "numismatics" instead of "coin collecting," will let them look at, but not touch, coins.

### SIGN OF SUPERFREAK:

Spends a ton of bills on a single coin.

# STAMP LOVERS

**ALSO KNOWN AS:**
*Stamp Collectors, Philatelists*

**JUST DON'T CALL THEM:**
*Fellatists*

**CORE BELIEF:**
*Good things come in small sizes.*

*"The fact that stamp collecting has long been the most popular hobby in the world, with over 16 million enthusiasts in the United States alone, is a good indication of how much fascination and appeal these colorful little pieces of gummed paper exert."*

—Robert Obojski, *A First Stamp Album for Beginners* (1984)

## WHO THEY ARE:

People of all ages and backgrounds who collect and/or study postage stamps. A careful distinction here: Philatelists needn't collect stamps to study them, while Stamp Lovers need not study stamps to collect them.

Most people don't give stamps a second thought, except to whine about how their cost rose two cents so that a courier can come to your house and deliver stuff for you, for free. Stamp Lovers, however, appreciate that the postage stamp is a tiny historical document, an art object, a cultural emblem, and a constant source of fascination and enjoyment.

Rough estimates put the number of stamp collectors in the United States at 20 million, mostly males. All of them would love to get their hands on a stamp as rare as the Swedish Treskilling Yellow, which at auction in 2010 hoped to garner a bid of $7.4 million.

If you're looking for a great stamp collection, ask the Queen of England: hers is estimated to be worth in excess of $150 million. You could also stop by the National Postal Museum in Washington, D.C., and see if John Lennon's childhood stamp album is on display—they've got it.

## HOW TO RECOGNIZE:

Their shopping cart at the arts and craft store is filled to the brim with archival albums (or better, "stockbooks" with clear plastic protective sheaths).

## TO BE FOUND:

Stamp Love is so huge, that the American Philatelic Society (APS) has to hold two conventions every year: the APS AmeriStamp Expo in winter and the APS StampShow in the summer.

## HERO:

U.S. President Franklin Delano Roosevelt was an avid stamp collector (as was then Secretary of the Interior, Harold Ickes). Reportedly, whenever the pressures of the office proved overwhelming for FDR, his secretary knew to get out his stamps and suggest he distract his mind for a while. Sounds nerdy, perhaps, but it sure beats what other presidents have done to relieve the pressure, wouldn't you say?

## THEIR IDEA OF FUN:

Looking through a "loupe" (magnifying glass) to look for watermarks, finer points of engraving, and potential errors that contribute to rarity and value.

## If You Have More Than Two, One's a Fake

The rarest U.S. stamp is not the one with the plane flying upside down: it's what's called the U.S. Franklin Z-Grill, printed in 1867. Peculiar to this stamp is a pattern of embossed squares, which was meant to absorb cancellation ink. (That way, cheapskates couldn't wash the ink off the canceled stamp and use it again, thus cheating Uncle Sam out of a penny.) What makes the stamp worth upward of $1 million is that there are only two known stamps of this kind in the world. Ben Franklin, who is on the stamp's face, would probably love knowing that.

## MOST DISTINCTIVE TRAITS:

An eye for detail, care and precision in the practice of their hobby.

## BIGGEST CONTROVERSY:

Apart from people who will always complain about what appears on a U.S. stamp (The Simpsons? Star Wars? Outrageous!), there are those who think that foreign-made "collectors' stamps" (sold in the United States, but with no postage value) cheapen and devalue the entire practice of studying, collecting, and appreciating stamps.

## BIGGEST MISCONCEPTION ABOUT:

That they are, like Numismatics, boring old grannies engaged in a dull, dust-covered hobby.

## WHAT YOU MAY HAVE IN COMMON:

A love of art on a small scale, interest in cultural and economic history, an affair with the mail carrier.

## BUZZWORDS:

A store or exhibition in which one buys or exchanges stamps is a "bourse"; a stamp issued primarily for collectors is a "speculative"; "tongs" are tweezers with which to handle stamps.

## SIGN OF FAN:

Buys commemorative "sheet" of stamps, frames prominently for den or office to convey gravitas.

## SIGN OF GEEK:

Frequently writes letters to the editor of *The American Philatelist* magazine.

## SIGN OF SUPERFREAK:

Plans vacation around annual London Festival of Stamps, an international exhibition celebrating "stamps, stamp design, and postal heritage."

# FASHION

- Trekkies
- Preppies
- Elves
- 501st Legionnaires
- Cosplayers
- Steampunkers
- Rennies
- Civil War Re-enactors

# TREKKIES

**ALSO KNOWN AS:**
*Trekkers*

**JUST DON'T CALL THEM:**
*Virgins*

**CORE BELIEF:**
*Even-numbered movies are good, while the odd-numbered ones suck.*

> *"Live long and prosper."*
> —Vulcan farewell, traditional

## WHO THEY ARE:

Trekkies, in case you've been hiding out on Ceti Alpha V, are devotees of *Star Trek*, a late-1960s science fiction TV show that ran for a mere three seasons but eventually inspired a multimillion-dollar franchise, giving birth to a series of movies, several TV spinoffs, and a 2009 "reboot" featuring a new, younger cast.

For some Trekkies, *Star Trek* is about camp, nostalgia, and guilty pleasure; for others, it's one of several science-fiction fantasies that stimulate their imaginations and give them pleasure. For many Trekkies, however, the show shares pantheon space with the works of Ray Bradbury, Philip Dick, and H.G. Wells: that is, exceptionally well-written fictions that speak to our times. *Star Trek* would not be what it is today without the characters and settings imagined by creator Gene Roddenbury or the scripts of the original series, provided by some of the best writers in television and science fiction.

## HOW TO RECOGNIZE:

Velour shirts, pointed ears, Klingon foreheads.

## Live Long and Prosper

A little-known fact outside the Trekkie community is where Mr. Spock's hand gesture for "Live long and prosper" comes from, and if you adduce your knowledge of this in conversation, you're sure to score points. Leonard Nimoy (like his co-star William Shatner) is a Jew, and when he was a child attending synagogue, his parents instructed him to avert his eyes from the presiding rabbi, lest he witness the presence of the Almighty. Naturally, Nimoy could not resist a peek, and he saw the rabbi extend raised palms with his fingers making a "V" shape. This hand gesture, in fact, may be found on Jewish headstones: it is a longstanding ceremonial gesture. So Nimoy stole it for his character Spock. The fact that the gesture resembles a "peace sign" surely enhanced its popularity when *Star Trek* aired in the mid-1960s.

## TO BE FOUND:

Most often, in the living rooms of everyday, normal men and women; often, but not always, at sci-fi conventions; and seldom in the basement of their parents' house.

## HEROES:

The crew.

## THEIR IDEA OF FUN:

*Star Trek*, unlike some other solitary hobbies or pursuits, is a communal experience and pleasure, so Trekkies enjoy enthusing about their favorite episodes or movies, critiquing and debating the latest incarnation of the *Star Trek* franchise, and feeling the camaraderie of fellow travelers. In that sense, *Star Trek* geeks and superfreaks are no different than sports fanatics.

## MOST DISTINCTIVE TRAITS:

They're rarely short on opinions about their favorite and least favorite aspects of *Star Trek*; there's always grist for discussion.

## BIGGEST CONTROVERSY:

Picard vs. Kirk; Q vs. Trelane, the Squire of Gothos; Data vs. Spock; Landru vs. M5.

## BIGGEST MISCONCEPTION ABOUT:

That they need (to quote an infamous William Shatner skit on *Saturday Night Live*) to "get a life."

## WHAT YOU MAY HAVE IN COMMON:

An interest in space technology and astronomy; support at work for an ethnically diverse team.

## BUZZWORDS:

phaser, tricorder, Tribble, Neutral Zone, transporter.

## SIGN OF FAN:

Owns movies or TV shows on DVD, dresses up as *Star Trek* character for Halloween.

## SIGN OF GEEK:

Trip to Las Vegas focuses not on gambling but on "The Star Trek Experience" exhibit at the Las Vegas Hilton; departing words to babysitter are "Yeoman, you have the helm"; dresses up as *Star Trek* character to attend convention.

## SIGN OF SUPERFREAK:

Drops $3,000 to own Diamond Select's replica of Captain Kirk's chair from bridge of Enterprise, insists on putting it in living room; dresses up as *Star Trek* character in daily life.

# PREPPIES

> *"Greed is good—greed works."*
>
> —Gordon Gekko, *Wall Street*

## WHO THEY ARE:

"Preparatory School Chic" is nothing new, but it was made new again in the early 1980s, when the election of conservative 1950s movie actor Ronald Reagan to the office of President coincided with the bestselling success of Lisa Birnbach's satirical *The Official Preppy Handbook*. "Preppie" quickly entered the popular culture lexicon as being synonymous not only with fashion but also with attitude, speech patterns, and sociopolitical status.

Clothing retailers such as J. Crew, L.L. Bean, and The Gap, as well as labels such as Lacoste, scrambled to become official outfitters of Preppiedom. In 2009, in a move of profound Preppie self-referentialism, Harvard University contracted with clothier Wearwolf Group to produce a line of "Preppy clothing," proceeds of which would go toward Harvard's undergraduate financial aid program.

To be sure, one can wear Preppie articles of clothing (boat shoes, loafers, polo shirts) or even preppie outfits without being a Preppie, just like college students can dress like homeless people and still return to the comforts of their dorms. Being a Preppie true blue (or pink and green) involves economic status and a sociological outlook.

How big a business is preppiedom? Ralph Lauren clears about $4 billion in revenue; L.L. Bean does a little over $1 billion; and Lacoste, Abercrombie & Fitch, and Tommy Hilfiger are still in the game. Tennis, anyone?

## HOW TO RECOGNIZE:

Tidy, well-groomed, upper-class appearance with hint of casual: chinos, khakis, Izod polo shirts, pearls on girls, loafers, letter sweaters, L.L. Bean "duck" boots, navy blazers, boat sneakers.

## TO BE FOUND:

Wherever one finds young people interested in adopting affectations of good breeding and wealth.

## HEROES:

Rich people, business moguls, P. Diddy, the Kennedys.

## THEIR IDEA OF FUN:

What they imagine to be the recreational pursuits of the wealthy: boating, backgammon, tennis, shopping, insulting the help.

## MOST DISTINCTIVE TRAIT:

Referring to parents either by their first names or as "Mater and Pater."

## BIGGEST CONTROVERSY:

Authenticity. At issue with the wearing of Preppie fashion is whether one dons the wardrobe to reflect Preppiedom, aspire to Preppiedom, or make an ironic critique of preppiedom: nothing distinguishes those three approaches. Of course, some people may dress Preppie because they like pink and green, but the question of intent and authenticity always lurks beneath the prettified surface.

### Preppie Sex Appeal

Traditionally, the response that Preppies most inspire in other people is a desire to beat them up. Preppies do, however, have some sex appeal. The female preppie, popularized in *Animal House* and its countless imitators, is the virginal Daddy's girl under whose icy exterior pounds a lustful heart and insatiable appetite for bad boys. The male Preppie aspires to a Jack Kennedy–style youth and vigor: the playboy scion, the brash aristocrat, the young gentleman of taste. Hey, whatever floats your skiff.

## BIGGEST MISCONCEPTION ABOUT:

That they are yuppies in training. Yuppies tend to work harder and be more ambitious. Also that because they dress rich, they have disposable income to buy everyone a round of drinks or treat for dinner—not always so.

**WHAT YOU MAY HAVE IN COMMON:**

A love of argyle.

**BUZZWORDS:**

Any word spoken with a clenched jaw.

**SIGN OF FAN:**

Chuckles at 2006 online video "Tea Partay," in which young WASPs rap about how Preppies live large.

**SIGN OF GEEK:**

Parents really did name him Biff.

**SIGN OF SUPERFREAK:**

Absolutely no sense of irony.

# ELVES

*"Elves are cool, man."*

—Orlando Bloom, actor and portrayer of the elf Legolas in the movie adaptation of *The Lord of the Rings* Trilogy

**WHO THEY ARE:**

People who adopt an elf persona or avatar for the purposes of Cosplay or games such as *World of Warcraft* (WOW), *Dungeons & Dragons, Runescape, Dark Age of Camelot*, and others.

In Germanic mythology, elves are diminutive Nature spirits. Some folklore divides elves into good and bad elves, divine or semi-divine elves, or even tall elves. Common to these traditions are an elf's pointed ears, magical powers, and strong connection to Nature and animals.

In gameplay and Cosplay, Elves tend to be archers, architects, and builders, and exemplars of bravery and loyalty. Although an elf and a dwarf fight side by side for the forces of good in *LOTR*, Elves may tend to distance themselves from their near-cousin Dwarves, whom they perceive as less intellectual, smelly, and crude. You would no more want to consider them the same thing as you would the Irish and the Scottish.

Tolkien developed a language of Elves called "Quenya," and while you will find several online dictionaries, phrase lists, and even translators for this magical tongue, know that "speaking Elvish" depends on what fictional universe you're talking about: different video games, books, movies, and fictional worlds can have their own version of Elvish.

## HOW TO RECOGNIZE:

Pointed ears, often wearing "mystical" crystal necklaces, forest green clothing.

## TO BE FOUND:

Cosplay, anime and manga conventions.

## HEROES:

Baker Ernest J. Keebler, Buddy the Elf (from the 2003 movie *Elf*), Hermey the Misfit Elf (who really wanted to be a dentist in the 1964 animated *Rudolph the Red-Nosed Reindeer*), and of course, Lord Oberon, mythological king of the elves.

## THEIR IDEA OF FUN:

Casting spells, exhibiting bravery, archery.

## MOST DISTINCTIVE TRAIT:

Spock ears.

## BIGGEST CONTROVERSY:

The preponderance of elf characters in very different video games and Cosplay can create confusion as to whether Elves are supposed to be magical, happy, creepy, on the Dark Side, or on the Light Side. Add to this, Will Ferrell as an elf, Dobby the House Elf from the *Harry Potter* books, and the Keebler Elves, and one imagines we'll soon see an Elf Anti-Defamation League to keep it all straight.

## That's "Elvish," Not "Elvis"

Author J.R.R. Tolkien wasn't content merely to create elf characters for his fantasy books: he took the time to create Elvish, an entire language. "Quenya" and "Sindarin" are varieties of Elvish, complete with grammar and phonology, in addition to vocabulary. To learn Elvish, consider consulting ELF, the Elvish Linguistic Fellowship *www.elvish.org*, an international organization dedicated to studying and learning Tolkien's invented languages. You'll be inscribing your wedding rings with charming Elvish sentiments in no time.

## BIGGEST MISCONCEPTION ABOUT:

Swoony British actor Orlando Bloom's portrayal of ass-kicking elf Legolas in *LOTR* may not have completely countered the prejudice that any guy who's into playing an elf is gay.

## WHAT YOU MAY HAVE IN COMMON:

Excellent woodshop skills, philanthropy, industriousness, treehouse.

## BUZZWORDS:

A "Dryad" is a totally smokin' hot green chick in World of Warcraft who gets it on with male elves.

## SIGN OF FAN:

Doesn't read "Twas the Night Before Christmas" to family, opts instead

for *Elfis: A Christmas Tale* (Price Stern
Sloan, 2006), about a Santa's helper
who knows how to rock.

## SIGN OF GEEK:
Uses E.L.F. cosmetics (Eyes, Lips,
Face) just because of the name.

## SIGN OF SUPERFREAK:
Rides Honda ELF motorcycle dressed
as elf en route to playing elf in *World
of Warcraft*.

# 501ST LEGIONNAIRES

**ALSO KNOWN AS:**

501st Legion, "Vader's Fist," Stormtroopers, Clone Army, Republic Army, Grand Army of the Republic

**JUST DON'T CALL THEM:**

Fanboys Who Like Dress-Up

**CORE BELIEF:**

Fun.

> *"We don't need to see his identification.*
> *These aren't the droids we're looking for.*
> *You can go about your business. Move along! Move along!"*

—Imperial Stormtrooper under the influence of The Force in the 1977 film,

*Star Wars: A New Hope*

## WHO THEY ARE:

Men and women who voluntarily and without financial compensation dress up as Imperial Stormtroopers (as well as other bad guys) from the *Star Wars* movies.

Founded in 1997 by two South Carolina *Star Wars* fans, the 501st Legion has approximately 4,700 members in forty countries. Legionnaires are contracted to appear at public or private events and, under agreement with Lucasfilm Ltd., charge nothing for their appearances (although, as their website says, they "enthusiastically welcome" donations to charity in lieu of payment).

All generations of *Star Wars* fans get a kick out of seeing these characters from their favorite movie step into the third dimension. What's interesting to see is that often little kids have no compunction about running up to Imperial Stormtroopers to have their photo taken with them, while those older fans who were kids when the original *Star Wars* came out tend to balk and get goose bumps at the sight of Vader's Army on patrol, fully armed!

## HOW TO RECOGNIZE:

The note-perfect replication of the Imperial Army's uniforms and equipment. The 501st doesn't permit ham-handed amateur attempts at costumes and gear.

## TO BE FOUND:

At charity, business, or personal events; providing security at the annual DragonCon (Atlanta, GA); appearing onstage with Weird Al Yankovic for performances of parody song "Yoda." Visit their website *www.501st.com* and you'll see their official trading cards, "off-duty" photo gallery, and 501st Imperial Cadet Training Manual (aka Kid's Activity Book).

## HEROES:

(Geek alert) Jedi Master Syfo-Dyas, who ordered the creation of the Clone Army from the Kaminoans; Lord Darth Vader.

## THEIR IDEA OF FUN:

Promoting interest in *Star Wars*, doing charity work, having fun, and oh yeah, crushing Rebel scum.

## MOST DISTINCTIVE TRAITS:

Accuracy, respect for the franchise, camaraderie, good sportsmanship.

## BIGGEST CONTROVERSY:

Lucasfilm Ltd. has an agreement with fans: they can engage in activities such as the 501st Legion, provided they don't make money off it. So technically, Lucas isn't crazy about the nonlicensed creation, buying, and/or selling of costumes that look so much like "the real thing" that the layman might think the 501st represents Lucasfilm Ltd. They don't.

## BIGGEST MISCONCEPTION ABOUT:

That they do this either because they like playing the Bad Guys or because they're *Star Wars* fans who are too embarrassed to have their identities revealed.

## WHAT YOU MAY HAVE IN COMMON:

Love of All Things Lucas, Halloween spirit, soft spot for bad guys, the belief that no detail is too small to escape the careful attention of the fan looking to recreate the fantasy in real life.

## BUZZWORDS:
The Legion, like the real military, is subdivided into Garrisons, Squads, Outposts, and Detachments.

## SIGN OF FAN:
Secures 501st as "security" for corporate awards function.

## SIGN OF GEEK:
At same function, asks Stormtrooper about joining the 501st.

## SIGN OF SUPERFREAK:
Seeks veteran benefits from federal government on grounds of service in Clone Wars.

# COSPLAYERS

**ALSO KNOWN AS:**
Otaku (that is, fans of Japanese comics, called "manga"), Role Players, Fantasy Fans, Science Fiction (or "SF") Fans

**JUST DON'T CALL THEM:**
Fantasy Freaks, Weirdos

**CORE BELIEF:**
One needn't always abide by the adage, "Be yourself."

*"Clothes make the man."*

—ancient proverb, popularly attributed to Shakespeare or Mark Twain

## WHO THEY ARE:

People of varying ages who engage in "costume play" ("cos" + "play"): a recreational form of dressing up as and pretending to be a fictional character, usually one from Japanese comics or animation, science fiction, video games, or the world of superheroes and superheroines. Hence, there are thousands of characters to choose from, and it's not unheard of for women to cosplay as male characters, and vice versa.

Dedicated Cosplayers see what they do as a form of public performance art: like a stage or film actor "inhabiting" a role, Cosplayers speak, walk, and act as their chosen character would. Think of them as avatars in the flesh.

Numbers don't lie! The largest Cosplay convention, the annual Anime Expo, attracts roughly 40,000 people every year (and by "people," we mean human beings dressed up as other creatures).

## HOW TO RECOGNIZE:

Look for capes, masks, swords, tails, big doe eyes, wild hair, and Lycra.

## TO BE FOUND:

Conventions of anime (Japanese animation), manga, and comics, especially the big ones: the annual San Diego Comic-Con and the semiannual Comiket market in Japan.

## HEROES:

The character of their choosing or invention: Superman, My Friend Totoro, Klingons, Princess Mononoke, etc.

## THEIR IDEA OF FUN:

Cosplay is not meant to be done in isolation, so a variety of social events let Cosplayers meet and enjoy each other's company: Cosplay cafés, Cosplay nights at dance clubs, Cosplay events at amusement parks.

## MOST DISTINCTIVE TRAIT:

Believing in make-believe.

## BIGGEST CONTROVERSY:

As with Civil War Re-enactors, Cosplayers can be casual dresser-uppers who do it just for fun, or they could be hardcore fans who obsess over the smallest detail and take issue with Cosplayers who adopt a more relaxed approach to costume and being in character. A not unpopular attitude—what some would call cynical posturing—is that anyone who can't make or obtain the most authentic costume possible shouldn't Cosplay because it gives Cosplaying a bad name.

## BIGGEST MISCONCEPTION ABOUT:

That dressing up as an anime character is somehow different from—and deserving of more opprobrium than—dressing up as a lion for Mardi Gras, dressing up as a Native American for a baseball game in Cleveland, or dressing up as Uncle Sam for a parade.

## WHAT YOU MAY HAVE IN COMMON:

Rich fantasy life; love of comics or science fiction; sewing skill.

## BUZZWORDS:

In Japan, people who like to photograph Cosplayers are "comeko." A "doller" dresses as an amine girl by wearing a head-covering mask. Also, Cosplayers of anime and manga characters classify themselves according to different types of those forms: e.g., "sentai," "Yuri," "Magical Girlfriend."

### Cosplay as Foreplay?

Anything involving fantasy, role play, and dress-up as Cosplay does is bound to arouse suspicions that its participants are really into it for the sex: that is, Cosplayers inhabit fictional characters so they can pretend that Doctor Who is getting it on with Princess Peach from Super Mario. This is kind of like accusing people who dress up for Halloween of witchcraft: while it can't be ruled out, it isn't necessarily the rule.

## SIGN OF FAN:

Attends Star Trek convention as Mr. Spock, doesn't break character to tell soda vendor that four dollars for a Sprite Zero is "illogical."

## SIGN OF GEEK:

Arranges Cosplay Bowling Night with friends, only to have argument over whether or not bowling shoes compromise costume authenticity.

## SIGN OF SUPERFREAK:

Travels to Japan for Comiket, wears costume on the entire plane ride.

# STEAMPUNKERS

**ALSO KNOWN AS:**
Steampunks

**JUST DON'T CALL THEM:**
Cyberpunks, Punks

**CORE BELIEF:**
Everything new is old again.

*"Remembering Yesterday's Tomorrows."*
—the title of an unpublished 2007 article writer Richard Morgan wrote for
the *New York Times* [but available online]

## WHO THEY ARE:

People with a hybrid fascination with nineteenth-century machines and fashion, and a sci-fi futuristic worldview.

Few things are more misleading than for Steampunks to have the word "punk" in their name, because you will never see a purple Mohawk or safety-pin piercing in the bunch. The term "Steampunk" is a joke few outsiders get: it's meant to spoof "cyberpunk," which combined futuristic elements within a gritty, industrial setting (think *Blade Runner*). Well, Steampunk went back to Victorian England for its industrial setting and adopted the mechanical fantasies of Jules Verne and H.G. Wells as their idea of science-futurism. Steampunks are fascinated with the past's notions of the future, and that fascination often extends to their building thing-a-ma-jiggies that look both old and futuristic, or to retooling modern things to look like they were built in a different century (past).

Steampunks will tell you that their subculture is about more than wearing bowler hats and tinkering with computer components: it's about graphic novels, literature, music, and art. It's a way of dressing differently but more spiffily than Punks, less gloomy than Goths, and more upper-class than Rivetheads.

Steampunks maintain a visually fascinating balance between nostalgia and futurama, Charles Dickens and Ralph McQuarrie, violins and synthesizers.

## HOW TO RECOGNIZE:

If Trinity from *The Matrix* was impregnated by a Victorian-era printing press, their love child would look like a Steampunk. Bizarre, yes, but there it is.

## TO BE FOUND:

At Lowe's or Home Depot, buying soldering irons and a mixed bag of metal fasteners and gears; renting *The League of Extraordinary Gentlemen, Brazil, Metropolis, Sherlock Holmes*; hammering and wiring in their garage or workroom; listening to online steampunk music channels.

## HEROES:

Jules Verne and H.G. Wells for their forward-thinking science-fantasy novels; contemporary writers like Michael Moorcock or K. W. Jeter; James Watt and Robert Fulton, for their work in steam technology.

## THEIR IDEA OF FUN:

Taking something mechanically or technologically obsolete (a typewriter, a turntable, an old sewing machine) and re-engineering it as art,

décor, conversation piece, or as part of a more modern appliance.

## MOST DISTINCTIVE TRAIT:

They tend to be hands-on do-it-yourselfers, tinkerers.

### Steampunk Youth

Steampunk may seem like another one of those subcultures that basically says to young people, "Let's dress up and get into weird stuff," but parents and teachers with an eye for applied learning can use Steampunk as a "teachable trend," to guide young interest in physics, automation, mechanical engineering, history, computers, and perhaps most importantly, making things with your own hands. That punk DIY work ethic comes to the rescue!

## BIGGEST CONTROVERSY:

If more people are going to become aware of Steampunk, it'll be through movies, and so far, major-release movies with a Steampunk vibe—*The League of Extraordinary Gentlemen, The Wild Wild West, Van Helsing,* assorted anime—have not done well at the box office (to say nothing of their artistic merits, or lack thereof). Steampunk is still waiting for its *Blade Runner.*

## BIGGEST MISCONCEPTION ABOUT:

Seldom are a Steampunker's interests split 50-50 between Victoriana and modern technology, so you're bound to err on one side or the other, identifying the person's primary interest.

## WHAT YOU MAY HAVE IN COMMON:

For men, curly waxed mustache; for women, hoop skirt and parasol.

## BUZZWORDS:

Old terms for modern things: e.g., robots are "automatons," cars are "horseless carriages," a men's clothing store is a "haberdashery."

## SIGN OF FAN:

While friends wear backward baseball caps, wears backward bowler.

## SIGN OF GEEK:

Takes old typewriter and reconfigures it to function as working computer keyboard.

## SIGN OF SUPERFREAK:

Five words: Steam-operated external hard drive.

# RENNIES

**ALSO KNOWN AS:**
Festies

**JUST DON'T CALL THEM:**
Comely Wenches, Sirrah, Yon Merry Fanboy

**CORE BELIEF:**
Faire's fair.

*"There were no utensils in medieval times, hence there are no utensils at Medieval Times. Would you like a refill on that Pepsi?"*

—Janeane Garofalo, *The Cable Guy* (1996, movie)

## WHO THEY ARE:

Men and women who dress in Renaissance-era clothing either to attend a Renaissance fair or because they are "actors" in a fair, festival, or other "medieval" function or organization.

"Renaissance nostalgia" concerns itself very little with historical accuracy or authenticity: many a Rennie and even more average people could not give you dates as to when the actual Renaissance took place (fourteenth–seventeenth century), where it began (Florence, Italy), or what major historical event defines its beginning (the Black Death). We do know that the term "Renaissance Man" means some smart or talented person who does a lot of different stuff, but we're also ready to apply the term to Brad Pitt or David Byrne. (That alone would make da Vinci vomit with rage.)

Also, Rennies are not "medieval": that period, aka the "Middle Ages," preceded the Renaissance. For better or for worse, the popular Rennie image projects things like King Arthur, jousting, lords and ladies, Maypoles and mandolins, turkey drumsticks, and cast iron steins. Apart from the music and face painting, there's little of the cultural explosion of ideas and art that characterized the actual Renaissance.

But no matter! Rennies wishest thou to be merry, stout yeoman! Art thou at all interested in crystal jewelry or dragons of pewter for thine cubicle?

---

## HOW TO RECOGNIZE:

Men typically have beards and look like they could ease up on the mutton; Women have either tousled or ribbon-braided hair and tend to skip merrily.

## TO BE FOUND:

King Richard's Faire (Renaissance Festival), Boston's "Medieval Manor" (a dinner theatre revue), and similar organizations and functions.

## HEROES:

Washington State touring company Ye Merrie Greenwood Players; the Medieval Fantasies Company of Virginia; and organizers of the Texas Renaissance Festival, which purports to be the largest such faire in the world.

## THEIR IDEA OF FUN:

A-maying, a-drumming, a-piping.

## MOST DISTINCTIVE TRAIT:

The state of their bodily and dental hygiene is markedly better than that of actual Renaissance men and women.

## BIGGEST CONTROVERSY:

Authenticity in appearance and character. Chances are, your average Rennie doesn't speak Middle English but instead just trills gaily in an English accent about "m'lords," "m'ladies," "thee," and "thou." Also, female Rennies tend to dress conspicuously slutty.

### Speaking of Majors . . .

People who pursue a curriculum of "general study" are, in a way, Rennie students. One of the key intellectual revolutions in the Renaissance was the influence of humanism on education: turning colleges and universities from vocational schools where you studied to be a doctor or a lawyer to "liberal arts" schools where you studied and later wished you'd become a doctor or lawyer.

## BIGGEST MISCONCEPTION ABOUT:

They're unacquainted with the health hazards endemic to the Renaissance period, as well as other things that made living in that time period not so hot.

## WHAT YOU MAY HAVE IN COMMON:

A Jethro Tull CD collection.

## BUZZWORDS:

Beer is "meade" or "grog"; "fool" is an official job title for a jester.

## SIGN OF FAN:

Expresses fondness for Michelangelo and da Vinci; buys fairy wings, a bodice, or a sword to wear at their local faire.

## SIGN OF GEEK:

Fire-eater at Faire on weekends.

## SIGN OF SUPERFREAK:

Joins Renaissance theater company, works knights and weekends.

# CIVIL WAR RE-ENACTORS

**ALSO KNOWN AS:**
*Civil War Recreationists*

**JUST DON'T CALL THEM:**
*Actors*

**CORE BELIEF:**
*The re-enactment of war is not meant to glorify or romanticize it, but to keep history alive and to cultivate an appreciation for the sacrifices made in the conflict.*

> *"It is altogether fitting and proper that we should do this."*
> —U.S. President Abraham Lincoln, Gettysburg Address

## WHO THEY ARE:

Men of varying ages who recreate battles and engagements of the United States Civil War (1861–1865), using replicas of uniforms and firearms.

Any subculture in which clothing plays a key component inevitably gives rise to stratified views on authenticity. Some Re-enactors are more relaxed in their adherence to authenticity of dress, firearms, or even language. It's not uncommon for disagreements to arise over the "correct" stitching in a jacket, the particular shade of gray or blue, or whether or not Re-enactors, while in character, may use words or slang terms not used in 1863.

Recreating battles in the U.S. Civil War was something actual veterans of the war did, at anniversary or commemorative events. The contemporary trend of re-enactment gained momentum in the 1980s and especially in the early 1990s with the popularity of Ken Burns's mini-series documentary *The Civil War*.

The Civil War is the most re-enacted conflict in the world, with participants even in Canada and Europe. Estimates put the number of Re-enactors in the United States at around 50,000.

## HOW TO RECOGNIZE:

The ones in the blue are the Union Army, and the ones in gray are the Confederates.

## TO BE FOUND:

Most often during some celebratory anniversary of a Civil War battle or engagement, occasionally on the Fourth of July.

## HEROES:

The heroes of the actual war, the identity of which depends on which side you favor: among them, Nathan Bedford Forrest and Robert E. Lee on the Confederate side; Lincoln, Grant, and Sherman on the Union side; and of course, the common soldiers.

## THEIR IDEA OF FUN:

Doing battle, win or lose; answering questions from onlookers; advising Hollywood on Civil War authenticity.

## MOST DISTINCTIVE TRAIT:

A willingness to pretend to die for one's country.

## BIGGEST CONTROVERSY:

Women who have an interest in Civil War re-enactment may find difficulty participating, since women in the nineteenth century weren't officially allowed in combat. Some re-enactment groups may allow women to dress up as men (not an unheard of practice in the original war); other groups may have their desire to maintain historical authenticity challenged by contemporary standards of inclusion and gender equity.

## War Onscreen

Curiously, no other war is re-enacted more than the U.S. Civil War, but the war is seldom re-enacted on film (exceptions include *Glory, Gettysburg, Gone with the Wind*). While American movies about the Vietnam War are arguably strongest in the American imagination, the Hollywood record for war movies is held by World War II. For a lighthearted treatment of war re-enactment, look up Season 5, Episode 1 of the animated show *American Dad!*, in which titular protagonist Stan Smith participates in a Vietnam re-enactment— at his local country club.

## BIGGEST MISCONCEPTION ABOUT:

That engaging in a pantomime version of war is a sign of immaturity and an inability to see the war for the horror that it was.

## WHAT YOU MAY HAVE IN COMMON:

Interest in history (military, cultural, social) and in keeping it alive and relevant, Civil War fascination, a musket collection.

## BUZZWORDS:

"Farbs" is a derogatory term among Re-enactors for people who have the afore-mentioned relaxed attitude about authenticity. "Progressives" are the hard-core authenticity buffs, and "Mainstream" represents the fat middle of the spectrum.

## SIGN OF FAN:

Participates in Re-enactment once, just for the experience.

## SIGN OF GEEK:

Dies every year at Gettysburg, or at least in an open field we're pretending is Gettysburg.

## SIGN OF SUPERFREAK:

Keeps Re-enactment uniform in better condition than business suits, has family Christmas photo done in style of Matthew Brady.

**ART**

- Local Thespians
- Slam Poets
- Suzukis
- Tattoo Artists
- Happening Artists
- B-Boys
- Yarn Bombers

# LOCAL THESPIANS

*"Oh, it offends me to the soul to hear a robustious periwig-pated fellow tear a passion to tatters, to very rags, to split the ears of the groundlings, who for the most part are capable of nothing but inexplicable dumb-shows and noise."*

—Hamlet's "Speak the speech" speech to the players of the play-within-the-play, Act 3, Scene 2

## WHO THEY ARE:

Men and women who may have "done a lot of theater in college" but had no interest in moving to New York, Chicago, or LA for the privilege of living hand-to-mouth while being an understudy and auditioning for tampon commercials.

The spectrum of Local Thespians is wide: at the low end is the self-confessed amateur who participates in a play "just to keep my hand in it" or, more plainly, just to have fun; midrange are the actors, directors, technicians, and company members who mount shows at your church, your high school auditorium, or your community center; and finally, far fewer, are the folks who are really going for it—joining an established theater troupe, winning awards, and building a CV that has more credits than you'd care to read.

Ironically, people at the low end can be as self-important and affected as people at the semi-professional end, and it's this pathetic reality that feeds comedies such as *Waiting for Guffman*.

All satire aside, local thespians perform a vital service to the community insofar as they selflessly dedicate their time and energy to provide people with an entertainment alternative to TV, video games, and porn. Not a few people go their entire lives without ever seeing live theater or even live music performance.

Even if you live in a large city with many theater offerings, not everyone can afford season tickets or front-row seats to watch The Play Everyone Knows. Some Local Thespians are the only people around who would mount a show by a local playwright, material that's challenging or provocative, or something for small children.

The American Association of Community Theatre (AACT) boasts 7,000 member theaters nationwide, putting on a total of 46,000 productions a year for about 86 million people. If anything, that's a lowball figure for a total national count, given that community theaters needn't be AACT members and that arts organizations may sponsor theater productions as part of their community programs.

## HOW TO RECOGNIZE:

They are busy making an extensive scrapbook of past shows (including playbill, photos, any reviews), to be left within easy reach of visiting friends and relatives.

## TO BE FOUND:

Posing for 8" × 10" headshots at shopping mall photographer;

holding up the family bathroom by doing their enunciation exercises in front of the mirror; corralling spouses into "reading with me," to learn lines; boring people at family reunions.

## HEROES:

Financial benefactors, paying audience members, local reviewers and press.

## THEIR IDEA OF FUN:

Discussing "the Craft" with colleagues.

## MOST DISTINCTIVE TRAIT:

A willingness to hand over large chunks of their lives for little to no money.

## BIGGEST CONTROVERSY:

Pre-casting of actors who are not so much talented as reliable.

### Act Up!

The local theater scene is more permeable than the local music, visual art, or dance scene, so if you have the time and interest to get involved in local theater, you may find it relatively easy to participate on some level, even if it's administrative or technical. And you might like it so much, you'll do it again!

## BIGGEST MISCONCEPTION ABOUT:

That they're hacks who overcharge you for an evening of mediocre entertainment. No doubt that's sometimes true, but it's true in part because of your too-high expectations and cynicism.

**WHAT YOU MAY HAVE IN COMMON:**
A belief in enlivening the community, a love of drama, the "itch" to perform.

**BUZZWORDS:**
"The boards" (the stage), "my process," "read-through."

**SIGN OF FAN:**
Appears in local production of *Our Town*.

**SIGN OF GEEK:**
Directs and appears in local production of *Our Town*.

**SIGN OF SUPERFREAK:**
Proudly tells bona fide actors about own acting and directing credits, including local *Daily Shopper* review of *Our Town*.

# SLAM POETS

**ALSO KNOWN AS:**

*Slammers*

**JUST DON'T CALL THEM:**

*Hacks*

**CORE BELIEFS:**

*Their contests are called "slams": these people resist the stereotype of the effete, dandified, pale-complexioned, academic wuss.*

> *"Poets are the unacknowledged legislators of the world."*
>
> —Percy Bysshe Shelley (1792–1822), poet

## WHO THEY ARE:

The "poetry slam" is a competitive event among poets of varying styles and ability levels. It's usually held in a coffeehouse or in a bar on a slow night. The response of judges and the audience rates the contestants. In most slams, the poet may not augment his or her recital with props, music, or public displays of nudity. The winning poet gets bragging rights, a free beer, and another line on their poet résumé.

There is no one type of Slam Poet. Depending on the venue or even the slam "theme," Slam Poets could be funny, moving, or reflective. Most often, however, they are expressive, voluble, and political. You may show up at a slam expecting to hear something along the lines of "I wandered lonely as a cloud," and instead you get "Cloud Loneliness As a Metaphor for Global Warming." Slam Poets believe that poets are tough enough to go head to head and take some blows from the judges or audience. Slam Poets welcome a vigorous response to their performance because it shows that poetry affects people.

## HOW TO RECOGNIZE:

Scratchy throat, knocking knees, always asking the bartender for one on the house in exchange for a poem.

## TO BE FOUND:

Poetry festivals, workshops, retreats, seminars, English departments.

## HERO:

Marc Smith, father of the poetry slam.

## THEIR IDEA OF FUN:

In all seriousness, it's contributing to the artistic life of the community by boosting literary performance.

## MOST DISTINCTIVE TRAIT:

Volume.

## BIGGEST CONTROVERSY:

The argument that poetry is not fodder for an *American Idol*-type throwdown, in which one person emerges a "winner." The poetry slam opponent has no problem with recitals or readings, and readily agrees that a poem comes alive when read aloud, and certainly the public benefits from hearing new work or even just poetry in general; however, a performance poetry contest can detract attention from the poem itself to reward the histrionics of whoever is onstage.

## BIGGEST MISCONCEPTION ABOUT:

The one Slam Poets have about themselves: that standing up in front of an audience and adding some rhetorical flourish or dramatic flair to their recital makes them "performance artists."

## WHAT YOU MAY HAVE IN COMMON:

A distaste for poetry that rhymes.

## Suit Your Slam

The beauty of the slam, like poetry, is that you can tailor it to your sensibility and taste. You don't have to rate the participants. (An "Anti-Slam" event in New York gives all participants "10s.") Make your slam suitable to whomever you want to welcome, and enjoy an evening of shared artistry—or shared amateurism. It's about having a good time.

## BUZZWORDS:

"Dub poetry" is a West Indian spoken-word tradition of poetry accompanied by reggae beats or music especially tailored to the poem. It ain't your college roommate shouting rhymes over Bob Marley.

## SIGN OF FAN:

Attends Poetry Slam.

## SIGN OF GEEK:

Attends Poetry Slam and actually pays attention.

## SIGN OF SUPERFREAK:

Participates in Poetry Slam, pays attention to other performers, blogs about win (or loss).

# SUZUKIS

**ALSO KNOWN AS:**
Students, teachers, or supporters of the "Suzuki Method"

**JUST DON'T CALL THEM:**
Brainwashed, Robotic Tots

**CORE BELIEF:**
Playing music builds character, and starting early is no sin.

> *"Teaching music is not my main purpose. I want to make good citizens. If children hear fine music from the day of their birth and learn to play it, they develop sensitivity, discipline, and endurance. They get a beautiful heart."*
>
> —Shin'ichi Suzuki (1898–1988)

## WHO THEY ARE:

Shinichi Suzuki was a Japanese violinist who noticed that small children learn and absorb language at an astonishing rate, including subtle nuances of diction and pronunciation. If children can learn so many words so early in life, Suzuki asked, why couldn't they learn to play a musical instrument—not only for fun or education, but to build character and a "noble heart"?

The popular image of Suzuki musicians is a classroom of cute little Japanese tots all playing "Twinkle, Twinkle, Little Star" on miniature violins: this, we Westerners think, must be where all those Asian musical prodigies come from.

But Suzuki wasn't trying to build a farm league for future Mozarts or even lifelong amateur musicians: rather, he saw how playing music instills discipline, character, and satisfaction that can last a lifetime. If playing music is so wonderful, thinks the Suzukite, why deprive it from children until the fifth or sixth grade?

Suzuki is a method, not a religion, and Suzuki principles may be integrated into a wide variety of musical pedagogy.

## HOW TO RECOGNIZE:

The Suzuki classroom has children: playing together, in a group; attending concerts and events as immersion into a musical environment; listening to sound recordings to understand and learn how a piece "goes," as opposed to teaching notation.

## TO BE FOUND:

Internationally, but primarily in Japan.

## HERO:

The Founder.

## THEIR IDEA OF FUN:

Creating the musical *environment* for children and young people to learn in: e.g., music "across the curriculum," listening to music every day (even prenatally), an emphasis on music as enjoyment and not the technical acquisition of motor skills.

## MOST DISTINCTIVE TRAIT:

The aspiration to fulfill founder Shin'ichi Suzuki's goal that music should develop a "beautiful heart."

## BIGGEST CONTROVERSY:

Children aged three to five, critics allege, are too young to be taught a musical instrument; the Suzuki Method, in its emphasis on playing by ear, produces musicians who can't read music; and playing in a group to mimic a sound recording looks too much like training parrots without imparting understanding or appreciation.

## BIGGEST MISCONCEPTION ABOUT:

That the Suzuki Method is disguised indoctrination into the virtues of conformity and mimicry of the group.

## WHAT YOU MAY HAVE IN COMMON:

A belief that children's lives are enhanced by music and especially by learning to play a musical instrument.

## BUZZWORDS:

Suzuki emphasized what he called "tonalization," which is the ability not just to put one's finger in the right place at the right time on the instrument, but also to learn how to produce a pleasant tone—much how we learn not only vocabulary, but also the range of vocal expressiveness in ordinary speech.

## SIGN OF FAN:

Begins education on violin, cello, piano, or flute before learning how to tie shoes.

## SIGN OF GEEK:

Surprised to learn that Master Suzuki evidently manufactured motorcycles.

## SIGN OF SUPERFREAK:

Refers to his or her own four children as a "quartet."

### Myth of Mozart

It's no irony that Suzuki developed variations on "Twinkle, Twinkle, Little Star" for his method, since the melody is attributed to Mozart, himself a musician at a young age. We think of Mozart as a young genius of composition, but Mozart aficionados will tell you that most of his works in his youth were highly imitative and derivative of popular composers of the day.

# TATTOO ARTISTS

**ALSO KNOWN AS:**
*Inkers, Skin Pounders*

**JUST DON'T CALL THEM:**
*Ex-cons, Art School Dropouts*

**CORE BELIEFS:**
*The body is a canvas to be beautified, and tattoos can be either purely decorative or emblematic of deep personal feelings and history.*

*"Show me a man with tattoo*
*and I'll show you a man with an interesting past."*
—author Jack London (1876–1916)

## WHO THEY ARE:

Men and women who work professionally to apply tattoos. By "professional," we mean someone who has been licensed by their state health department to give tattoos and who has completed an apprenticeship at a licensed tattoo parlor. Licensing requirements vary, state to state. No U.S. state outright bans tattoos, but to be sure, you're likely to find more tattoo parlors in California than in Wyoming.

The Tattoo Artist cannot be simply a good artist: he or she needs to be someone who knows customer service and has excellent bedside manner. After all, this art hurts, only gets one shot for application, and is pretty much permanent. It's a big decision, and one that not a few people rush into.

The website *www.ustattoostudios.com* lists more than 500 parlors across the country, and if you're as good as New York's star tattoo artist Paul Booth, you just might be able to clear $450,000 a year.

## HOW TO RECOGNIZE:

They're usually billboards for their own line of work.

## TO BE FOUND:

Major cities (in states that allow tattoo parlors, anyway), college towns, blue-collar neighborhoods.

## HEROES:

Mark Machado, aka "Mr. Cartoon"; Kat vonD, star of *LA Ink*, at least for showing a national audience that tattoo artists are not necessarily thugs and skeevy low-lifes; and Ami James of *Miami Ink*.

## THEIR IDEA OF FUN:

No different from an artist contracted to paint a portrait or commissioned to do a landscape or mural: they love a happy, satisfied customer.

## MOST DISTINCTIVE TRAIT:

Head to toe in stories.

## BIGGEST CONTROVERSY:

The perennial push-pull between people who dismiss tattoos as a once-rebellious fad now gone hopelessly mainstream and people who insist that tattoos retain their aura of biker, prison, tough guy, rebel, outsider chic.

## BIGGEST MISCONCEPTION ABOUT:

That subcutaneous ink is the only artistic medium they can work in, or that they're not real "artists." No doubt, there are plenty of amateurs out there producing terrible work, but the real pros are experts and often visual artists outside the parlor.

## WHAT YOU MAY HAVE IN COMMON:

Affection for tribal markings, punk rock, motorcycles, Rockabilly, hot rods, S&M, and listening to people tell stories from their lives.

## BUZZWORDS:

Tattoos are also called "ink" or "tats"; a "B-Back" is a potential customer who says "I need to hit the ATM, I'll be right back" and never returns; and someone covered head to toe in tats is a "Showcase."

## SIGN OF FAN:

Watches *LA Ink* TV show, offers studious critique of tattoo work to the annoyance of friends.

## SIGN OF GEEK:

Is inspired by tattoo culture to draw tattoo designs, develop portfolio, share with friends who bring them to tattoo parlor for application.

## SIGN OF SUPERFREAK:

Goes for license, apprenticeship, and full-time job at parlor; gets scores of tattoos strictly for credibility.

### *Tattoo You?*

What distinguishes the Tattoo Artist from other artists is that while they consult with and advise customers, as artists they work at the customer's behest. Tattoo Artists may want to pull their hair out the next time someone asks for a flaming skull or a butterfly over their butt cheeks, but that's their job, and they need to do it well and with a good disposition.

# HAPPENING ARTISTS

**ALSO KNOWN AS:**
*Performance Artists, Anti-Artists, Installation Artists*

**JUST DON'T CALL THEM:**
*Exhibitionists, Crackpots, Hacks, Charlatans*

**CORE BELIEF:**
*Art is three-dimensional, often interactive, experiential, and needn't conform to conventional notions of performance, entertainment, or the conveyance of a "message."*

*"Art is what you can get away with."*

—artist Andy Warhol (1928–1977)

## WHO THEY ARE:

Artists who turn art into an experience, and vice versa.

The Happenings art movement can be traced back to American Allan Kaprow (1927–2006), who may have picked up some contact mojo from the Abtract Expressionists as they exploded traditional notions of art after World War II. Kaprow engineered more than 200 "Happenings" in his art career and is seen as an inspiration to such avant-garde movements as Fluxus and installation art.

What makes a Happening? Well, something happening. In other words, the art is not a static object, assuming a passive role in relation to the viewer; rather, art becomes experiential, and that experience can be challenging, disturbing, mystifying, hilarious, or just plain odd. Happenings may draw on theater, music, dance, audience interaction, or any kind of artistic expression or media. The only thing is, unlike paintings or sculpture, you can't experience Happenings by reading about them: you need to be there, literally, as the Happening is happening.

## HOW TO RECOGNIZE:

Let's say you see a guy through an art gallery window, and his face is covered with honey and gold leaf. He's cradling a dead rabbit in his arms, whispering into its ear. He has an iron slab shackled to his foot. That's artist Joseph Bueys (1921–1986), performing his 1965 Happening, *How to Explain Pictures to a Dead Hare*.

## TO BE FOUND:

Teaching graduate-level art at a college or university, marrying into money, exhibiting in European countries that don't seem to mind this sort of thing.

## HEROES:

Joseph Bueys (whom you've never heard of), Yoko Ono (whom you have heard of, but for other reasons), Wolf Vostell (who was German).

## THEIR IDEA OF FUN:

Challenging your preconceived notions of what art is.

## MOST DISTINCTIVE TRAITS:

Low threshold of shame, inscrutability.

## BIGGEST CONTROVERSY:

We're all pretty much agreed that painting involves applying paint to some kind of surface, usually canvas. Ditto on the assertion that music involves musical instruments. The defining characteristic of "Happenings," however, is that they defy definition: they could be anything, anywhere. Supporters see that as a boon and a gateway to creative expression, while critics see it as a flaw that opens the floodgates of pseudo-artistic quackery.

## BIGGEST MISCONCEPTION ABOUT:

That they don't possess other traditional art-related skills.

## WHAT YOU MAY HAVE IN COMMON:

Married to a pathological need for attention; a shared address with one's parents; obscurity.

## What's Happening?

If, after reading about art Happenings, it sounds like something that you could do . . . maybe that's part of the point. Other forms of art—classical sculpture, fine art portraiture, ballet—show off the formidable skills of the artist and seem to say, "Admire me, because you couldn't do this in a million years." Happenings, however, may shake your mind loose of traditional thinking so that you say, "Hey, maybe I could become an artist, too."

## BUZZWORDS:

"Fluxus," an art movement with crossover in Happenings, is taken from the Latin word "to flow," because they blend and flow several art forms together.

## SIGN OF FAN:

Happens upon Happening and happens to enjoy it.

## SIGN OF GEEK:

Rejects two- and three-dimensional artwork in favor of Happenings.

## SIGN OF SUPERFREAK:

Becomes Happening artist and submits, for BFA thesis, entire life as ongoing Happening.

# B-BOYS

**JUST DON'T CALL THEM:**

*Breakdancers (This term, while not offensive or inaccurate, is seen by the B-community as outdated and unhip.)*

**CORE BELIEF:**

*No different from other forms of dance: a premium is placed on fidelity to prescribed moves, originality, physical and emotional expressiveness, and dedication to one's craft.*

> *"There is only the dance."*
>
> —poet T.S. Eliot (1888–1965), "Burnt Norton"

## WHO THEY ARE:

Practitioners of an acrobatic dance style performed to Hip-Hop music, involving quick, full-body movement: leaps, rotations, spins, and fancy footwork.

A musical "break" is an interlude in which the main flow of the piece temporarily stops for either a percussive element or an instrumental solo. DJs loop together and remix these "breaks" to provide a rhythmic backbeat against which B-boys dance, or "breakdance."

B-boys have come a long way from the late '70s-era New York City, when they reportedly used dancing as a means to settle gang disputes or just decide where to go later to shoot at one another. Today, B-boys continually expand the boundaries of breakdancing beyond a limited bag of tricks: as a result, being a B-boy (or B-girl) is more of an aesthetic and style of expression than an adherence to a proscribed series of steps and positions.

And fortunately, true breaking requires a precision and technical excellence that is beyond the ability of most pop singer-dancers who wish to appropriate it.

## HOW TO RECOGNIZE:

Performing dance feats of seemingly impossible speed, physical strength, and agility.

## TO BE FOUND:

City parks or playgrounds, street corners, church halls, gymnasiums: wherever space permits for an exhibition, practice, or contest. Often, B-Boys and B-Girls may be found in urban communities that are socio-economically depressed, dance being a ready alternative to drugs, gangs, or violence.

## HEROES:

Ronnie Abaldonado (aka Ronnie Boy) is a veteran winner of international B-boy competition Red Bull BC-1; other names that frequently pop up on online top 10 lists are Hong 10, Physicx, Darkness, and Cico.

## THEIR IDEA OF FUN:

Competition, studying other people's moves and either adapting them or taking them as their own.

## MOST DISTINCTIVE TRAITS:

Speed, agility, flexibility, balance, passion—all the things you'd expect in a dancer of any kind.

## BIGGEST CONTROVERSY:

B-Girls, and gender inequity when it comes to media exposure, promotion, and support for female breakers.

## BIGGEST MISCONCEPTION ABOUT:

That they cannot dance in any other style, a canard repeatedly disproven on the competition dance show *So You Think You Can Dance?*

## WHAT YOU MAY HAVE IN COMMON:

Love of Hip-Hop music.

## BUZZWORDS:

"Power" moves involve gravity-defying spins and rotations, "blowup" is a rapid-fire aggregate of difficult moves intended to decimate the competition, and "burn" moves are comic or obscene moves intended to humiliate the competition.

## SIGN OF FAN:

Does the "robot dance" and floor spin at high school reunion or wedding.

## SIGN OF GEEK:

Takes lessons in breaking from local dance school, youth center, or at home on DVD.

## SIGN OF SUPERFREAK:

Competes, wins, earns nickname.

### B-Boys Gone International

When breakdancing achieved mainstream awareness in the 1980s, it was seen as the provenance of African Americans—not so, today. As the 2008 documentary *Planet B-Boy* demonstrates, formidable challenges are made to American B-Boys from Japan, France, and Korea. Thanks to worldwide distribution of B-boy videos via YouTube, aspirants from every country on Earth can toss out their VHS copy of the 1984 movie *Breakin'* and learn from more current masters of the art.

# YARN BOMBERS

**ALSO KNOWN AS:**
*Knitters, Knittas, Graffitti Knitters, Yarnstormers*

**JUST DON'T CALL THEM:**
*Grandmas, Knit-Wits, Makers of Unwanted Christmas Presents*

**CORE BELIEF:**
*Knit One, Purl Two.*

> *"I take my knitting everywhere to take the edge off of moments that would otherwise drive me stark raving mad."*
>
> —Stephanie Pearl-McPhee, *At Knit's End: Meditations for Women Who Knit Too Much (Storey Publishing, 2005)*

## WHO THEY ARE:

Often anonymous knitters who decorate public spaces and objects with knitted coverings, as a way of enlivening sterile or colorless environments.

A Yarn Bomber, for example, may knit a covering for a cold metal door handle or attempt to drape a traffic light pole. Tree branches, bicycle seats, statues—nothing is safe!

As makers of graffiti or public art, Yarn Bombers are particularly susceptible to vandalism and theft: their work has a more transient quality than spray painted words or images.

Knitting has long been a favored pastime in America, and according to the Craft Yarn Council of America, approximately 53 million American women in 2005 (36 percent of the American female population) know how to knit and/or crochet: this is a 51 percent increase, the Council reported, over the past ten years.)

How and why this wholesome activity crossed the threshold into bold statements of public art and "graffiti" is difficult to say, but surely the recent emergence of Rhode Island–based artist Dave Cole has had some influence. In 2009, Cole and a team of twenty-five traveled to Melbourne, Australia, to undertake a massive Yarn Bomb exhibit on a large bridge. Reports of other

Yarn Bombings have come in from New Jersey to Texas. Who knows when and where these mad knitters will strike next?

## HOW TO RECOGNIZE:

Audible clicking sound of needles in nighttime urban environment; suspects mostly female, between eighteen and thirty-four, with agility necessary to climb public structures.

## TO BE FOUND:

Mill stores, yarn outlets, fabric stores, knitting circles.

## HEROES:

Mom, Nana, American footballer Rosie Grier (who showed that even tough guys can enjoy needlepoint), and collective Bombing group Knitta in Houston, TX.

## THEIR IDEA OF FUN:

Adding splashes of color, warmth, and whimsy to otherwise drab and soulless environments.

## MOST DISTINCTIVE TRAIT:

The ability to tackle projects of size, such as a utility "pole warmer" or a giant hat for a bus stop kiosk.

## BIGGEST CONTROVERSY:

It may be beautiful, but it's still illegal.

## Who Might Be the Famous Face of Yarn Bombing?

Could one of the following celebrities be a closet Yarn Bomber? Actress Scarlett Johansson loves to knit, as does Sarah Jessica Parker (reportedly taught by *Sex and the City* costar Kristin Davis), and British comedienne Tracey Ullman has coauthored the knitting instructional book *Knit 2 Together* (STC Craft, 2006) with friend and Los Angeles yarn store owner Mel Clark. Actresses Uma Thurman, Catherine Zeta-Jones, and Julia Roberts also have the bug. Roberts might be the safest bet, given her role in the movie *The Friday Night Knitting Club*. We're on to you girls!

## BIGGEST MISCONCEPTION ABOUT:

That they're just faux-artsy hipsters who think public decoration is radical and, like, totally random, you know?

## WHAT YOU MAY HAVE IN COMMON:

The belief that gifts made by hand are the only gifts given with love.

## BUZZWORDS:

"Crochet" is making fabric from yarn and thread, using a crochet hook; "needlepoint" is yarn-embroidered canvas; a "skein" is a ball of yarn measured in grams; and yarn thickness is delineated in "weight."

### SIGN OF FAN:

Discovered near Yarn Bomb, innocently reading *VogueKnitting* magazine.

### SIGN OF GEEK:

Buys knitting needles with light-up tips to knit in the movie theater; ends up knitting covering for drink holder.

### SIGN OF SUPERFREAK:

Has calculated bodily dimension of Statue of Liberty—'nuff said.

# FOOD AND DRINK

- Vegans
- Oenophiles
- Locavores
- Macrobioticists
- Homebrewers
- Raw Food Nuts

# VEGANS

**ALSO KNOWN AS:**
Hippies, Granola Heads, Veggies, The Tofu Crowd, Californians

**JUST DON'T CALL THEM:**
Food Nazis

**CORE BELIEF:**
Because Americans live in an environment of such abundant food choices, the privilege of choice should actually be exercised.

> *"Nothing will benefit human health and increase chances for survival of life on Earth as much as the evolution to a vegetarian diet."*
>
> —Albert Einstein

## WHO THEY ARE:

While vegetarians eliminate animal flesh from their diet, Vegans (pronounced VEE-gans) avoid eating animal flesh and, whenever possible or practical, animal products, be it food such as milk, honey, or cheese, or clothing made from animals. The key words here are "whenever possible or practical": one can easily avoid wearing genuine fur but not so easily ordinary fabrics made from animal skin or hair. Also, you may be surprised to learn that some fast food restaurants fry potatoes in beef tallow and that animal cartilage can be found in medicine. Even basic gelatin is extracted from animal cartilage. A Vegan's decision not to eat meat or animal products could be related to attitudes concerning cruelty to animals, or the fact that it's simply more efficient and ecologically sound to grow vegetables than to sink a megaton of feed, chemicals, and water into a cow so that we can all wear suede and contract E. coli. Veganism is not a religion, but just as there is a spectrum of orthodoxy within a religion, there is a range of practices within the freedom not to eat animals.

A 2008 survey by Harris Interactive of American adults estimates that 4.2 million Vegans are in the United States. That's enough people to create a metropolitan center slightly smaller than the greater San Francisco-Oakland-Freemont area.

And no—they don't all live there already.

## HOW TO RECOGNIZE:

Usually slender with good skin; females may be unshaven in more than one place; seldom seen wearing Armani; weighing "firm" or "extra firm" tofu options at health food store.

## TO BE FOUND:

At farmer's markets, natural food markets, protest rallies, college campuses and university towns; eating by themselves at family reunions.

## HEROES:

Themselves; Donald Watson, founder of the Vegan Society.

## THEIR IDEA OF FUN:

Finding a restaurant where they can eat something other than salad, and where they don't make every soup with chicken broth. Vegans are also often enthusiastic cooks and chefs.

## MOST DISTINCTIVE TRAIT:

They know where all the best Indian, Korean, Japanese, and Thai restaurants are.

## BIGGEST CONTROVERSY:

Because veganism deviates so much from the American food-eating norm, carnivores delight in trying to trip them up: "If you're opposed to the use of animals for human enjoyment, why do you wear leather shoes?" The fact is, Veganism is as diverse as Christianity or Republicanism. Rather than mock it, non-vegans might try understanding it or learning from it.

## BIGGEST MISCONCEPTION ABOUT:

That they're humorless ascetics who "don't enjoy food" and insist on killing everyone else's food buzz. Some vegans' diets and lifestyles are restricted not by choice but by allergies, religion, or a sense of decency.

## WHAT YOU MAY HAVE IN COMMON:

An interest in sustainable agriculture and eco-friendly practices; opposition to veal; opposition to animal cruelty.

## BUZZWORDS:

"Ovo-vegans" eat eggs; "lacto-vegans" consume milk and milk products.

## SIGN OF FAN:

Avoids eating animals or animal products, whenever possible or convenient.

## SIGN OF GEEK:

Doesn't eat animals or animal products ever, happy to tell you so.

## SIGN OF SUPERFREAK:

Doesn't eat candied cherries because they contain cochineal, which is red coloring made from a ground-up insect (no kidding).

# OENOPHILES

**ALSO KNOWN AS:**
Wine lovers and/or collectors

**JUST DON'T CALL THEM:**
Wine Snobs, Cork Dorks, Rich Bastards

**CORE BELIEF:**
Life is too short for bad wine.

*"If anyone orders Merlot, I'm leaving.
I am NOT drinking any f\*\*king Merlot!"*

—Miles Raymond in 2004 film *Sideways*

## WHO THEY ARE:

Oenophiles [ē-nə-fī(-ə)ls\] are wine lovers, literally, as the word comes from the Greek word for love (philia) and wine (oinos). Americans drink some 753 million gallons of wine a year—and as that number grows every year, so does the number of its aspiring connoisseurs. Oenophilia is not an inexpensive addiction; while you may find bottles of Trader Joe's $3 Red in the temperature-regulated wine cellars of oenophiles down on their luck, most are prepared to spend hundreds, thousands, even millions of dollars on just the right vintage.

It's an obsession that offers a virtually endless source of variety, nuance, and surprise. Each year brings new wines to discover and enjoy, and each year enhances the flavor and fullness of the best wines.

## HOW TO RECOGNIZE:

Swirling glass, inserting nose in glass, eyeing glass in the light—basically taking five minutes to take a first sip, and then spitting it out.

## TO BE FOUND:

Wineries, art and wine festivals, tasting fundraisers, wine clubs.

## HEROES:

Dom Perignon, the Benedictine monk who invented champagne; Thomas Jefferson, who planted the first vineyard in America at Monticello.

## THEIR IDEA OF FUN:

Chatting up sommeliers; bargaining with wine merchants; touring vineyards; advising friends, family, and strangers alike on the pros and cons of various varietals.

## MOST DISTINCTIVE TRAITS:

While most people are interested only in showing you their hobbies, enthusiasms, and avocations, wine lovers are interested in *sharing* it with you. They also know what to order with what you're eating.

## BIGGEST CONTROVERSIES:

Cork, the traditional stopper of bottled wine, allows wine to breathe and age, but may also contain a contaminant called 2,4,6-trichloroanasole (TCA), affecting flavor. Vintners pressure cork makers to improve their product or else go to Stelvin-type closures (aka "screw-tops"). Switzerland uses 15 million Stelvin closures per year; other countries (including the United States) are slower to buck tradition.

## BIGGEST MISCONCEPTION ABOUT:

That they only drink the most *expensive* wine they pride themselves on drinking the *best* wine.

## WHAT YOU MAY HAVE IN COMMON:

A fondness for good food, good drink, good company.

## BUZZWORDS:

"Plonk" (U.K. slang for cheap wine), "nose" or "bouquet" (smell), "notes" (elements of taste), "body" (consistency).

## SIGN OF FAN:

Attends wine tastings, wine tours, wine vacations.

## SIGN OF GEEK:

Is on a first-name basis with the owner of the local wine store, conspicuously leaves *Wine Spectator* out on the coffee table.

## SIGN OF SUPERFREAK:

Rents room at hotel hosting wine auction, because car won't hold night's purchases in one trip.

### Superstar Vinters

You aren't really rich and famous enough until you have your own vineyard. Bob Dylan, Gerard Depardieu, Ernie Els, Mario Andretti, and Sting all boast their own wineries—from Napa to Anjou. The biggest big name in wine is Francis Ford Coppola, whose wine empire now includes all of Inglenook.

# LOCAVORES

**ALSO KNOWN AS:**
*Microfarmers*

**JUST DON'T CALL THEM:**
*Locos, Food Nuts, Food Nazis, Earthy-Crunchy Types*

**CORE BELIEF:**
*Local food doesn't just taste good: buying it shows good taste.*

*"The Slow Food Movement is a very positive one. Organics, artisanal cheeses, making things the old way—that can only be good."*

—star chef Anthony Bourdain (1956– )

## WHO THEY ARE:

People who believe that the freshest, healthiest, and best food is local: that is, obtained either through one's own garden, a community garden, or a farmers market or nearby farm.

Someone eating locally grown food whenever practical or possible may do so for reasons having to do with environmentalism, a desire to support the local economy, or an interest in food whose origins you can see, smell, and ask questions about.

The National Directory of Farmers Markets, which the U.S. Department of Agriculture started in 1994, reports that the years 2008 to 2009 saw a 13 percent increase in the number of farmers markets nationwide, for a total of 5,274. As the green movement continues to hit home for Americans (see entry for Urban Homesteaders), the practice of "microfarming" gains traction. Microfarming is the use of one's own property or separate purchased property for the creation of a small farm, sometimes even with a small amount of animals such as chickens or goats for milk.

## HOW TO RECOGNIZE:

By where you'll never see them: in the supermarket's canned or frozen vegetable aisle.

**TO BE FOUND:**

Among eco-freaks, white liberals, four-star chefs, nutritionists.

**HERO:**

First Lady Michelle Obama scored one for the Locavores when she oversaw the planting of a vegetable garden on the White House grounds.

**THEIR IDEA OF FUN:**

Cultivating friendships with the people who cultivate their food.

**MOST DISTINCTIVE TRAIT:**

As hokey and touchy-feely as it sounds, the emotional and psychological connection they have to what they eat. Until you grow your own food, you can't know how gratifying it is.

**BIGGEST CONTROVERSY:**

Locavores who extend their preference for locally grown produce to a rejection of any foodstuff that is imported from outside the United States or even from outside his or her own state.

**BIGGEST MISCONCEPTION ABOUT:**

That Locavores are part of a "movement," a term used frequently by the media and by some Locavores themselves. To some people, calling Locavorism a "movement" suggests that it's advancing a political agendum and is attempting to brainwash unbelievers.

**WHAT YOU MAY HAVE IN COMMON:**

Concern about pesticides or whatever regulations (or absence thereof) govern the growing of avocados in Chile.

**BUZZWORDS:**

High-minded, college-educated Locavores are "Locallectuals."

**SIGN OF FAN:**

Frequents farmers market, encourages friends and family to do likewise.

**SIGN OF GEEK:**

Will eat out only at restaurants who buy local produce or work with local farms.

**SIGN OF SUPERFREAK:**

Will eat only what occurs naturally within a five-mile radius of living space.

# MACROBIOTICISTS

**ALSO KNOWN AS:**
Macrobiotics, Hippies, Californians

**JUST DON'T CALL THEM:**
Slow Chewers, Food Flakes, Crunchies

**CORE BELIEFS:**
Balance, health, love of food.

*"You are what you eat."*

— American nutritionist Dr. Victor Lindlahr (1895–1969)

## WHO THEY ARE:

Advocates or practitioners of macrobiotics, a diet that in a thumbnail description emphasizes grains and avoidance of processed foods. Macrobioticists share some dietary practices with Vegans, but depending on the degree to which one pursues macrobiotics, some macrobiotic diets may include fish or even meat.

Macrobioticists believe that what you feed your body has a profound influence not only on your physical health but also on your sense of well-being and spiritual balance. In other words, the macrobiotic philosophy runs contrary to virtually every aspect of workaday American diets, which place a premium on speed of preparation and eating, flavor over health content, style over substance.

Your mother would certainly approve of one central tenet of macrobiotics: that you should chew your food slowly and thoroughly before you swallow. Some Macrobioticists count how many times they chew each bite of food, which may strike you as a little extreme when being served Jell-O. The point, however, is to develop a keen sensitivity to food and its effect on the body, spirit, and mind.

If that sounds more like a religion than a diet, you're not far off: Macrobioticism is by no means a cult, but for some it can be a philosophy that guides and governs one's life. For what purpose? Some Macrobioticists will tell you that the practice simply leads to good health; others will argue that macrobiotics helps prevent cancer or other illnesses.

Like vegetarianism or veganism, macrobiotics encompasses a broad spectrum and level of practice, which makes it all the harder for carnivores and fast-food lovers to make fun of them.

If you're curious (or just need a vacation in a nice rustic setting), look up the Kushi Institute of Becket, MA, which has been educating people about macrobiotics for more than twenty years. They offer a variety of programs in diet, health, and personal renewal.

## HOW TO RECOGNIZE:
Upturned nose in vicinity of what you're eating.

## TO BE FOUND:
Squinting at ingredient labels, dropping paychecks at health food stores.

## HEROES:
Famous Macrobioticists include John Lennon and Yoko Ono, Bob Weir of The Grateful Dead, Sting, Madonna.

## THEIR IDEA OF FUN:
Making cooking as fun as possible to compensate for what they're making.

## MOST DISTINCTIVE TRAIT:
Annoyingly healthy.

## BIGGEST CONTROVERSY:
Varying levels and degrees of practice inevitably feeds elitism within ranks.

## BIGGEST MISCONCEPTION ABOUT:
None of their food tastes any good; that their diet is 100 percent purely macrobiotic; that they don't partake in other unhealthy habits, like smoking or avoiding exercise.

## WHAT YOU MAY HAVE IN COMMON:
An interest in not contaminating your body with chemicals, preservatives, and carcinogens; irritation that there's nothing good to eat on that 100-mile highway trip; vegetarianism; plot in community garden.

## BUZZWORDS:
Foods are classified according to "yin" and "yang," the point being to achieve harmony and balance in the diet. The designation of yin and yang is based on a food's density, composition, effect on the body, and other factors.

## SIGN OF FAN:
Opts for side of quinoa instead of large fries.

## SIGN OF GEEK:
Subscribes to *Macrobiotics Today* magazine, gets you gift subscription.

## SIGN OF SUPERFREAK:
Organizes pantry so that all the "yin" is on the left and all the "yang" is on the right.

# HOMEBREWERS

**ALSO KNOWN AS:**
Hopheads

**JUST DON'T CALL THEM:**
Sam Adams, Mr. Science, Mr. Wizard

**CORE BELIEFS:**
Things taste better when you make them yourself—or at least they can taste better; life is too short to drink lousy beer; recipes were made to be tinkered with.

> *"Beer is proof that God loves us and wants us to be happy."*
>
> —Ben Franklin [apocryphal]

## WHO THEY ARE:

Making a successful batch of beer at home is easy, but it's far easier to mess up: a few degrees off here, too much or too little of ingredients there, and what you waited two months to crack open tastes like liquid death. Making beer at home gives you a renewed appreciation for people and companies who are able to do it well, on any scale. While making your own beer doesn't save you a tremendous amount of money, compared to buying it in the store, anything you make with your own hands in the kitchen by definition tastes better. Homebrewing will also open up to you the possibilities of taste, aroma, color, and enjoyment.

The Homebrewers Association of America counted 750,000 U.S. homebrewers in 2009, along with 800 homebrewing clubs and 300 homebrew competitions. Despite these numbers, two U.S. states (Mississippi, Alabama) still consider homebrewing illegal. Oklahoma legalized homebrewing in 2010.

## HOW TO RECOGNIZE:

They are turning kitchens and basements into giant science experiments.

## TO BE FOUND:

Often, among scientists and engineers, or people who enjoy weighing things and checking temperatures and making notes on data.

## HEROES:

Believe it or not, there is such a thing as a "beer sommelier" and schools that confer such professional status: these are the fine chefs of the gourmet beer world. One of the hotter ones is author Christina Perozzi of Los Angeles, CA, founder of the website Beerforchicks .com. Apologies, Simon Beveridge of Australia and Jens Piferoen of Maryland!

## THEIR IDEA OF FUN:

Trading recipes; shopping at farmers markets for blueberries and raspberries, to make ale; experimentation.

## MOST DISTINCTIVE TRAITS:

Their sensitivity to nuances of flavor, color, and aroma in beer doesn't come across as effete as that of wine lovers; their willingness to try or taste something new instead of professing a lifelong allegiance to some crap in a can.

## BIGGEST CONTROVERSY:

Diversity breeds contempt. With so many types of beer and various ways of making it, you're bound to encounter disagreements over methods, ingredients, and taste—and since everyone in the discussion is drinking beer, beware of blows breaking out.

## BIGGEST MISCONCEPTION ABOUT:

That they won't drink or can't enjoy "regular beer" out of a can or bottle.

## Drinking in Further Research

See if there is a homebrewing association in your area. There may even be smaller, more intimate gatherings of neighborhood Homebrewers: guys who just want to have people sample their latest batch, trade recipes, and talk shop. Your local wine and beer store may have information about groups or events related to homebrewing, and you may even be able to pick up a copy of *Brew Your Own* magazine.

## WHAT YOU MAY HAVE IN COMMON:

A preference to enjoy flavor in alcoholic beverages.

## BUZZWORDS:

Stout, lager, "real ale," hydrometer, fermometer, bock, eisbock, doppelbock, hellerbock.

## SIGN OF FAN:

Helps Homebrewer friend bottle and drink his latest batch.

## SIGN OF GEEK:

Takes up homebrewing, persists in the face of failure.

## SIGN OF SUPERFREAK:

Buys everyone a round, but insists that it must be Extra Dark Chocolate Triple Beaverwood Hellenbock, made in some dude's basement in Palo Alto.

# RAW FOOD NUTS

**ALSO KNOWN AS:**
*Raw Bourgeois*

**JUST DON'T CALL THEM:**
*People Who Can't Cook*

**CORE BELIEF:**
*Cooking depletes some foods of natural enzymes that are there to help digestion and the absorption of nutrition.*

> *"The rest of the world lives to eat, while I eat to live."*
>
> —Socrates

## WHO THEY ARE:

People who prefer, whenever practical or possible, to put raw foods at the bottom of their personal food pyramid, making it the foundation of their diets. Typically, the Raw Food Nut aims to have about 75 percent of his or her diet be raw fruits and vegetables, nuts and seeds, and raw grains.

The raw food diet may be a rejection of the high degree of processed foods in the American diet, or it may be pursued as an ancillary to a regimen of exercise or spiritual practice. As sensible and beneficial as a raw food diet sounds, it isn't for everybody. Children, anemics, and women who are pregnant, nursing, or suffering from osteoporosis are not ideal candidates for the raw food diet. This isn't to say, of course, that the diets of such individuals wouldn't improve with a little more raw food, but anyone should consult with their doctor before making any change to their diet.

## HOW TO RECOGNIZE:

Clues include healthy skin and complexion, regularity, high energy level, weight loss.

## TO BE FOUND:

Among vegans and vegetarians, life-extension fanatics, nutritionists, and people with the money and resources to have access to raw food three meals a day.

## HEROES:

Natural diet proponent Euell Gibbons (1911–1975), as well as reported raw food celebrities Woody Harrelson, David Bowie, and Demi Moore.

## THEIR IDEA OF FUN:

Juicing vegetables, dehydrating fruit.

## MOST DISTINCTIVE TRAIT:

Extensive knowledge of plants, herbs, algae, and seaweed and their nutritional benefits.

## BIGGEST CONTROVERSY:

The degree to which the long-term health claims of the raw food diet are borne out by scientific research and anecdotal evidence. While raw food is certainly healthier than processed food, it's not definitively superior to cooked food, nor has it been established that cooked food increases toxins in the body resulting in disease and sickness.

## BIGGEST MISCONCEPTION ABOUT:

Similar to vegans or macrobioticists, that they don't "enjoy food" and that their chosen diet is a model of inconvenience and impracticality.

## WHAT YOU MAY HAVE IN COMMON:

An interest in: weaning your diet from sodium, saturated fats, and preservatives; detoxification of the body; weight loss; reducing your risk of diabetes or heart disease.

## Apart from the Apple . . .

If you reread the Book of Genesis in the Hebrew Bible, you'll note that in the Garden of Eden, Adam and Eve did not eat meat. They also didn't have so much as a wok. Some Raw Food Nuts extrapolate from this scenario the assertion that in God's ideal community, a raw food diet was the order of the day. Then again, a man and his wife walked around naked all the time, and even raw food restaurants have a policy of "No shirt, no shoes, no service."

## BUZZWORDS:

"Salmonella" is a blanket term for a wide variety of microbacteria that can cause diarrhea; infection; and, in rare instances, death. Food that has not been sufficiently cleaned or cooked may harbor the bacteria.

## SIGN OF FAN:

Snacks exclusively on fruits and vegetables, buys juicer.

## SIGN OF GEEK:

Takes vegetable side dishes such as carrots, peas, or broccoli uncooked; considers seaweed.

## SIGN OF SUPERFREAK:

Typical dinner is beef tartare, sashimi, double helping of sunflower seeds.

# LIFESTYLES

- Bohemians
- Nudists
- Homeschoolers
- Hoarders
- Trustafarians
- Urban Homesteaders
- Survivalists
- Houseboaters
- Bilderbergers
- Dumpster Divers

# BOHEMIANS

**ALSO KNOWN AS:**
Bohos, Bobos (bourgeois bohemians)

**JUST DON'T CALL THEM:**
A resident or native of the former Kingdom of Bohemia, currently known as the Czech Republic

**CORE BELIEF:**
An inversion of mainstream values: the elite individual is not the well-dressed, moneyed, conventional, savvy man or woman of business. Instead, the exact opposite figure is lauded.

> *"Well, isn't Bohemia a place where everyone is as good as everyone else—and must not a waiter be a little less than a waiter to be a good bohemian?"*
>
> —Djuna Barnes (1892–1982), author

## WHO THEY ARE:

In the most general sense, Bohemians are people who pursue an alternative lifestyle with interests in the arts, the intelligentsia, low-rent living, and a kind of creative cool. Bohemians are starving artists and free-thinkers, contrarians and iconoclasts. Think people with college degrees who look like they're homeless.

The term "Bohemian" is slippery: since the late nineteenth century, the word has been used to refer to everyone from painters and newspaper reporters to junkies and revolutionaries. Not only does that make a Bohemian hard to define, it also makes it easy for any yahoo to claim Bohemian status.

Originally, "Bohemians" were what the French called gypsy immigrants. The term expanded to include artists like the Impressionists, free love advocates, or any creative type whose rejection of materialism was either willful or involuntary. In the 1990s, fashion icons Kate Moss and Sienna Miller were credited with being at the vanguard of "bohemian chic," which is where we get distressed jeans that cost $250.

## HOW TO RECOGNIZE:

The Bohemian look leans decidedly toward the scraggly and the worn: peasant skirts, second-hand clothes, loose lines, and the artfully mismatched.

## TO BE FOUND:

College campuses, low-rent "ethnic" communities where twenty-somethings aggregate, artist colonies, art schools, progressive towns and cities (e.g., Cambridge, MA; Ann Arbor, MI; Madison, WI; San Francisco, CA).

## HERO:

Author Henri Murger, whose 1845 short fiction work *Scenes of the Bohemian Life* became the opera *La Bohème* by Giacomo Puccini, which became the megahit musical *Rent,* by Jonathan Larson.

## THEIR IDEA OF FUN:

Writing or sketching in cafés, food shopping in "ethnic" markets, watching foreign and non-Hollywood movies, loitering and lounging, scoring freebies, living off coffee and weed, disconcerting their parents.

## MOST DISTINCTIVE TRAIT:

An air of both superiority and unwashedness.

## BIGGEST CONTROVERSY:

Accusations and suspicions of phoniness, especially when the Bohemian look or outlook is adopted by someone of wealth, privilege, or celebrity (see Trustafarian).

## BIGGEST MISCONCEPTION ABOUT:

A pervasive "reverse prejudice" that assumes that all artists, creative types, and members of the intelligentsia must be or at least look like Bohemians in order to project or embody authenticity.

## WHAT YOU MAY HAVE IN COMMON:

Impecuniousness, creativity, nonconformity.

## BUZZWORDS:

"Indie," "relevant," "the Man," "bourgeois."

## SIGN OF FAN:

Grows facial or leg hair, doesn't wear underpants, takes pottery class, complains about landlord hassling for rent.

## SIGN OF GEEK:

Purposefully buys second-hand eyeglasses or ones with heavy frames, wears heavy scarf, tries to convince landlord to accept pottery as rent.

## SIGN OF SUPERFREAK:

Eviction compels crashing in pottery studio, can't wait to tell friends.

# NUDISTS

*"The man and his wife were naked, and they felt no shame."*
—Genesis 2:25, *The Bible*

## WHO THEY ARE:

Nudism, as a practice, is at least as old as the Garden of Eden, where the world's first couple was naked and unashamed: indeed, some Nudists will cite this passage in arguing that the naked body is nothing to be embarrassed about, and that nudism is a choice about lifestyle, not about sex.

For many Nudists, being naked is just one component of a comprehensive approach to health, philosophy, human interaction, and even politics and religion. In the early twentieth century in Germany, Nudists also believed strongly in the health benefits of exercising outdoors in the sunlight and in adhering to a vegetarian diet. Even today, in the United Kingdom, people draw a careful distinction between people who embrace Nudism as part of a larger lifestyle choice ("Naturists") and the ordinary "Nudist" who simply elects to go without clothes.

Tallying Nudists in America may be fun, but it's not easy, given the number of casual, part-time, or non-confessed Nudists. The American Association for Nude Recreation claims about 50,000 members in the United States, Canada, and Mexico. In 1993, the Treehouse Fun Ranch of Devoe, California, held their annual Nude Chili Cookoff and counted no fewer than 2,000 participants. That's hot!

## HOW TO RECOGNIZE:

If you see a woman in public who is totally unclothed, you are looking at a Nudist; if the woman is only partially clothed, you are in Europe.

## TO BE FOUND:

The United States has many parks, beaches, and recreational areas that are designated either Nudist or "Clothing Optional" (CO). There are about 100 nude beaches in America alone.

## HERO:

Even though he was the "villain" on the first *Survivor*, Richard Hatch was probably America's first exposure (pun intended) to someone who elected to go naked because he simply felt more comfortable doing so.

## THEIR IDEA OF FUN:

If you can have fun doing it with clothes on, chances are it's still fun in the nude. The past ten years or so has seen the rise, too, of naked marathons, bicycle races, protests, and performance art.

## MOST DISTINCTIVE TRAIT:

Respect. Unlike some guys in bathing suits at the beach, nudists know it's impolite to stare.

## BIGGEST CONTROVERSY:

Their freedom to have their own space, be it part of a beach or park or resort.

## Okay, Let's Talk about Sex

The sex appeal of the Nudist is not to be found so much in their naked bodies—which, like those of most clothed Americans, are not in peak physical condition—but in the fact that they literally are comfortable in their own skin. Anyone who has achieved that advanced stage of evolution is attractive no matter what they look like.

## BIGGEST MISCONCEPTION ABOUT:

That they're pervs, exhibitionists, hippies, sex addicts.

## WHAT YOU MAY HAVE IN COMMON:

An enjoyment of walking around your own house or apartment naked.

## BUZZWORDS:

They're now called "naturalist clubs," not "Nudist colonies."

## SIGN OF FAN:

Skinny-dipping, occasional nude sunbathing.

## SIGN OF GEEK:

Has sticker for nude beach on car.

## SIGN OF SUPERFREAK:

Answers door in the nude, petitions for "clothing optional" office, never fails to remind health club manager that Greek Olympians trained and competed naked.

# HOMESCHOOLERS

**ALSO KNOWN AS:**
*Home Schoolkids, graduates of Mom University*

**JUST DON'T CALL THEM:**
*Shut-Ins, Agoraphobics, Religious Nuts*

**CORE BELIEF:**
*Education begins at home.*

*"Home Sweet Homeschool."*

## WHO THEY ARE:

Parents who elect to teach their children at home instead of at a public or private school.

Being taught at home is nothing new: it is, after all, what American settlers and pioneers did. Today, the decision to homeschool children is not one made lightly, and the reasons for doing so are various. Parents may disagree with elements of the school curriculum, school performance may be substandard, or there may be issues of religion or learning disabilities involved. Statistically, most homeschooling parents simply believe they can give their children a better education at home. State regulations and requirements vary, and it's certainly possible for homeschooled kids to apply to and get into college.

In 2001, the U.S. Census estimated that roughly 2 million American children were schooled at home, projecting the numbers to increase 10 to 15 percent every year.

## HOW TO RECOGNIZE:

They don't show up at the prom, and they don't need anyone to help carry their books home.

## TO BE FOUND:

In households in which at least one of the parents is not working outside the home.

## HEROES:

Abraham Lincoln, George Washington, Franklin Delano Roosevelt, Winston Churchill, Charles Dickens, Mark Twain, and Frank Lloyd Wright all received no formal education in childhood and adolescence.

## THEIR IDEA OF FUN:

Feeling secure, as a parent, that their children's teachers love them, support them, and are always willing to tutor them outside of class time.

## MOST DISTINCTIVE TRAITS:

People who pursue a path this alternative usually have or must develop strength of character and courage of conviction.

## BIGGEST CONTROVERSY:

The debate over the socialization of homeschooled children. Proponents argue that homeschooled kids socialize with peers in study groups and social settings "after school," and that the social setting of a conventional school is beset with peer pressure, bullying, gossip, and values parents don't want their children to share or be exposed to.

## BIGGEST MISCONCEPTION ABOUT:

That having no team athletic programs or traditional school clubs in which they may participate deprives children of social and emotional growth. While these arguments may hold some water, it's undeniably true that the "homeschool" is less likely to have drug dealers and bullies.

## WHAT YOU MAY HAVE IN COMMON:

Dissatisfaction with your local public or private school, frustration with education bureaucracy, desire to teach and guide children.

## BUZZWORDS:

An "autodidact" is someone who is self-taught; a "boxed curriculum" is packaged learning materials for use in homeschooling; "NHEN" is the National Home Education Network; "HEM" is *Home Education Magazine*.

## SIGN OF FAN:

Homeschools kids for elementary level; child raids fridge to bring teacher apple.

## SIGN OF GEEK:

Homeschools to secondary school level; child discovers she cannot "play hooky" by staying home.

## SIGN OF SUPERFREAK:

Disciplines child in homeschool class by writing note home to parent.

# HOARDERS

**ALSO KNOWN AS:**
*Collectors, Obsessive Gatherers*

**JUST DON'T CALL THEM:**
*Junkaholics, Crazy Cat Ladies*

**CORE BELIEF:**
*Safety in numbers (and sheer volume).*

*"Less isn't more: more is more."*

## WHO THEY ARE:

People for whom the accumulation of material things serves an emotional and psychological need. That's putting a kind spin on an often highly unsanitary obsession/compulsion.

If you don't have a Hoarder in the family, you may have seen them on a "nightly news magazine" program or the Lifetime Network: folks whose homes look like they've been decorated with a dump truck—boxes overflowing, knickknacks in stacks, and not an inch of room on the floor for the faint of heart to pass out.

What gives? Obsessive hoarding typically serves an emotional or psychological insecurity about imminent danger, threats to security, or the notion that any day now, some catastrophe will make us all glad that we saved all these paper clips, empty water jugs, used sweatshirts, and broken treadmills.

Hoarders need not hoard "useless" objects: they may also hoard pets (cats, dogs, birds), money (bills hidden in a safe or mattress), food and drink, or items of sentimental value (papers from elementary school, photos, childhood toys). What distinguishes hoarding from collecting is that the latter discriminates with respect to more universal value or utility. A pronounced unwillingness to part with or discard items that you haven't touched or looked at in years may be a sign of crossing the line into compulsion.

## HOW TO RECOGNIZE:

Take a peek through their house windows: if you can't see anything for all the crap in the way—Bingo.

## TO BE FOUND:

People who have experienced poverty or financial setbacks may be especially prone to hoarding. The elderly, who often feel that life is increasingly beyond their control and that things and people are taken away from them, may also compensate by hoarding.

## HERO:

King Solomon leaps to mind: that dude had it *all*.

## THEIR IDEA OF FUN:

Flea markets, yard sales, liquidation sales, the "free" section on Craigslist, dumpster diving, curbside collecting.

## MOST DISTINCTIVE TRAIT:

Very hard to buy a gift for the person who has everything.

## BIGGEST CONTROVERSY:

Part of what makes "too much of anything a bad thing" is that anything in terrific volume will eventually sprout mold, attract insects, or interfere with one's ability to find the house bathroom.

## BIGGEST MISCONCEPTION ABOUT:

That they're incurably nuts. Hoarding is an obsessive/compulsive disorder and is treatable with therapy or medication.

## WHAT YOU MAY HAVE IN COMMON:

A collection of all your partner's love letters from years ago (it's just that the Hoarder keeps his or hers under a mammoth pyramid of other crap).

## BUZZWORDS:

"Mine!"

## SIGN OF FAN:

Admits that personal collection or store of cherished objects is "getting a little out of hand."

## SIGN OF GEEK:

Doesn't recognize half of the stuff in collection.

## SIGN OF SUPERFREAK:

Leases storage unit as living space because you can't even get the front door of that house open anymore.

# TRUSTAFARIANS

**ALSO KNOWN AS:**

*Weekend Toker, Trust Fund Hippie, Suburban Slummer, Poorgeoisie*

**JUST DON'T CALL THEM:**

*Spoiled Rich Kid, Yuppie Punk, Poser*

**CORE BELIEFS:**

*You can have your cake and eat it, too, and it's not only possible but socially and culturally okay to lead two lives.*

*[Insert poignant Grateful Dead lyrics here]*

—The Grateful Dead

## WHO THEY ARE:

The word "Trustafarian," while a spoof on "Rastafarian" (a member of a Jamaican religious movement, for whom smoking marijuana is a spiritual practice), could refer to any middle-class kid or moneyed young adult who walks the line between a hippie lifestyle and his or her white bread roots. The Trustafarian may not be aware of his or her nature, or that there's anything wrong with smoking a bone and then hiding the evidence when Mom and Dad visit for the weekend.

American Trustafarians often settle together in seemingly Bohemian neighborhoods with exclusive rent; hotspots around the country include Brooklyn, San Fransisco, and Boulder. And while they may blend into the background of metropolitan Americana, they know that their faded denim was likely purchased for the price of a Wal-Mart shopping spree.

While it's true that "Trustas" are shallow posers compared to their "Rasta" cousins, you can't be too hard on them: most people would rather play it safe than take the rebel thing all the way. Adolescence and college are times for the Trustafarian to thrive, so live and let live.

## HOW TO RECOGNIZE:

Look for the kid who only has one or two markers of hipster cred: e.g., the Bob Marley T-shirt among a drawerful of Polo shirts; the Grateful Dead poster cheek by jowl with those inspirational posters you find in corporate coffee rooms; the pot leaf pendant easily hidden under clothing.

## TO BE FOUND:

Prep schools, college, and universities, urban "ethnic" communities gentrified by recent college graduates and artists, Spring Break.

## HERO:

George Vanderbilt, the world's first Trustafarian—even though he was born in the 1860s.

## THEIR IDEA OF FUN:

Taking a walk on the mild side. The Trustafarian's interest in sticking it to the Man is not unlike the Native American practice of "counting coup": riding up close to the enemy, smacking him on the head, and galloping quickly and safely away on the idea that hurting your opponent's pride is tantamount to causing them serious injury.

## MOST DISTINCTIVE TRAIT:

Their deluded belief that they're rebels, punks, mavericks.

## BIGGEST CONTROVERSY:

The respectable haircut they got right before Thanksgiving break; the nice clothes at the back of their closet; the fact that they bought weed with birthday money from Nana.

### Careful Who You Trust

Sure, the Trustafarian seems like a cool dude or chick to know, 'cause they're your contact for scoring some weed. The only problem is, cops and narcs target the Trustafarian as an easy mark, because your middle-class stoner pal will roll over on you faster than the boulder in *Indiana Jones*.

## BIGGEST MISCONCEPTION ABOUT:

That they'll never amount to anything. Chances are good to excellent that they'll ditch the stoner persona as soon as circumstances require it for their own advancement.

## WHAT YOU MAY HAVE IN COMMON:

Most people want to be cool and still play by the rules.

## BUZZWORDS:

"Dude!"

## SIGN OF FAN:

Gets parents to buy a car without checking GPA.

## SIGN OF GEEK:

Holds a part-time, unpaid internship for several years after grad school while parents cover living costs—weed included.

## SIGN OF SUPERFREAK:

Buys T-shirts for the price of a department-store suit jacket.

# URBAN HOMESTEADERS

**ALSO KNOWN AS:**
Green Thumbs, Hippies

**JUST DON'T CALL THEM:**
Eco-Freaks, Martha Stewart

**CORE BELIEF:**
Charity toward the earth begins at home.

*"In order to live off a garden, you have to practically live in it."*
— cartoonist and wit Frank McKinney Hubbard (1868–1930)

## WHO THEY ARE:

Urban or suburban homeowners who, in their drive to reduce their "carbon footprint," push the boundaries of environmentalism.

If industry is slow to adopt "green measures," Urban Homesteaders bring the fight to the home front: fewer federal regulations and lawyers to deal with, and the only limits are to one's passion and imagination.

Insulate the windows! Toss out the TV! If it's yellow, let it mellow, and if it's brown, flush it down! The Urban Homesteader leaves no corner of the house uncut or untouched by his or her green thumbprint.

Urban Homesteaders are chronic canners and passionate about preserves, and they may be occasional bathers in the interests of saving water. Publications such as *The Tightwad Gazette* and *ecohome* magazine help the Urban Homesteader locate green contractors, low-flow showerheads, and solar-panel systems.

Statistics from LEED (the Leadership in Energy and Environmental Design) building certification system indicate that their projects to date have used $10 billion of "green materials," an industry expected to grow to $100 billion by 2020.

## HOW TO RECOGNIZE:

Dirt under fingernails, canned preserves in basement or cellar, compost in backyard, solar panels on roof, stationary bicycle hooked up to power television.

## TO BE FOUND:

Gardening in either backyard or front yard, on roof measuring space for solar panels, shopping for hybrid family cars.

## HERO:

Actor and green activist Ed Begley, Jr., whose TV show *Living with Ed* on the Planet Green channel chronicled his urban homesteading obsession.

## THEIR IDEA OF FUN:

Spending a few hours to save a few pennies (oh, and the earth, of course).

## MOST DISTINCTIVE TRAITS:

Working knowledge of personal water and kilowatt consumption; familiarity with what is recyclable and compostable; has calculated contribution to the 208 million tons of municipal solid waste Americans generate each year.

## BIGGEST CONTROVERSY:

If there's no limit to how much energy you can save, there's no limit to how much energy (and money) you can spend, greening your home.

## BIGGEST MISCONCEPTION ABOUT:

That the amount of money Urban Homesteaders spend retro-fitting their home with green technology cannot possibly be lower than what the green technologies save.

## WHAT YOU MAY HAVE IN COMMON:

Environmental concern, love of gardening and home cooking from scratch, neighbors who are sick of all the free eggplant you give them from your garden.

## BUZZWORDS:

The "zero-energy house" produces as much energy as it consumes. Also called "passive houses."

## SIGN OF FAN:

Starts vegetable and herb garden in backyard, grows dandelions just to make homemade wine.

## SIGN OF GEEK:

Dad's traditional policing of the thermostat ("I put it there for a reason!") extends into water use, light use, and recycling.

## SIGN OF SUPERFREAK:

Ultra-strict eco-standards in home drive college graduate kids out of the house, leaving parents to celebrate.

# SURVIVALISTS

**ALSO KNOWN AS:**
*Outdoorsmen, Rugged Individualists, Mountain Mikes*

**JUST DON'T CALL THEM:**
*Redneck Lunatics, Paranoid Apocalyptics*

**CORE BELIEF:**
*Be prepared (or at least be standing next to someone who is).*

*"In the struggle for survival, the fittest win out at the expense of their rivals because they succeed in adapting themselves best to their environment."*

—Charles Darwin (1809–1882)

## WHO THEY ARE:

Survivalists are men or women who train and equip themselves for survival in inhospitable circumstances.

The Survivalist believes—and rightly so—that modern civilization has rendered people soft and stupid, with no idea which star is the North Star and why we would need to know that anyway. The Survivalist need not be a Luddite, rejecting electronic gadgetry as something that compromises a person's independence, but they surely know what to do when there's no cell signal or the batteries in just about anything run out.

While some Survivalists foresee their skills called upon in the event of Armageddon, alien invasion, or the emergence of world government, other less fantastic scenarios put people in the Survivalist frame of mind: economic recession, terrorist attacks, viral epidemics, and natural disasters.

Hence, some Survivalists talk about their knowledge and skills as "emergency preparedness," which gives off less of a crazy mountain man vibe.

## HOW TO RECOGNIZE:

Water purification kit in their pantry, compass on their keychain.

## TO BE FOUND:

Stockpiling canned goods and MREs (meals-ready-to-eat), reflecting on what to do if any given situation takes a turn for the worse.

## HEROES:

Frontiersmen such as Daniel Boone or Davy Crockett, John Rambo (see movie *First Blood*), MacGyver (late-1980s action TV star known for resourcefulness).

## THEIR IDEA OF FUN:

Equipment shopping at Eastern Mountain Sports, L.L. Bean, or military surplus stores; singing along to Gloria Gaynor's "I Will Survive."

## MOST DISTINCTIVE TRAITS:

Resourcefulness, inventiveness, alertness, and willingness to secure protein in places you don't even want to know.

## BIGGEST CONTROVERSY:

The relatively few people who give survivalism a bad name: i.e., recluses and fringe-element extremists who consider stockpiling weapons a necessary component of survival. Unfortunately, these folks get all the press (usually when they're involved with something bad happening).

## BIGGEST MISCONCEPTION ABOUT:

That their skills are a manifestation of their insecurity and fear, and that such skills are unnecessary, given the probability of someone experiencing a prolonged catastrophe.

## WHAT YOU MAY HAVE IN COMMON:

Independent streak, self-reliance, love of making things, desire to test one's limits and endurance.

## BUZZWORDS:

"Urban Survivalism" refers to surviving in the city or suburbs, in the event of a natural disaster or some other major calamity such as a prolonged power outage; "Financial Survivalism" is skillful management of assets and investments, in case of world economic collapse; and "Military Survivalism" is arming oneself in the event of martial law or anarchy.

## SIGN OF FAN:

Watches *Man vs. Wild* on Discovery Channel.

## SIGN OF GEEK:

Buys DVDs of *Man vs. Wild*.

## SIGN OF SUPERFREAK:

Takes DVDs of *Man vs. Wild* into wild and watches them, having constructed a functioning DVD player out of pine cones, moss, and somehow human urine.

# HOUSEBOATERS

**ALSO KNOWN AS:**
*Sea Dogs, Salty Dogs, Retirees*

**JUST DON'T CALL THEM:**
*Waterfront Freeloaders, Water Squatters*

**CORE BELIEF:**
*Boat Sweet Home*

> *"It's marketed as a boat, it's sold as a boat,
> well, if it's a boat it's a boat."*
>
> —Virginia Boating Law Administrator Charlie Sledd
> (article, the *Capital* newspaper, 8/17/08)

## WHO THEY ARE:

Men and women whose permanent or full-time residence is, technically, a boat: that is, a structure that floats on water.

Houseboats need not be powered to function as a boat: they may be moored permanently in a marina, on a lake, or on some other body of water.

Fundamentally, Houseboaters are people who, when they say they want a house on the water, they really want a house on the water. Their reasons are various: a houseboat affords comfortable living and may be less expensive than an apartment or house on the ground; a houseboat may serve as temporary living quarters, while the occupant is looking for a house in the area; or it may just be plain fun to live on a boat all the time.

But is a houseboat a boat or a house? If Sonny Crockett, the detective from TV's *Miami Vice*, lives permanently on a sailboat, is he living in a houseboat? And what about rich people who live on yachts? What about houseboats that aren't shaped like boats?

If this sounds like splitting hairs, skip to the "Controversy" section.

The popularity of houseboats in America took hold in the years following World War II and continues to this day. You may see more elaborate and funky examples of houseboats on cable television programs about unusual homes and living spaces.

Of course, professional sailors and fishers live on boats, but they're out at sea. Houseboating provides a balanced alternative to that salty life for people who love both land and water.

## HOW TO RECOGNIZE:

Some boats have windows: Houseboats have window boxes full of flowers. Some boats have tackle boxes: Houseboats have mailboxes. Some boats have First Mates: Houseboaters may be on their Second or Third Mates.

## TO BE FOUND:

Lake and oceanfront properties; marinas and docks; coastal cities and towns.

### Film Flimsy on Houseboat Culture

The 1958 romantic comedy *Houseboat* starring Cary Grant and Sophia Loren does indeed feature a houseboat and all the hilarity that may ensue when rearing a family on one, but you may come away romanced more by the two glamorous stars than by the boat itself.

## HEROES:

David Gilmour, guitarist and singer for the rock group Pink Floyd, has a houseboat that contains its own recording studio, and the fictional action hero MacGyver lived on a houseboat. C'mon, can you possibly get cooler than that?

## THEIR IDEA OF FUN:

Showing off their homes, because chances are, they're more interesting per square inch than your home or apartment on land; and if Houseboaters don't like the scenery, they can start up the motor and move the whole house.

## MOST DISTINCTIVE TRAIT:

Usually neighborly but respectful of privacy (for being in such close proximity to other Houseboaters).

## BIGGEST CONTROVERSY:

Cities and states may not have regulations governing houseboats. As a result, Houseboaters may escape some real estate taxes and get waterfront property in the bargain. Too many houseboats in one area, and now we get into the issue of human waste disposal. Because many houseboats run on gasoline generators, there are carbon monoxide emissions, which may prove harmful to the environment and to the Houseboater.

## BIGGEST MISCONCEPTION ABOUT:

That they're social dropouts, hippies, and/or druggies.

## WHAT YOU MAY HAVE IN COMMON:

Love of the water, salt in your blood.

## BUZZWORDS:

A "barge" houseboat is a flat-bottomed boat, a "pontoon" houseboat is like a barge but rests on two buoyant cylindrical tubes, and "cruisers" are built for more speed and fewer people.

## SIGN OF FAN:

Sleeps on boat when it functions as "doghouse."

## SIGN OF GEEK:

Keeps houseboat permanently moored at marina (and is permanently mired in debt).

## SIGN OF SUPERFREAK:

Business card identifies homes as "New York, Paris, London, Pacific Ocean."

# BILDERBERGERS

**ALSO KNOWN AS:**
Members of the Bilderberg Group, Attendees of the Bilderberg Conference

**JUST DON'T CALL THEM:**
Members of ZOG, The Illuminati, The Trilateral Commission, the New World Order

**CORE BELIEF:**
Cooperation among nations—but . . . to what end? [cue music]

*"No comment."*

—the official Bilderberg member response

## WHO THEY ARE:

People—mostly men—who attend an annual invitation-only conference of major figures of politics and business from Europe, the United Kingdom, and the United States. The conference retains its name from its original meeting place in 1954, the Hotel de Bilderberg in the Netherlands.

The original purpose of the inaugural Bilderberg Conference was to promote "Atlanticism": that is, to brainstorm and discuss ways in which the United States and Europe could develop shared interests, goals, and understanding.

That, anyway, is the *stated* purpose. There isn't a Bilderberg Conference website that spells out who gets to go this year and what they're all planning to talk about. Reporters aren't allowed into the Conference, and any one of the roughly 100 annual attendees may not even reveal that they attended.

This absence of information about what goes on at the Bilderberg Conference has inspired many a theorist's imagination to run wild and accuse Bilderbergers of plotting world domination, world government, and what to do concerning the imminent alien colonization of Earth.

## HOW TO RECOGNIZE:

Wikipedia does have a list of attendees who have admitted to or have been identified as attending.

## TO BE FOUND:

Wherever the Conference is held, which could be anywhere in Europe, the U.K., or even the United States. Past U.S. locations have been in Georgia (1957, 1997), Virginia (1964, 2002, 2008), Vermont (1971), New Jersey (1978), and New York (1985, 1990).

## HERO:

Founder Józef Retinger (1888–1960), a Polish political advisor who founded what later became the European Union.

## THEIR IDEA OF FUN:

Keeping the world guessing.

## MOST DISTINCTIVE TRAITS:

They're the kind of people who don't drive their own cars, who don't drive in cars (just limousines), who don't carry much money because they don't do their own shopping or have to pay for meals, and who don't carry business cards because everyone already knows who they are.

## BIGGEST CONTROVERSY:

That what onlookers call secrecy, the Bilderberg Conference calls privacy.

## BIGGEST MISCONCEPTION ABOUT:

That being a Western group means being anti-Eastern; that the combined presence of business leaders and government officials implies collusion between the two toward policies that are mutually beneficial and contrary to the best interests of ordinary people.

## WHAT YOU MAY HAVE IN COMMON:

A reluctance to tell your spouse where you were last weekend, who you were with, and what you were doing.

## BUZZWORDS:

"No pictures, please," "I'm here as a tourist."

## SIGN OF FAN:

Knows someone whose cousin once worked for a company headed by someone who may or may not have been invited one year, hard to say.

## SIGN OF GEEK:

Camps out at Conference location with telephoto lens, and when security "escorts" him off the property, shouts "Roswell!"

## SIGN OF SUPERFREAK:

Isn't at liberty to tell you where or how he obtained the 2002 Bilderberg Conference table napkin that's framed in his den.

# DUMPSTER DIVERS

**ALSO KNOWN AS:**
*Bargain Hunters, Dump Diggers*

**JUST DON'T CALL THEM:**
*Garbage Pickers, Vultures, Parasites*

**CORE BELIEF:**
*In a country as materialistic and wasteful as America, "thrown out" is not as bad as it sounds.*

*"One man's trash is another man's treasure."*

—Anonymous

## WHO THEY ARE:

People who scavenge what others discard. We're not talking here about indigent people who literally explore dumpsters and trash bins for food with the fewest ants on it: "Dumpster Diver" may apply to anyone who looks first in someone else's material things before buying new. In this light, the Dumpster Diver may be seen as a necessary contributor to the ecological greening of America.

Naturally, this subculture looks first for what is free, but they are also willing to spend money on the second-hand, the used, or the item in need of small repairs.

Unless you have worked a summer on a sanitation truck or have volunteered at a Goodwill store, you cannot appreciate what some people throw away: indeed, some people throw things out not because they're broken or old or damaged, but because they've replaced them with newer things.

Americans represent 5 percent of the world's population, but somehow we generate 30 percent of the world's trash. Odds are, somewhere in that 30 percent are things worth keeping, and they're there for the pickings!

## HOW TO RECOGNIZE:

The day or night before "trash day," they drive around the neighborhood in their minivans or flat-bed pickup trucks; they also know when college kids in town leave for the summer, emptying their rentals curbside.

## TO BE FOUND:
City or town dumps, recycling centers, flea markets, garage sales, estate sales, auctions, consignment stores, second-hand shops.

## HEROES:
Saint Vincent de Paul, Goodwill, the Salvation Army.

## THEIR IDEA OF FUN:
Waiting until you sip your tea to reveal that the entire serving set was found in the trash.

## MOST DISTINCTIVE TRAITS:
Eye for potential, resale value, collectible value, ease with which something can be fixed.

## BIGGEST CONTROVERSY:
That bringing home stuff from the trash, the dump, or someone else's yard sale may also bring home mold, bacteria, insect larvae, and who knows what else.

## BIGGEST MISCONCEPTION ABOUT:
That they're poor, cheap, unhygienic, and don't recognize or appreciate quality.

## WHAT YOU MAY HAVE IN COMMON:
Limited budget, junk fetish, "free" fetish, fix-it ability, love of haggling.

### Dumpstering and the Law
Before you head out and dive headfirst into dumpsters looking for treasure, you seriously might want to consult your local police department about relevant laws and regulations. You may see an attractive dumpster next to a corporate office, but by diving into it, you may be trespassing on private property. If anything, local law enforcement can give you an idea as to how rigorously they enforce laws regarding Dumpster Diving.

## BUZZWORDS:
A "Freegan" is either an anti-consumerist or environmentalist who tries to reduce his or her "economic footprint" as much as possible and is likely to partake of Dumpster Diving, also known as "shopping at D-Mart."

## SIGN OF FAN:
Brings a load to the town dump, comes home with half a load.

## SIGN OF GEEK:
Drives an empty van or truck for no other reason than to hold pickings discovered while traveling.

## SIGN OF SUPERFREAK:
See the entry for "Hoarder," or watch the History Channel's show *American Pickers*.

# MUSIC

- "Ring"-Nuts
- KISS Army
- Punk Rockers
- Audiophiles
- Goths
- Rockabillies
- Grungers
- Rivetheads
- New Romantics
- Beatlemaniacs
- Dance Partiers
- Deadheads
- Phish Heads
- Rappers

# "RING"-NUTS

**ALSO KNOWN AS:**
Wagnerites

**JUST DON'T CALL THEM:**
Nazi Music Lovers (see Misconception section)

**CORE BELIEF:**
Fifteen hours of music represents a bottomless well of enjoyment, in which no detail is too small to be appreciated for its genius.

> *"I write music with an exclamation point!"*
> —Richard Wagner (1813–1883)

## WHO THEY ARE:

People who have an extraordinary devotion to or fascination with an operatic tetralogy by German composer Richard Wagner [VAHG-ner] officially titled *Der Ring des Nibelungen* but more commonly referred to as "The Ring Cycle."

Why focus obsessively on one—that is to say, four—operas? The nearest pop culture analogy would be to ask why rockers are particularly fond of Lynyrd Skynyrd's "Free Bird" (nine minutes long) or Led Zeppelin's "Stairway to Heaven" (almost eight minutes): it's great music, difficult to perform, and its unusual length enhances its legendary status.

Space here does not permit an appropriate explication of why and how Wagner's four operas represent a mammoth achievement in composition and performance. "The Ring Cycle," simply, is one of the most challenging operas for any orchestra or opera company to perform. Wagner intended all four operas to be performed together, so you'll need to block out on your calendar four nights at the opera at a total of about fifteen hours of music. Take that, Jimmy Page.

## HOW TO RECOGNIZE:

Endowed with what the Germans call (no kidding) "sitzfleisch," meaning sufficient strength in the butt to sit for long periods of time.

## TO BE FOUND:

Opera houses, symphony halls, the classical section of music stores, (and for women) shopping for helmeted horns with blonde braids to dress up as a Valkyrie.

## HERO:

Herr Maestro Wagner.

## THEIR IDEA OF FUN:

Giving comparative fifteen-hour listens to each of the many CD recordings of "The Ring Cycle."

## MOST DISTINCTIVE TRAIT:

A supernatural ability, in a symphony hall or opera house, to hold one's bladder.

## BIGGEST CONTROVERSY:

Besides quality of performance? Some orchestras or companies present individual operas from the tetralogy, which "Ring"-Nuts frown on.

## BIGGEST MISCONCEPTION ABOUT:

That adoration of Wagner makes them Nazis. Wagner had his own ideas about Jews, which, along with his music, may have made him appealing to Adolf Hitler. Wagner suffers to this day from associations with a man who rose to power roughly half a century after his death. All one can say is: Music is music, and

Hitler liked dogs and vegetarianism, too, but that doesn't mean all vegan dog lovers are fascists.

## WHAT YOU MAY HAVE IN COMMON:

An affection for the Bugs Bunny cartoon "What's Opera Doc?" in which Elmer Fudd and Bugs portray characters from "The Ring Cycle" and sing to its most famous melodies ("The Ride of the Valkyries" becoming "Kill the Wabbit").

## BUZZWORDS:

A "Valkyrie" (val-KEER-ee) is a figure from Norse mythology whose main job was to decide, on the battlefield, who lived and who died.

## SIGN OF FAN:

Has one "Ring Cycle" recording on CD, saves up (and girds up) to take in a four-night performance.

## SIGN OF GEEK:

Has more CDs of "Ring Cycle" than you have of The Beatles; takes in every performance of "Ring Cycle" in immediate area.

## SIGN OF SUPERFREAK:

Ready for this? In emulation of Deadheads, travels the world specifically to take in performances of "Ring Cycle."

# KISS ARMY

**ALSO KNOWN AS:**
White dudes and their chicks

**JUST DON'T CALL THEM:**
Knights/Kids in the Service of Satan; Fallen Star Wagon Hitchers; Gene Simmons Greed Enablers; Bygone Era Nostalgia Lovers; Rock Bottom Feeders

**CORE BELIEFS:**
Spectacle over substance; volume over value; vox populi over critical opinion; and rockin' classic tunes.

> *"You wanted the best and you got the best!*
> *The hottest band in the world—KISS!"*
>
> —KISS concert introduction

## WHO THEY ARE:

Devotees of the American glam rock band KISS (1973–⸮). The idea for a "KISS Army" originated with a fan, who commandeered a college radio station and played KISS records nonstop. This event still holds the record for most KISS songs ever played on a single radio station. Unfortunately, the designation of a fan base as an "army," coupled with the Gestapo lightning bolts in the band's logo, contributed to the parental misperception that KISS was out to recruit and corrupt the youth of America. That, and the fact that Gene Simmons's character is called "The Demon," so that must mean he's Satan.

In fact, the predominate theme in KISS music is not devil worship, anarchy, killing your parents or yourself: it's hot chicks and partying.

The band continues to tour and make appearances, albeit not as much or as often as in their glory days. Original members guitarist Ace Frehley and drummer Peter Criss have long since been replaced by other, younger musicians sporting their makeup. Look soon for the day when the entire line-up is replaced, and the brand—excuse me, the band—goes on indefinitely.

When he's not counting how many women he's slept with, Gene Simmons keeps track of the more than 3,000 licenses for KISS merchandise. Live Nation Merchandise, which oversees the KISS brand, claims the band's income over the past thirty-five years from merchandise is about, oh, half a billion dollars. Lick *that* up!

## HOW TO RECOGNIZE:

They are indistinguishable from the band (apart from the quality of the makeup job).

## TO BE FOUND:

Wherever authentic KISS products are sold.

## HEROES:

Gene, Paul, Ace, and Peter, plus those two guys who dress up like Ace and Peter.

## THEIR IDEA OF FUN:

Concerts, conventions, cover band concerts, cover convention concert bands, and buying KISS stuff.

## MOST DISTINCTIVE TRAIT:

Not all rock fans are willing to "party ev-er-y day," or at least pass out trying.

## BIGGEST CONTROVERSY:

The quality of the music. Members of the KISS Army will argue that their band is about more than music: it's performance, it's theater, it's entertainment. They might also point out that not every Rolling Stones album is a winner, either. They'll surely quote gold record stats to every critic you cite who says KISS sucks.

## BIGGEST MISCONCEPTION ABOUT:

That members of the KISS Army are fools perennially separated from their money. While some KISS products seem exploitative at first blush (okay, second or third, too—e.g., the KISS casket that doubles as a cooler), KISS fans probably spend the same amount of money as you spend on your own personal luxury items (or groceries).

## WHAT YOU MAY HAVE IN COMMON:

A love of fireworks and carny tricks.

## BUZZWORDS:

Demon, Star Child, Space Ace, Cat Man (i.e., the band's personae).

## SIGN OF FAN:

Attends KISS concert wearing KISS makeup.

## SIGN OF GEEK:

Attends KISS convention wearing KISS makeup as part of KISS cover band.

## SIGN OF SUPERFREAK:

Attends own wedding wearing KISS makeup.

# PUNK ROCKERS

**ALSO KNOWN AS:**
*Punks, Punkettes, Riot Grrrls (post-punk feminists)*

**JUST DON'T CALL THEM:**
*Skinheads (a totally different scene)*

**CORE BELIEFS:**
*Primal expression, unadorned music, authenticity, directness, and brutal honesty reign.*

*"Don't accept the old order: get rid of it."*

—John Lydon, aka "Johnny Rotten," lead singer of The Sex Pistols

## WHO THEY ARE:

Devotees or performers of punk music.

"Punk" originated in late 1970s England as an emerging style of music, fashion, and philosophy. At the time, the dominant music form was Disco, whose aesthetic was glittery high fashion and whose music was characterized by synthesized beats, string orchestration, and cattle calls to "get down and boogie." Punk was the reactionary bitch-slap to Disco, not only with its garish, low-rent wardrobe (torn shirts and jeans, studs and piercings, oddball haircuts) but also with its aggressive, three-chord guitar-and-drum musical attack. Disco had sapped 1960s-era rock of its social commentary and personal expression. Punk put it all back, celebrating the amateur musician over the Disco balladeer.

Punk's dyed Mohawk haircuts and safety-pin earrings of the 1970s and early 1980s may have faded away, but the musical form never has, inspiring new generations of "post-punk" bands: many who remain obscure (willfully or otherwise) and some who have achieved mainstream success, such as Green Day.

As more time goes by, "punk music" becomes harder to define, just as the spectrum of "rock," "country," and "blues" continues to widen. Some Punk Rockers would tell you that punk is all about attitude, anyway, but time has a way of changing attitudes, too.

## HOW TO RECOGNIZE:
Ramones or CBGB T-shirt, bright-colored hair dye, Dr. Martens boots.

## TO BE FOUND:
Sulking, moshing, posing for photos with tourists, adopting British slang ("wanker," "gob").

## HEROES:
Veterans The Sex Pistols, The Damned, Iggy Pop and The Stooges, Patti Smith ("Godmother of Punk"), The Ramones, and The Clash; more underground legends Black Flag and Hüsker Dü; and contemporary stars Offspring, Bad Religion, Social Distortion.

## THEIR IDEA OF FUN:
Thrashing, slam dancing (aka bashing into one another on dance floor), collecting early punk concert posters and memorabilia.

## MOST DISTINCTIVE TRAIT:
Volume, in both music and clothing.

## BIGGEST CONTROVERSY:
Punk was founded on youth, aggression, shock, and revolutionary rebellion— all things very hard to maintain as one reaches middle age. Also, punk's premium on street cred authenticity has been challenged since Green Day became a Broadway musical sensation and The Stooges were enshrined in a museum (of rock, no less).

## BIGGEST MISCONCEPTION ABOUT:
That punk fans are social malcontents arrested in a fantasy of adolescent rebellion, and that punk bands are amateurs who would only stop playing if you put sheet music in front of them.

## WHAT YOU MAY HAVE IN COMMON:
A belief in the ethic of DIY, or "do-it-yourself."

## BUZZWORDS:
"Anarchy" (symbolized by encircled letter A), "cow punk" (a punk-country music hybrid), "gutterpunks" (indigent street punks who panhandle), "pogoing" (jumping up and down like a pogo stick at concerts).

## SIGN OF FAN:
Owns seminal punk vinyl: *Horses* (Patti Smith), The Clash's eponymous debut, and *Never Mind the Bollocks Here's the Sex Pistols*.

## SIGN OF GEEK:
Applies silver spray paint to leather jacket and Dr. Martens, torn between nipple stud and dog collar.

## SIGN OF SUPERFREAK:
Gets tattoo of Black Flag logo on arm, starts band, spits at appreciative audience.

# AUDIOPHILES

> *"The first duty of love is to listen."*
> —Theologian Paul Tillich (1886–1965)

## WHO THEY ARE:

People (usually men) who can spend more on equipment to listen to music than on the music itself.

The advent of the mp3 and iPod revealed that the average consumer will gladly sacrifice some degree of sound quality in exchange for convenience and portability—not so the Audiophile, who wishes to get as close to the sound of live performance without actually hiring people to play and sing in his living room.

The cost of the audiophile entertainment system is limited only by what one is willing to spend: even stereo cables can run into the thousands of dollars. Companies such as Odyssey Audio will tempt the newbie with a budget $1,500 entry-level system, but beware of getting hooked! The first song is always free!

## HOW TO RECOGNIZE:

The "listening room" in their home or apartment has been specially designed or arranged to provide optimum fidelity, with walls and windows that are likely soundproofed.

## TO BE FOUND:

Reading *Stereophile* magazine or the online magazine *Audiophilia*; debating the merits of one particular cable over another.

## HEROES:

While you respect names like Sony, Aiwa, or Bose, Audiophiles give props to Bang & Olufsun, Canton, MartinLogan, Oracle, and KR Audio.

## THEIR IDEA OF FUN:

Listening, relistening, comparing and contrasting, discussing and debating results, then listening again.

## MOST DISTINCTIVE TRAIT:

Their taste in music tends to be as diverse as a gourmand's is in food.

## BIGGEST CONTROVERSY:

Novice or self-declared audiophiles—like aficionados of anything (wine, coffee, cars, etc.)—can fall into the facile belief that quality is directly proportional to price: that is, if a set of speakers or even a mere cable costs thousands of dollars, it must be better than less expensive alternatives. Some manufacturers of audiophile equipment have been accused of abetting this belief by marketing their products to promise ever-so-nuanced improvements in sound quality in exchange for a kid's college fund.

## BIGGEST MISCONCEPTION ABOUT:

That they prefer home listening to live performance; that they're philosophically opposed to iPods; that they know more about stereo equipment than about music itself.

## WHAT YOU MAY HAVE IN COMMON:

Disposable income, love of music, an ear for fine distinctions in vocal and instrumental performances, occasional or total preference of vinyl over CD, ability to decipher sophisticated instruction manuals.

## BUZZWORDS:

FLAC stands for "free lossless audio compression," a method of data formatting and coding that provides more audio "integrity" than an mp3; DVD-Audios and Super Audio CDs are discs that deliver more audio depth and range—kind of like Blu-Ray for music.

## SIGN OF FAN:

Drops $1,000 on handcrafted set of speakers.

## SIGN OF GEEK:

Drops everything to read review of $5,000 stereo cable on online fan forum.

## SIGN OF SUPERFREAK:

Drops dead when multimillion-dollar sound system produces a level of audio integrity that the human ear was never engineered to listen to.

# GOTHS

**ALSO KNOWN AS:**
Goth Rockers, Death Punks

**JUST DON'T CALL THEM:**
PIBs (People in Black), Ghouls

**CORE BELIEF:**
Once you've had black, there's no going back.

*"Whatever doesn't kill you makes you stranger."*

—Unknown, but paraphrased from Friedrich Nietzsche's remark that whatever did not kill him made him stronger

## WHO THEY ARE:

Thankfully, the people we identify as Goths are in no way affiliated with the barbaric Germanic tribe of Goths who plundered the Roman Empire in A.D. 377. If they were, mall cops would have a lot more to worry about.

Goths emerged in late-1970s England as the black sheep of punk, blossoming into wider popularity in the early 1980s, primarily through bands such as The Cure, The Cult, Jesus and Mary Chain, Siouxsie and the Banshees, Cocteau Twins, and more. Dominant themes were a macabre interest in death, Victorian nostalgia, vampiric clothing, and undertones of sadomasochism (e.g., an erotic appeal of chains, studs, piercings).

The more popular that Goth or any subculture becomes, the more variants and subgroups emerge, increasing internecine contention over Goth authenticity. Undeniably, however, Goth begins with the color black, worn in a way that projects *The Addams Family* as opposed to high fashion or Bohemianism.

## HOW TO RECOGNIZE:

They wear so much black, light and time actually bend around them.

## TO BE FOUND:

Loitering in cemeteries and shopping malls, Cosplaying, dressing up as normal kids for Halloween.

## HEROES:

Various, but include: Marilyn Manson; Robert Smith (The Cure); Gothic writers such as Lord Byron, Horace Walpole, Poe, Anne Rice, Donna Tartt.

## THEIR IDEA OF FUN:

Getting together in groups and creating pockets of depression at the shopping mall, donut shop, music store, or cemetery.

## MOST DISTINCTIVE TRAIT:

Glowering expression.

## BIGGEST CONTROVERSY:

Because the shooters behind the 1999 massacre at Colorado's Columbine High School were reportedly members of a Goth cadre (later reported to be untrue), popular perception equated Goths' macabre outlook with murderous intent. Of course, coroners are interested in death, too, but parents don't worry much about them.

## BIGGEST MISCONCEPTION ABOUT:

That their choice in fashion, makeup, music, and attitude is nothing more than an infantile expression of a desperate need for attention.

## WHAT YOU MAY HAVE IN COMMON:

Black eyeliner, purple lipstick, black lace, Dr. Martens boots.

---

### Can I Major in Goth Studies?

Early twentieth-century American literature has a subgenre that may be of interest to the untutored Goth south of the Mason-Dixon line: "Southern Gothic" fiction writers include William Faulkner, Flannery O'Connor, and Truman Capote. While you won't find protagonists with heavy black eye shadow here, you will find emphasis on the supernatural and the grotesque, usually with a moralistic condemnation of bigotry and prejudice.

---

## BUZZWORDS:

A "Net Goth" participates in Goth culture only online, a "Mansonite" is a devotee of Marilyn Manson, and a Goth air of superiority is being "Gother-than-thou."

## SIGN OF FAN:

Dyes hair black, paints fingernails and toenails black, starts reading British Romantic poetry in graveyards.

## SIGN OF GEEK:

Has more black in wardrobe than Hassidic rabbi, lets younger siblings raid closet in preparation for Halloween.

## SIGN OF SUPERFREAK:

Applies for summer internship at funeral home.

# ROCKABILLIES

**ALSO KNOWN AS:**
*Retro Hipsters, Guys 'n' Dolls, Greasers*

**JUST DON'T CALL THEM:**
*Musical Hicks, Rockin' Rubes*

**CORE BELIEF:**
*Swing, Daddy-O!*

> *"That rockabilly sound wasn't as simple as I thought it was."*
> —singer-songwriter Carl Perkins (1932–1988)

## WHO THEY ARE:

Devotees of a music genre that combines early rock and roll with country, or "hillbilly," music: hence, "rockabilly."

Rockabilly has a rich history dating back to the 1950s, but the rockabilly subculture—or Rockabilly Revival—begins with an American group that had to go to England to be successful enough to get a hit song in the United States: The Stray Cats, an early 1980s trio fronted by guitarist Brian Setzer.

Their hair in '50s-era pompadours and their hep-cat rockin' sound divided between drums, guitar, and an upright bass, The Stray Cats had a touch of the new about them: copious tattoos, a badass vibe, and a sneer of punk aggression in even their most upbeat hits (e.g., "Rock This Town," "Sexy and Seventeen").

Outside of music, Rockabillies today are associated most strongly with hot rod culture: vintage 1950s drag racers, fuzzy dice, flaming skulls and eight balls, and chicks who look like a cross between Ellie Mae Clampett and Bettie Page. Brian Setzer is still alive and kicking, introducing an element of big band swing into his rockabilly persona with The Brian Setzer Orchestra.

Rockabilly has broad appeal: consider that Carl Perkins's "Blue Suede Shoes" was the first million-selling country hit to cross over to both the pop and R&B charts.

## HOW TO RECOGNIZE:

Males are usually rail-thin, smokers, greasy fingernails from mechanic work; Females usually wearing Capri pants, Poodle skirts, blood-red lipstick, and may have more tats than their dudes.

## TO BE FOUND:

Vintage car conventions and festivals, rockabilly concerts.

## HEROES:

Carl Perkins, Wanda Jackson, Brian Setzer, artist Ed "Big Daddy" Roth.

## THEIR IDEA OF FUN:

Jumpin' and jivin', drag racing.

## MOST DISTINCTIVE TRAIT:

Conformity to gender stereotypes (macho guys, sultry gals) without being violently aggressive or meretriciously slutty.

## BIGGEST CONTROVERSY:

Relative to the punk, Goth, or metal crowd, Rockabillies are pretty benign. Arguably, the biggest controversy concerning them is that outside of the American South, you're not likely to hear contemporary rockabilly bands on the radio.

## BIGGEST MISCONCEPTION ABOUT:

That they're stuck in the 1950s, in a rigid and arcane music form. See "Buzzwords" for the current evolution of Rockabilly.

---

### Rockabilly Is as Rockabilly Does

That the difference between Rockabilly and what gets labeled "country rock" is that the former is more danceable, swingable, and sticks to a short spectrum of subjects: fast cars, fast women, hard times, and good times.

---

## WHAT YOU MAY HAVE IN COMMON:

A love of either early country or rock and roll.

## BUZZWORDS:

Rockabilly has informed several splinter musical genres, including "Gothabilly," "Punkabilly," and "Psychobilly," the latter of which infuses rockabilly with elements of horror, sci-fi, and even surf music.

## SIGN OF FAN:

Content to buy CDs, attend custom car conventions, apply Brylcreem to hair.

## SIGN OF GEEK:

Gets copious arm tats of black cats, eight balls, flaming skulls, hot rods.

## SIGN OF SUPERFREAK:

Becomes mechanic by day, upright bass player by night, '50s retro freak all the time.

# GRUNGERS

**JUST DON'T CALL THEM:**
*Posers, Sell-Outs, Old Hat, Irrelevant*

**CORE BELIEFS:**
*Honesty, directness, simplicity, emotivity.*

*"Pure grunge! Pure noise! Pure shit!"*

—Mark Arm of band Mudhoney, describing his then-band Mr. Epp and the Calculations to Seattle zine *Desperate Times*, in what is cited as the first use of the term "grunge"

## WHO THEY ARE:

Devotees or practitioners of a mid-1980s punk/hard rock hybrid, popularly thought of as originating in Seattle, WA.

Every nascent music form is a reaction to a pre-existing one, adding to and subtracting from a set of influences. In the case of Grunge, musicians were reacting against the flashy aesthetic of mid-'80s New Wave, as well as heavy metal's feathered hair, shredding arpeggio guitars, and tight Spandex. Grungers drew on punk's raw energy (while toning down its nihilistic theatrics) and borrowed a dash of introspective angst from indie rock. Instead of donning uniforms of Goth black, studded leather, or baggy pants with backward baseball caps, Grungers performed in whatever they woke up in that morning—usually the plaid shirts of lumbering communities of the American Northwest.

The twin-headed mainstream spawn of Grunge were Pearl Jam and Nirvana, with dozens of less successful relatives in their tree. When Nirvana frontman Kurt Cobain shot himself dead in 1994, the mainstream media tried to spin his suicide as "The Day the Music Died" for Generation X, stretching to compare his passing to the murder of John Lennon, fourteen years earlier.

## HOW TO RECOGNIZE:

Uncombed hair, unshaven faces, torn jeans, plaid shirts, sullen demeanor.

## TO BE FOUND:

Basements, garages, at which parental cries of "turn it down" are directed.

## HEROES:

The most famous are Kurt Cobain and Eddie Vedder, but having more current and remotely known examples improves your grunge cred rating.

## THEIR IDEA OF FUN:

Spinning the straw of self-absorbed high school poetry into thrashingly hard music gold.

## MOST DISTINCTIVE TRAITS:

High volume, high energy, possibly high bandmates.

## BIGGEST CONTROVERSY:

That the genre died too young from overexposure in the media and the moneying mainstreaming of key players.

## BIGGEST MISCONCEPTION ABOUT:

That too much success killed Kurt Cobain. Alas, Cobain had more urgent problems: manic depression and heroin addiction. Almost two centuries earlier, twenty-five-year-old Romantic poet John Keats was said to have died not from tuberculosis but from a broken heart over bad reviews. Nice stories, but just that—stories.

## WHAT YOU MAY HAVE IN COMMON:

DIY attitude, garage band or punk aesthetic, tinnitus.

## BUZZWORDS:

In 1992, Sub Pop Records underling Megan Jasper played the *New York Times* and Britain's *Sky* magazine for fools, releasing to both a bogus list of "grunge speak." Jasper's prank was meant to irritate mainstream media looking to scoop what "the kids" were into. Example: Jasper claimed that grunge slang for "hanging out" was "swingin' on the flippety-flop."

## SIGN OF FAN:

Grunge stalwarts on heavy iPod rotation: Nirvana, Pearl Jam, Soundgarden, Mudhoney, Alice in Chains.

## SIGN OF GEEK:

Playlist features more esoteric Grunge bands: Mono Men, Green River, Hammerbox, Screaming Trees.

## SIGN OF SUPERFREAK:

Forms Grunge tribute band, available for alt-weddings, punk bar mitzvahs, and anti-corporate functions.

# RIVETHEADS

**ALSO KNOWN AS:**
*Fans of industrial music*

**JUST DON'T CALL THEM:**
*Goths*

**CORE BELIEFS:**
*Music should be progressive and forward-looking, experimental and reflective of the technological age in which we live; too much of mainstream music is either stuck in idle (latching on to whatever trend is current) or in reverse (indulging a superficial nostalgia for the past).*

*"I want to be a machine."*

—American artist Andy Warhol (1928–1987)

## WHO THEY ARE:

People who are fans or performers of industrial music, a late-twentieth-century experimental rock music form characterized by harsh dissonance, heavy percussive elements, and subject matter that is intentionally transgressive.

Industrial music performers typically borrow imagery and fashion from totalitarian or fascist regimes as a way either of opposing such philosophies or projecting an image of power and authority.

The term "Rivethead" is not new: it's long been used to describe either workers on an automobile assembly or workers who use a type of metal fastener (the "rivet") to build steel frames of buildings and other structures. The term serves a double meaning, as to be "riveted" is to be inextricably attached to or fascinated with something.

## HOW TO RECOGNIZE:

Males—Imagine a less androgynous Goth with a factory day job: i.e., a militaristic or industrial macho look, camo or leather pants, heavy boots, plus goggles or even a gas mask; Females—Picture a Goth chick with less makeup and less of a death vibe: i.e., black leather, stiletto heels, military accoutrements, sort of a junior dominatrix.

## TO BE FOUND:

At industrial music raves.

## HEROES:

In addition to a host of underground artists, more recognizable names such as Kraftwerk and Frank Zappa.

## THEIR IDEA OF FUN:

Shopping at the Army & Navy Surplus stores, BDSM shops, tattoo and piercing parlors, and the dark end of the makeup counter.

## MOST DISTINCTIVE TRAITS:

Openness to experimentation, innovation; aggression, assertiveness; Goth scorn.

## BIGGEST CONTROVERSY:

That their adoption of militaristic clothing and industrial bands' appropriation of totalitarian symbolism (see the band Laibach) represents a set of political views or affiliates them with groups like Skinheads, Neo-Nazis, or even nihilistic Punks. It's all about fashion, music, and striking a pose meant to unnerve Mom and Dad, so take it easy, Homeland Security.

## BIGGEST MISCONCEPTION ABOUT:

That their penchant for black, leather, rebellion, tattoos, and transgressiveness in any way affiliates them with Goths. It's kind of like grouping together the kids in the drama club and the kids

from metalshop because they go to the same school.

## WHAT YOU MAY HAVE IN COMMON:

CDs by Kraftwerk, although technically they're Electro-Industrial.

## BUZZWORDS:

"EBM" is Electronic Body Music, or industrial music you can dance to.

### Live It, Rivet, Dare It, Wear It

The Rivethead preoccupation with fashion is inescapably related to their anxiety over being confused for subcultures they profess to hate: Goths, Punks, Cyber-Punks, Metalheads, Death Rockers, etc. The fact that so many subcultures claim black as their color of choice contributes to the confusion. Hence, Rivetheads emphasize a military or mechanical look.

## SIGN OF FAN:

Music playlist at work heavy with extended Industrial tracks, makes him/her more productive.

## SIGN OF GEEK:

Scouts out warehouse and factory district for potential Rivet Rave.

## SIGN OF SUPERFREAK:

Elects to learn drums, by which he means synthesized percussion pads and a series of metal barrels struck with sledgehammers.

# NEW ROMANTICS

**ALSO KNOWN AS:**
New Wavers

**JUST DON'T CALL THEM:**
'80s One-Hit Wonders

**CORE BELIEF:**
Girls (and boys) just want to have fun.

> *"Hey hey! What's this I see? I thought this was a party! Let's dance!"*
> —Ren McCormack (played by Kevin Bacon), *Footloose* (1984)

## WHO THEY ARE:

Devotees and performers of an early 1980s music trend out of England. The New Romantics sound was upbeat synthesizer pop, engineered for dancing and the top 10 hit list.

The musical dawn of the 1980s saw Disco in its death throes, with fans and critics alike eager for the Next Big Thing: it came in the form of a "Second British Invasion," accelerated by a new medium called MTV. New Romantic bands who took most advantage of the music video form achieved the biggest success: Duran Duran's record sales are neck-and-neck with the likes of music legend Bob Dylan at 70 million albums and singles worldwide.

But as music trends go, New Wave was short-lived, dying out mid-decade as the airwaves were dominated by Bruce Springsteen, Madonna, The Police, Prince, and U2.

The New Romantics fashion sense borrowed heavily from the androgyny of David Bowie and the feathered look of glam rockers such as Roxy Music and The New York Dolls. Today, it's seen as virtually synonymous with "the '80s look": angular shapes, pastel and neon colors, dashing, daring, and all dolled up.

And call the songs one-hit wonders if you wish, but they maintain a strong appeal among the demographic designated in the early 1990s as "Generation

X" (which was also the name of the band Billy Idol was in, prior to his solo success).

## HOW TO RECOGNIZE:

"Quiff" hairdo, suitjackets with padded shoulders (for boys *and* girls).

## TO BE FOUND:

DJing the "Eighties Lunch" on your local radio station; attending "'80s night" at bar, night club, or bowling alley.

## HEROES:

Musical fashion plates David Bowie, Bryan Ferry, Boy George, Adam Ant.

## THEIR IDEA OF FUN:

Reaping the wild wind (cf. Ultravox), tumbling 4 ya (cf. Culture Club), standing and delivering (cf. Adam and the Ants), feeling fascination (cf. The Human League).

## MOST DISTINCTIVE TRAIT:

Now middle-aged.

## BIGGEST CONTROVERSY:

That the New Romantics abetted the popular belief that "rock is dead," replacing skilled musicians with synthesized instruments and operators who pushed buttons. (Witness the keyboard playing in A Flock of Seagulls' video "I Ran.") Bear in mind, however, that some people will always think rock died with Jimi Hendrix.

## BIGGEST MISCONCEPTION ABOUT:

That they still have, and listen to, New Romantic music on the original vinyl.

## WHAT YOU MAY HAVE IN COMMON:

An attachment to mousse and other hair products; an electronic drum kit and "keytar" (electronic keyboard slung over shoulder).

## BUZZWORDS:

The "safety dance," from a song of the same title by Men Without Hats, involves an abrupt curving of the arms into an "S" formation. As with all things New Romantic, watch the video.

## SIGN OF FAN:

Listens to New Romantic music for fun or a goof, notes that some of it has held up over time.

## SIGN OF GEEK:

Listens to New Romantic music without irony or realization that most of it hasn't held up over time.

## SIGN OF SUPERFREAK:

Forms '80s New Romantic tribute band and just makes cool songs sound worse.

# BEATLEMANIACS

**ALSO KNOWN AS:**
*Beatlefans, Lennonists, McCartneyites*

**JUST DON'T CALL THEM:**
*Dinosaur Lovers, Old Farts*

**CORE BELIEF:**
*All you need is love.*

> *"Me auntie used to say, 'The guitar's all right for a hobby,*
> *but it won't earn you any money!'"*
>
> —John Lennon (1940–1980)

## WHO THEY ARE:

Lifelong, diehard fans of The Beatles, a 1960s-era British quartet of pop singer-songwriters John Lennon (1940–1980), Paul McCartney (1942– ), George Harrison (1943–2001), and Ringo Starr (born Richard Starkey, 1940– ). Eight years as a band, twelve albums made, and they changed the world.

The handy thing about Beatlemaniacs is that they can translate groaning bookshelves of scholarship about The Beatles into shorthand explanations of why the group is so enduringly special. This humble band of boys with no formal music education has sold more albums in the United States than any other musical artist; they have had more number one albums in the United Kingdom than any other artist; and their 1965 ballad "Yesterday" is the most covered song ever, with more than 3,000 recorded versions. The list of achievements, like the final chord of "A Day in the Life," goes on and on.

What distinguishes the Beatlemaniac from the average fan is a lifelong dedication that transcends just buying the CDs. The Beatlemaniac finds the Fab Four an endless wellspring of inspiration and fascination, as well as enjoyment. If a new book comes out, they read it. If a bootleg or unauthorized mash-up hits the web, they download it.

Even the diehard dedication of "Deadheads," "Phishheads," and Jimmy Buffet's "Parrotheads" cannot compare to Beatlemaniacs, who have resources and references aplenty to tell them what instrument was used on what song and how said song was written and where and why and with whom. (Example: McCartney wrote "Hey Jude," the longest song then to top the British charts at more than seven minutes, as a cheer-up tune for Lennon's son Julian during John's divorce, and the song's fade-out chorus—Na, na, na na!—is longer than the verse.)

## HOW TO RECOGNIZE:

They indoctrinate their young, as early as *in utero*, to The Beatles catalog; they're also the only tourists braving traffic at Abbey Road to get the perfect picture.

## TO BE FOUND:

Since 1974, a Beatles "Fest" convention has been held in the New York area, bringing together tons of fans, Beatle memorabilia, and B-list Beatle celebs.

## HEROES:

Besides the obvious: producer George Martin, engineer Geoff Emerick, manager Brian Epstein.

## THEIR IDEAS OF FUN:

Playing the video game, The Beatles: Rock Band; making pilgrimages to England.

## MOST DISTINCTIVE TRAIT:

Tendency to lapse into English accent (aka the "Linda McCartney Syndrome").

## BIGGEST CONTROVERSIES:

Whether or not Yoko broke up The Beatles is old hat. Current arguments concern the handling of the catalog, the quality of the 2009 remastered albums, and when or if the megatonnage of Beatle bootlegs should be officially released.

## BIGGEST MISCONCEPTION ABOUT:

That they are sworn enemies of The Rolling Stones.

## WHAT YOU MAY HAVE IN COMMON:

A love of hook-laden, upbeat pop.

## BUZZWORDS:

"Fab" and "gear" (Beatlemania-era slang for "cool"); moptops.

## SIGN OF FAN:

Sings along with every song in the car and at home.

## SIGN OF GEEK:

Sings Paul's harmony parts, just to impress the hell out of you.

## SIGN OF SUPERFREAK:

Learns to play Paul's bass lines left-handed; gladly dedicates time to give comparative listen to bootleg takes eight and nine of "Strawberry Fields Forever"; blogs findings.

# DANCE PARTIERS

*"I'm on the list, they just forgot to write my name down."*

*"I know the owner."*

*"It's just me and my friend Ben Franklin."*

(Or just about anything that will get them past the doorman.)

## WHO THEY ARE:

Young people who attend organized or improvised dance parties or festivals, formerly known as Raves.

In the late 1980s and 1990s, "Raves" got (some would say, earned) a bad reputation for being dance parties where teenagers could listen to industrial music, play with glowsticks, drop Ecstasy, and spend the evening feeling each other. Police crackdowns and media hysteria inspired the trend to call a rose by another name, hence the plethora of alternate terms:

**Squat Parties**—Impromptu or hastily planned dance events held at abandoned or unused buildings, with location and time relayed through cell phones, Twitter, or similar media to avoid attention of police.

**Free Parties**—Don't show up without your wallet: the "free" refers to freedom from the controls and regulations of a licensed dance environment: so while you're not invited or encouraged to do drugs, there are no bouncers or security to hassle you either—hence the reason why police and parents frown on such events.

**Acid House or Trance Parties—**
Dance events in which the music is of a particular genre of house music emphasizing hypnotic, wordless, repetitive rhythms.

Perhaps as a way to dignify or restore a positive image to their "scene," some Dance Partiers defend their dance activities as a movement whose primary virtues are peace, love, happiness, respect, inclusiveness, and other good stuff.

To be fair, Dance Parties need not be illegal or secret. Student organizations, youth clubs, and even churches may organize their own version of Dance Parties as a way to discourage young people from attending the illicit ones.

## HOW TO RECOGNIZE:

Wrists heavy with colored admission bracelets; constantly checking cell phone or BlackBerry for updates to Party locations and times; sweat stains on clothing.

## TO BE FOUND:

Among teens, young adults, and people whose time and money have yet to be sapped by parenthood.

## HEROES:

DJs (or, more currently, "MP3Js"), who can develop cult followings to rival the artists they play.

## THEIR IDEA OF FUN:

Yelling over the music; searching for friends through the ambient fog or soap suds; inventing alibis to use on Mom and Dad; pleading with police to just "be cool."

## MOST DISTINCTIVE TRAIT:

Ability to move quickly: on the dance floor, or out the nearest exit when Narcs show up.

## BIGGEST CONTROVERSY:

Fly-by-night Dance Parties don't consider themselves legally obligated to provide clean chairs, clean bathrooms, or even a clean alley in which to throw up. They will not be held responsible for missing or stolen personal items or for any other circumstance that relates to your physical, mental, or emotional health.

## BIGGEST MISCONCEPTION ABOUT:

That they're all high on Ecstasy, ketamine, amphetamines, cocaine, or Red Bull spiked with vodka.

## WHAT YOU MAY HAVE IN COMMON:

Ignorance of formal dance steps; short record of "juvey"; tinnitus, hangover, and/or laryngitis.

## BUZZWORDS:

A "superclub" is a night club or dance club that occupies several stories of a single building, or else occupies square footage usually reserved for a football field.

## Safety Dance

Clubbing or Dance Partying overseas can carry some risk: terrorists see dance clubs as an easy way to target large groups of innocent, unsuspecting victims. Domestic Dance Partying carries more of a risk of fire safety, so as soon as you walk in the door, acquaint yourself with the exits.

### SIGN OF FAN:
Considers going out to one dance club "clubbing."

### SIGN OF GEEK:
Designates certain days of the week for Dance Partying, such as only days whose name ends in "-day."

### SIGN OF SUPERFREAK:
Photos of vacation to Ibiza are all blurry and uneven cell phone shots, owing to near-total time spent at Dance Parties.

# DEADHEADS

**ALSO KNOWN AS:**
Dead Freaks, Dead Fans

**JUST DON'T CALL THEM:**
Old Farts and Young Hippie Wannabes

**CORE BELIEF:**
Music as communal experience.

*Any retrospective reference to the length and strangeness of the "trip."*

## WHO THEY ARE:

Fans of The Grateful Dead, a San Francisco-based band who combined American blues, folk, and psychedelic rock into their own unique sound, often embellished with jamming and improvisation.

Between their genesis in 1965 and their dissolution thirty years later upon the death of de facto leader Jerry Garcia, The Dead performed more than 2,000 concerts—which averages out to about seventy-five gigs a year. Favoring road performance over aiming for mainstream radio airplay, The Dead quickly became a "cult band" followed around the country by loyal fans.

By the late 1970s and early 1980s, Deadheads started selling their own band merchandise (or other wares) at concerts, as a way of generating travel money. Most bands would have nipped this practice in the bud, but the Dead—known to nip a few buds themselves—were cool with it, as they were with fans recording bootlegs of Dead shows.

Sure, Deadheads all look like hippie stoners, starry-eyed and tie-dyed riff raff, bearded and pony-tailed or dreadlocked, but what of it? Go to a Goth concert, a metal concert, or an old-time big band concert and see how heterogeneous the crowds are there.

## HOW TO RECOGNIZE:

On their cars, backpacks, or dorm room walls, you will see one of the following: a red, white, and blue skull with a lightning bolt through it; a chorus line of rainbow-colored dancing bears; a skull adorned with roses; an Uncle Sam skeleton; a jester skeleton with a flute; dancing terrapin turtles; or Jerry Garcia.

## TO BE FOUND:

Currently, at Phish concerts, that band having assumed some of the mantle of worship among Deadheads post-1995.

## HEROES:

The band: aka Tom Constanten, Jerry Garcia, Donna Jean Godchaux, Keith Godchaux, Mickey Hart, Bruce Hornsby, Bill Kreutzmann, Phil Lesh, Ron "Pigpen" McKernan, Brent Mydland, Bob Weir, Vince Welnick.

## THEIR IDEA OF FUN:

Truckin'.

## MOST DISTINCTIVE TRAITS:

The tie-dye shirt, the peasant skirt, the uncombed hair (Deadhead bedhead?), the laid-back vibe.

## BIGGEST CONTROVERSY:

Identifying at what point The Dead "stopped bein' The Dead, man." Who you ask and what answer they give will clue you in to what level of Deadhead they are. Was it when the band left San Fran? Was it when they scored their one-and-only number one hit with "Touch of Gray"? Was it when Jerry died? The debate continues.

## BIGGEST MISCONCEPTION ABOUT:

That there's no middle ground between the longtime, hippie-styled, road-travelin' fan and the just-got-on-board, yuppie college kid who likes the band but knows very little about them.

### Archival Dead

Usually, literary authors leave their "archives" to a college or university, but The Grateful Dead may be the first band to do so. In 2008, the Dead donated a treasure trove of audio and video recordings, plus memorabilia and merchandise, to the University of California at Santa Cruz. Since you can no longer go to a Dead concert, at least you can pile into a van and make a road trip pilgrimage to the UCSC archives.

## WHAT YOU MAY HAVE IN COMMON:

A love of American music (bluegrass, jazz, folk); an interest in long, extended guitar or drum jams; a "weed connection."

## BUZZWORDS:

"Wookies" are hirsute, scraggly Deadheads (note the spelling change to avoid legal problems with Lucasfilm Ltd.); "Wharf Rats" are Deadheads who help each other stay clean and sober; "Spinners" use Dead music in religious services . . . well, in their religion anyway: The Church of Unlimited Devotion.

## SIGN OF FAN:

Digs the Dead, has a few CDs, maybe a bumper sticker.

## SIGN OF GEEK:

Has held on to all his Dead bootlegs on audio cassette.

## SIGN OF SUPERFREAK:

All his bootleg Dead audio cassettes were made on location, although he seriously can't remember taping any of them, dude.

# PHISH HEADS

**ALSO KNOWN AS:**
Phish Fans, Phish Phans, Phish Phriends, Phish Phamily (Get it yet?)

**JUST DON'T CALL THEM:**
Deadhead Wannabes

**CORE BELIEF:**
No Bogarting.

*"Each of our 900 shows so far was different—maybe that's what*
*makes the fans come back to our gigs time and again. And that they're*
*always part of the show. Phish concerts are a communal experience."*
—Phish keyboardist Page McConnell (1963– )

## WHO THEY ARE:

Fans of the multigenre jam band Phish.

The band Phish began life, unironically, as a Grateful Dead cover band at the University of Vermont in 1983. Since then the band has evolved into a kind of "reincarnated Dead," playing original music, jamming, touring, cultivating a loyal fan base, and emulating the same musical and performance virtues of the 1960s band that inspired them.

With more than twenty officially released albums under their belts, Phish has been on-again, off-again over the years and remains a going concern at this writing.

Being a Phish Fan (or Phan) doesn't carry the same contrarian, counter-culture cred that being a Deadhead did for the hippies of the 1960s: it's more or less saying you're laid-back, kind of earthy-crunchy, probably pro-environment and liberal, young, activist, white, and cool with the Dave Matthews Band as well.

Both Phish and the Dead are all about live shows, are cool with fans recording and trading bootlegs, and have been known to have fans follow them on tour around the country. So what's the difference? Basically, Phish has more of a jazz flavor, while the Dead has more of a folk flavor.

## HOW TO RECOGNIZE:
Picture a Deadhead, but not as grungy and too young to remember a President before Ronald Reagan.

## TO BE FOUND:
Eating Ben & Jerry's "Phish Food" flavor ice cream (because "Cherry Garcia" is sold out).

## HEROES:
Band members Trey Anastasio, Mike Gordon, Jon Fishman, Page McConnell; former members Marc Daubert and Jeff Holdsworth; and Chris Kuroda (aka CK5), the dude who runs the light show at concerts.

## THEIR IDEA OF FUN:
The unorthodoxy of the band, who change set lists from concert to concert, have been known to announce impromptu performances in unusual locations, and who sell soundboard recordings via their website, *www.phish.com*.

## MOST DISTINCTIVE TRAIT:
Enjoyment of band's latest escapades and performances enhanced by short-term memory loss, so it all seems new.

## BIGGEST CONTROVERSY:
Haters who think of Phish as being a step above The Monkees (i.e., a highly derivative band who cannot hold a candle to their inspiration), as well as a lame outlet for middle-class white kids to indulge in hippie nostalgia.

## BIGGEST MISCONCEPTION ABOUT:
The above controversy, which originates among people who likely have never seen the group in concert and own none of their CDs (or bootlegs).

## WHAT YOU MAY HAVE IN COMMON:
Hippie nostalgia, relaxed personal hygiene, leg and/or facial hair, disaffection toward "classic rock" FM radio format, love of music jams, Grateful Dead bootleg collection.

## BUZZWORDS:
The "Phish Fellowship" is a fan organization dedicated to the clean and sober appreciation of live performances, and the "Phish Green Crew" are fans who volunteer to pick up trash and other detritus after a concert.

## SIGN OF FAN:
Circulates petition to have Phish play at college.

## SIGN OF GEEK:
Attends college near upcoming Phish concert.

## SIGN OF SUPERFREAK:
Loves Phish music so much, is actually inspired to listen to jazz.

# RAPPERS

> *"Love will make a dog howl in rhyme."*
>
> —British Renaissance dramatist Francis Beaumont (1584–1616)

## WHO THEY ARE:

Practitioners of a spoken-word style of musical expression that achieved its biggest mainstream success in the early 1980s and is now associated most strongly with hip-hop music.

Rap—as a rhythmic verbal execution against a strong background beat—has deep roots in African-American culture, going all the way back to the era of American slavery. Arguably, the rapidly improvised nonsense lyrics of "scat" that appear in Jazz are a form of rapping, but to most people of a certain age, the 1979 hit song "Rapper's Delight" by The Sugarhill Gang was the opening salvo in rap's campaign. In the early 1980s, music magazines such as *Rolling Stone* started writing about black kids in Washington, D.C. challenging each other to rap contests and creating a brazen new trend in music.

Jump ahead thirty years to the present: "Rap" is more a verb than a noun, the preferred noun being "Hip-Hop." Rapping continues to be a rich wellspring of creativity and innovation. It's no longer a joke for white people to rap (unless it's Madonna, rapping about her soy lattés), and rap has fused with other music forms to create grime (Hip-Hop and Garage), rapcore (Hip-Hop, punk, funk) and rap metal.

## HOW TO RECOGNIZE:

Among men: casual, usually loose-fitting dress; sunglasses indoors; baseball cap askew on head; conspicuous neck and hand jewelry. Among women: flashier, usually tight-fitting dress; awkward use of hand "gang signals"; more of a tendency than men to relapse into actual singing.

## TO BE FOUND:

Always with a notebook, ready to rock a rhyme.

## HEROES:

Too numerous to mention, too invidious to suggest.

## THEIR IDEA OF FUN:

Chumping the style of sucker MCs.

## MOST DISTINCTIVE TRAIT:

Originality.

## BIGGEST CONTROVERSY:

Any African-American music form has aroused suspicion and fear from the Caucasian community. Jazz, Blues, Rock and Roll, Rap: they've all been accused of promoting hedonism, rebelliousness, a laxity of morals, and a celebration of sins such as lust and avarice. Rap's "rap" is encouraging violence and misogyny, but if anything is "old school," it's this tired canard. The scene is now far too varied to be so pigeonholed.

### Race to Rap

White people can rap: Eminem, The Beastie Boys, Slug, and at least a few more. Strangely, though, there are few more powerful conveyers of "whiteness" than rap. The ultimate rap insult, in fact, is to call someone "Vanilla Ice," the first white mainstream rapper.

## BIGGEST MISCONCEPTION ABOUT:

That melodic singing is harder than rapping. Sophisticated rapping requires formidable vocal/breathing technique.

## WHAT YOU MAY HAVE IN COMMON:

An interest in busting a move.

## BUZZWORDS:

"Freestylin'" is improvisational rapping and likely takes place in the context of a Rap Contest. Rappers may take to rhythmic insulting of one another, known in African-American oral tradition as "the dozens."

## SIGN OF FAN:

Raps along to lyrics of favorite Hip-Hop songs.

## SIGN OF GEEK:

Mixes own beats, pens own rhymes, shares with friends.

## SIGN OF SUPERFREAK:

Braves Rap Contest and wins, fool.

# SPORTS AND GAMES

- Jan Ken Pon Players
- MMORPGers
- Dungeon Masters
- Jugglers
- Bodybuilders
- Yoginis
- Skaters
- Spelunkers
- Rodeoers
- Thru-Hikers
- NASCAR Fans
- Marathoners

# JAN KEN PON PLAYERS

**ALSO KNOWN AS:**

*Players of Rock-Paper-Scissors, aka Janken, Rochambeau*

**JUST DON'T CALL THEM:**

*People who don't know how to toss a coin or make up their minds*

**CORE BELIEF:**

*The determination of Jan Ken Pon is absolute, irrefutable, and eternally binding.*

> *"One, two, three times, shoot!"*
>
> *"Ro! Cham! Beau!"*
>
> *"Ching, Chang, Chong!"*
>
> *"Rock, Paper, Scissors, Shoot!"*
>
> —Traditional

## WHO THEY ARE:

Players of an ancient hand game recognized cross-culturally as a means of selection: e.g., who goes first, who gets the last piece of pie, who has to walk the dog, who is awesomest. While there is some element of strategy and probability to the game (e.g., scissors is considered the least likely choice), Jan Ken Pon is seen as a fair and impartial method of selection between two or more people.

As evidence that any game or hobby can achieve official organizational status, there is both a USA Rock Paper Scissors League (founded 2006) and a World Rock Paper Scissors Society (originally founded in England as the "Paper Stone Scissors Club," in 1842—yes, 1842).

The appeal to Jan Ken Pon Players is that the game can be played anywhere, any time, for any reason, and with no game pieces beyond what's at the end of your wrist. The rules are so simple, they arguably transcend language—until you get into a debate as to whether Paper "wraps" Rock or Rock beats Paper to a pulp.

## HOW TO RECOGNIZE:

Pumping fists at chest level, releasing into hand gesture.

## TO BE FOUND:

Wherever disputes need to be settled, either on the playground or, no kidding, in federal court—see the 2006 case *Avista Management vs. Wausau Underwriters*.

## HERO:

Cody Lombardo, who holds the Guinness World Record as the winner of the world's largest Jan Ken Pon tournament (more than 1,100 participants), held at a high school in Ottawa, Canada.

## THEIR IDEA OF FUN:

Going two for three, five for seven, or just about all day long.

## MOST DISTINCTIVE TRAIT:

Nostalgia for simplicity and innocence of childhood.

## BIGGEST CONTROVERSY:

Some players add a fourth hand option, "Dynamite" (by extending the thumb or index finger), and debate continues as to whether dynamite blows up paper or paper pinches the dynamite fuse.

## BIGGEST MISCONCEPTION ABOUT:

That people who do not play for recreation—who actually rely on the game as a means of making decisions or settling disputes—are too ignorant or immature to employ reason or argument as a decider.

## WHAT YOU MAY HAVE IN COMMON:

A willingness to let chance (with a dash of strategy) decide matters.

## BUZZWORDS:

Japanese players "psych out" an opponent by shouting out, as they release their hand, what gesture they will deal, the strategy being that the opponent will instinctively react with the appropriate gesture: e.g., paper to cover rock—only to be confronted by scissors. Gotcha!

## SIGN OF FAN:

Settles any and all domestic disputes by means of Jan Ken Pon.

## SIGN OF GEEK:

Studies *The Official Rock Paper Scissors Strategy Guide* (Simon and Schuster, 2004, by Douglas and Graham Walker).

## SIGN OF SUPERFREAK:

Participates and kicks ass in the annual USA Rock Paper Scissors League Jan Ken Pon Championship.

# MMORPGERS

**ALSO KNOWN AS:**

*Massively Multiplayer Online Role-Playing Gamers*

**JUST DON'T CALL THEM:**

*Avatards*

**CORE BELIEF:**

*The game is life; the game never ends; therefore life never ends when you're playing the game.*

> *"Unfortunately, no one can be told what the Matrix is. You have to see it for yourself."*
>
> —Morpheus, *The Matrix* (movie, 1999)

## WHO THEY ARE:

Devotees of video games in whose virtual world more than one participant may play simultaneously, the goal being a shared play experience. Popular games include *World of Warcraft, Call of Duty, Everquest, Ultima Online, Bioshock, Mass Effect,* and *Dragon Age.*

To the MMORPGer, the single-player video game in which you blow up pixilated alien spacecraft is not only antiquated but dull as dishwater because you're all alone and nothing more than the muzzle of a laser gun. There's no story, no plot, no engagement between "press to start" and "game over."

Role-playing games, in contrast, allow the player to create his or her own character, and the multiplayer angle gives the player a sense of community, as well as of continuity.

Fans of the single-player video game will play the same for as long as they last, before they get blown up or their time runs out. MMORPGers will play one of their games for years, without ever reaching an "end" or "winning," because it's about more than winning or reaching a high score.

At last count, *World of Warcraft* had more than 11 million subscribers. Can that many elves and battle-axe-wielding heroes be wrong?

## HOW TO RECOGNIZE:

They look nothing like their avatars.

## TO BE FOUND:

Glued to the computer while other kids are outdoors playing sports.

## HEROES:

*WOW* creators Bill Petras and Kevin Beardslee, game programmers, makers of sequels.

## THEIR IDEA OF FUN:

Playing the next generation version of their favorite game, because unlike movies, MMORPG sequels are usually better than the original.

## MOST DISTINCTIVE TRAIT:

Loyalty to the game.

## BIGGEST CONTROVERSY:

Depends on the game, but can include: avatars (i.e., players) using objectionable language or behaviors within the game; the trading of virtual game items for actual money; the influence of violence within the game; and the debate over whether gaming overall mimics the addictiveness of substance abuse.

## BIGGEST MISCONCEPTION ABOUT:

That more so than the stereotypical video game player, MMORPGers are socially inept losers who have to live in a fantasy world of their own making. Yeah—and golfers don't know anything about being a team player.

## WHAT YOU MAY HAVE IN COMMON:

Interest in the interactivity potential of the Internet or entertainment; good hand-eye coordination; active imagination.

## BUZZWORDS:

"Kiting" is running from an opponent to avoid injury, while still trying to cause it damage; "grinding" is staying in one spot to slay opponents for a long time; and "RTM" advises newbie players to "Read the manual" (aka "RTFM").

## SIGN OF FAN:

Gets obsessed with *Call of Duty* or *World of Warcraft*; makes parents concerned.

## SIGN OF GEEK:

Starts dating girl but never meets her because she's an Elf Priestess on *WOW* (anyway, he's pretty *sure* she's a girl . . . ).

## SIGN OF SUPERFREAK:

Marries Elf Priestess in virtual wedding, virtually no one shows up.

# DUNGEON MASTERS

**ALSO KNOWN AS:**
DM, Games Master, Games Operations Director, Referee, Storyteller, God

**JUST DON'T CALL THEM:**
Master Baiters

**CORE BELIEF:**
Longstanding rules and spontaneous imagination can peacefully coexist in the D&D universe.

> *"I am the master of fantasy."*
>
> —French poet Arthur Rimbaud (1854–1891),
> from *Une Saison En Enfer (A Season in Hell)*

## WHO THEY ARE:

Players of fantasy role-playing game *Dungeons & Dragons* who elect to play Dungeon Master, or the controller/storyteller of the game.

The DM describes what the other players see and hear, as they make their way through the game. The DM also acts as referee, and like all refs, is subject to disputation and allegations of blindness or insanity.

Each *D&D* game, known as an "adventure," may follow the framework of a prescribed "module," or the DM, given sufficient preparation time, may construct a module of his or her own imagining.

Being the ultimate controller and narrator of the adventure does not mean the DM is wholly impartial, unbiased, and infallible. The Greek mythmakers knew that Zeus and his ilk could make mistakes, and even Yahweh of The Holy Bible has preferences (Abel over Cain, Joseph over his brothers). No game or adventure is perfect, but that's what creates excitement, surprises, and fun.

According to the website Wizards of the Coast (the game's publisher), about four million Americans play *D&D* every *month*. In addition to the traditional game, *D&D* enjoys an online version to accommodate more techno-savvy elves and warlocks.

## HOW TO RECOGNIZE:

Usually males, often so appointed for their imaginative prowess, organizational ability, and superhuman knowledge of rules of the game.

## TO BE FOUND:

Wearing the star-covered robes and wizard hat his Mom agreed to make for him in exchange for repainting and organizing the shed.

## HEROES:

Game founders and developers Gary Gygax and Dave Arneson; Gandalf; Dumbledore; Zeus.

## THEIR IDEA OF FUN:

Reviewing game rules in *Player's Handbook, Dungeon Master's Guide,* and *Monster Manual.*

## MOST DISTINCTIVE TRAIT:

A knowledge of game rules that, were it translated into tort law, would make them Clarence Darrow.

## BIGGEST CONTROVERSY:

Since the game's inception in the mid-1970s, D&D has been suspected of indoctrinating young people in Satanic or demonic rituals and beliefs. Parental outcry prompted TSR, the makers of D&D, to remove all game references to "demons" and "devils" in the second edition of the game, *Advanced Dungeons & Dragons* (AD&D).

## BIGGEST MISCONCEPTION ABOUT:

That they enjoy playing God. As Jim Carrey learned in the movie *Bruce Almighty,* being the architect of the universe has its privileges but it also means you're the recipient of people's cries of unfairness and are accused of arbitrary favoritism.

## WHAT YOU MAY HAVE IN COMMON:

Love of *The Hobbit* or *The Lord of the Rings*; penchant for things medieval; rich fantasy life.

## BUZZWORDS:

Strength, Dexterity, Constitution, Intelligence, Wisdom, and Charisma: "ability," or the six natural traits that define and determine your D&D character, before game play begins; "melee" is characters in direct combat; "d" is shorthand for "die" or "dice": players use a polyhedral die in game play.

## SIGN OF FAN:

Follows prescribed modules, but needs to consult reference for some decisions.

## SIGN OF GEEK:

Invents own modules, never needs to consult reference for storytelling or arbitration.

## SIGN OF SUPERFREAK:

Submits Dungeon Mastery in job interview as proof of managerial skills.

# JUGGLERS

**ALSO KNOWN AS:**

*Toss Jugglers, Club Swingers, Passers (types of juggling)*

**JUST DON'T CALL THEM:**

*Clowns, Thrower-Uppers*

**CORE BELIEF:**

*Keep 'em in the air.*

*"Life is a struggle if you can't juggle."*

—Anonymous

## WHO THEY ARE:

Dynamic, aerial manipulators of various objects for purposes of entertainment or competition. (Boy, when you put it like that, jugglers sound kind of boring, huh?)

No giggling please, but juggling really is an ancient art, tracing itself back to many countries in Africa, Asia, and Europe. Always popular as entertainment—except to those who considered it a form of magic and witchcraft—juggling is popularly thought of as something done with spherical objects: rubber balls, apples, hand grenades. Even today, on TV and in movies, the shorthand way of identifying the lovable male clown character is to have him pick up three random objects and do a little juggle.

The transition from juggling rubber balls to flaming torches to bowling balls and chainsaws has developed an elite world of juggling, and the rise of both the International Jugglers' Association and the World Juggling Federation.

Juggling's appeal may be that unlike lion taming or trapeze artistry, the entry-level skill set (keeping three balls in the air) can be easily learned by people of all ages.

## HOW TO RECOGNIZE:

Seldom recognizable by face, jugglers distinguish themselves by what and how they juggle.

## TO BE FOUND:

In more places than the circus: in Renaissance Faires, carnivals, kids' parties, sidewalks, *America's Got Talent*, magic shows, college campuses, cabaret shows, *Cirque Du Soleil* . . .

## HEROES:

Las Vegas performer Anthony Gatto, Michael Moschen, Jason Garfield.

## THEIR IDEA OF FUN:

Surfing the Internet Juggling Database: a trove of information about juggling events and appearances, juggling techniques, and juggling online forums.

## MOST DISTINCTIVE TRAIT:

Hand-eye coordination.

## BIGGEST CONTROVERSY:

Yes, even in juggling, there is controversy: the schism is between those who juggle purely for entertainment and those who do it for sport or to win competitions.

## BIGGEST MISCONCEPTION ABOUT:

Acrobats convey strength, and magicians convey mystery and intelligence. Jugglers tend to project "goofy," despite the intelligence and physical ability that elite juggling requires.

## WHAT YOU MAY HAVE IN COMMON:

An appreciation for entertainment that doesn't require lasers and fireworks, massive sets or props, or elaborate production values.

## BUZZWORDS:

"Antipodism" is lying on your back and juggling with your feet; "siteswap" is a mathematical notation system for describing juggling moves; a "diabolo" is a double-cup object juggled on a string.

### Feet on the Road, Balls in the Air

"Joggling" is juggling while jogging. Every year, the International Juggling Association holds a variety of road races under the rubric of the World Joggling Championship, with distances ranging from 100 meters to five kilometers. Participants have been known to juggle clubs, but the word on the street is that three balls are the easiest and best "props" for the course.

## SIGN OF FAN:

Keeps three tennis balls or Hackysacks in the car when going to family functions, in case tots or the elderly need to be amused.

## SIGN OF GEEK:

Forms college juggling club, secures on-campus gigs as entertainment everyone can agree on and not be offended by.

## SIGN OF SUPERFREAK:

Juggles full-time at *Cirque Du Soleil*, teaching position, and private parties.

# BODYBUILDERS

**ALSO KNOWN AS:**
Muscle Heads, Iron Pumpers, Hypertrophists

**JUST DON'T CALL THEM:**
"Hans and Franz" (a late 1980s Saturday Night Live duo parodying Arnold Schwarzenegger, known for saying, "Ve're going tuh pump [clap] you up!")

**CORE BELIEF:**
No pain, no gain.

> "The resistance that you fight physically in the gym and the resistance that you fight in life can only build a strong character."
> —Arnold Schwarzenegger (1947– )

## WHO THEY ARE:

Men—and, to a lesser extent, women—who pursue physical fitness through muscular development.

Typically, Bodybuilders are weightlifters, working out not primarily for strength and endurance (although this is key) but for a balanced hypertrophic "body sculpture." Advanced Bodybuilders may compete for "professional" status through bodybuilding competitions, such as those sanctioned by the International Federation of Body Building (IFBB).

Between the late 1970s and the early 1980s, male action movie stars went from being slim (Burt Reynolds, Steve McQueen) to being ripped (Arnold, Stallone, Van Damme): thus, the era of 1950s fitness icons Charles Atlas and Jack LaLanne evolved into a bulked-up period in which even rock singers such as Bruce Springsteen and Tina Turner started showing off their biceps.

While weight training remains popular, heavy-duty bodybuilding has suffered a taint of controversy related to the use of steroids, and changing ideals of human beauty have shifted away from someone who looks like they could dead-lift a bison.

Nevertheless, Bodybuilders still walk (or lumber) among us, albeit to varying degrees of "pumpitude."

## HOW TO RECOGNIZE:

Necks the size of your waist, forearms the size of your thighs, veins the size of your fingers. Not known for wearing loose-fitting clothing.

## TO BE FOUND:

In the free-weight section of the health club; on "Muscle Beach" (in either Santa Monica or Venice, California); carrying depth charge-size containers of protein powder out of GNC stores; at the tailor, having their clothing taken out to fit their expanding frames.

## HEROES:

Arnold, Charles Atlas, Jack LaLanne, Sergio Oliva, Kellie Everts, Steve Reeves.

## THEIR IDEA OF FUN:

Similar to Marathoners, Bodybuilders enjoy taking a methodical approach to pushing their bodies through the threshold of pain into a refreshing waterfall of endorphins.

## MOST DISTINCTIVE TRAITS:

Bulk, low body fat, zero body hair, and an eerie tendency to be uniformly tan all year round.

## BIGGEST CONTROVERSY:

Besides allegations of steroid use, Bodybuilding is a particular kind of physical health: that is, it may or may not be suitable for you. Your own health may require a focus on aerobic exercise or aspects of your diet. Before you start pumping, discuss it with your doctor.

## BIGGEST MISCONCEPTION ABOUT:

That they're all on steroids.

## WHAT YOU MAY HAVE IN COMMON:

An interest in not being obese when young or atrophied when old.

## BUZZWORDS:

"isotonic" (e.g., free weights), "isokinetic" (e.g., Nautilus machines), "isometric" (yoga).

## SIGN OF FAN:

Subscribes to *Men's Health*, tapes up workout charts in basement, memorizes names of major muscles (biceps, triceps, deltoids, etc.).

## SIGN OF GEEK:

Subscribes to *Muscle and Fitness*, memorizes neck muscles such as "sternocleidomastoid," has to throw out T-shirt collection.

## SIGN OF SUPERFREAK:

Waxes body, competes in contests, and when posing seriously looks like muscles will explode.

# YOGINIS

**ALSO KNOWN AS:**
Yogaholics, Yogis

**JUST DON'T CALL THEM:**
Gumby, Yogi Bear

**CORE BELIEFS:**
Very diverse, depending on the yogi. Yoga can be a deeply spiritual and transcendent practice or it can be exercise, and anything in between on any given day of the week.

*"The state of severance of union with sorrow
is known by the name of yoga."*

—*Bhaghavad Gita*

## WHO THEY ARE:

People who swear by yoga as either a simple method of exercise or as a totally revolutionary approach to opening your mind and your inner spirit. Fundamentally, yoga practitioners believe that yoga heightens your sensitivity to your body and its connection to your breath and your spirit. You do what you can the best you can: if you cannot put the flat of your foot gently against the back of your head, you are not "failing." This aspect of yoga alone attracts people young and old.

While yoga is nothing new, the merchandising and mainstream watering-down of yoga is. In its Indian roots, yoga is more than just stretching: it's achieving a mental and physical unification (one definition of the word "yoga" is "to unite") so as to lead a more fulfilling and centered life. Yoga has things to say about diet, philosophy, speech, and how we relate to others. While not a religion, yoga is most certainly a way of life for millions of people around the world.

Then, of course, you've got the middle-aged mom who does it only on Tuesday nights at that nice center downtown.

As of 2008, *Yoga* magazine reported that 15.8 million American adults practice yoga and that the U.S. yoga market was worth $5.7 billion annually. That number sounds just about right when single classes can run anywhere from free (at a community center) to several hundred dollars (at that elite spa).

## HOW TO RECOGNIZE:
T-shirts with Indian symbols, cropped pants, and mat-bags.

## TO BE FOUND:
Shopping for sorghum at your local (yet prohibitively expensive) health food market; taking up space in the park; getting their hands painted with Indian designs (mehndi); sending you mandala flair on Facebook.

## HERO:
Reed Richards of The Fantastic Four.

## THEIR IDEA OF FUN:
Combining the ethereal experience of opening the fifth chakra with sweating like a stuck pig.

## MOST DISTINCTIVE TRAIT:
They will bend over backwards for a friend (or anybody, quite frankly).

## BIGGEST CONTROVERSY:
The twain between people for whom yoga is a way of life and people for whom it's simply a status symbol.

## BIGGEST MISCONCEPTION ABOUT:
That they're all peaceful, centered, mystical people. You can do yoga and still be an asshat. It's just that unlike bodybuilding, yoga may help you become *less* of an asshat.

## WHAT YOU MAY HAVE IN COMMON:
A penchant for working out in a room whose thermostat is set to somewhere around "the surface of Mars"; a love for deep relaxation.

## BUZZWORDS:
There are Indian terms for every move, every position, even different kinds of breathing. A few major ones: "bikram yoga" is doing yoga in a highly heated room; "kundalini yoga" is intensely physical-mental discipline yoga; and "asanas" are yoga postures. (Skip the "downward dog" jokes, we've all heard them.)

## SIGN OF FAN:
Takes yoga class, likes it.

## SIGN OF GEEK:
Goes on yoga retreat, loves it.

## SIGN OF SUPERFREAK:
Is getting it on with the yoga instructor, in ways that would both shock and impress you

# SKATERS

**ALSO KNOWN AS:**
*Skateboarders*

**JUST DON'T CALL THEM:**
*Punks*

**CORE BELIEF:**
*Hang loose (which, among surfers, is expressed with the "shaka sign": extend the thumb and pinky finger while keeping the other three fingers curled).*

> *"I consider skateboarding an art form, a lifestyle, and a sport."*
>
> —Professional American Skateboarder Tony Hawk (1968– )

## WHO THEY ARE:

Mostly young adult males who ride skateboards for sport, recreation, transportation, or combinations thereof.

The image of the skateboarder has changed—or evolved—over the roughly half-century of the skateboard's popularity. You'd be hard pressed to make a case that today's Skater is a juvenile delinquent, a troublemaker, a punk: chances are better that he's a decent kid who rides his board to school and has dreams of either competing professionally or opening his own skateboard graphic design business.

This isn't to say, however, that skating has totally lost its edge. In the 1950s, leather-clad Brando wannabes had their motorcycles; in the 1960s, the British Mods had their scooters; and in the 1970s, Skaters went from being California surfers who needed something to glide on when the waves weren't happening to teenagers across America swerving and dodging sidewalk traffic as if the rules just didn't apply to them. No surprise that when the opening credits of *The Simpsons* introduced Bart to America, he went sailing out of school detention on a skateboard.

Back in the day (i.e., 1970s–'80s), Skaters spent their week's allowance on a "banana board" (a skateboard of polypropylene) or a simple board made of plywood. Now, thanks to progress and the evolution of skateboarding, kids can now drop their summer job income on boards that cost more than their cell phone, iTouch, and custom sneakers combined.

## HOW TO RECOGNIZE:

Grace over speed, style over difficulty, and fun and safety aren't mutually exclusive.

## TO BE FOUND:

Skate parks, sidewalks, gliding down outdoor stair handrails.

## HERO:

Tony Hawk.

## THEIR IDEA OF FUN:

Learning "tricks," decorating their boards with stickers, laughing at other skaters' epic fails and asking, "Dude, are you okay?"

## MOST DISTINCTIVE TRAIT:

The smart ones have reinforced knees, elbows, and skulls.

## BIGGEST CONTROVERSY:

Cities and towns big and small have Skaters and legislators who wonder what to do with them. Skaters without a skate park tend to (to put it kindly) execute some "wear and tear" on local public places, sometimes disturbing pedestrians. If a city or town decides to build a skate park, local Skaters may not be consulted on design, which may lead them to conclude that it's "too little, too late, too lame."

## BIGGEST MISCONCEPTION ABOUT:

That skaters are all alike: grungy low-lifes prone to injury and up to no good. Fact is, your kid is more likely to get hurt (and hurt worse) playing contact sports in school.

## WHAT YOU MAY HAVE IN COMMON:

An interest in "boardsports": e.g., snowboarding, mountainboarding, surfing, windsurfing.

## BUZZWORDS:

Mostly confined to maneuvers and "tricks." Fundamentals include the "Ollie" (becoming airborne with feet still on board and hands free), the "kickflip" (a 360-degree spin), and "grinds" (riding the board on some structure, such as a handrail).

## SIGN OF FAN:

Buys plywood skateboard, skates to and from class.

## SIGN OF GEEK:

Invests in expensive board, watches videos of skating tricks on YouTube, goes to skate park.

## SIGN OF SUPERFREAK:

Tries skating trick he's never heard of before and ends up breaking bones he's never heard of before.

# SPELUNKERS

**ALSO KNOWN AS:**
*Cave Explorers, Cave Divers*

**JUST DON'T CALL THEM:**
*Kerplunkers, Spelunkheads, Speleologists (i.e., scientists who study caves)*

**CORE BELIEF:**
*The truth is down there.*

*"I want to borrow it. For, uh . . . spelunking."*

—Bruce Wayne (Christian Bale) explaining why he wants a Batsuit prototype, *Batman Begins* (movie, 2005)

## WHO THEY ARE:

Interior rock climbers.

Humankind's interest in spelunking, or "cave diving," began when the first early cave-dwelling humanoid took one wrong step. Since then, spelunkers have enjoyed penetrating hearts of darkness in Mother Earth, exploring its hidden recesses, braving its uneven interior topography, and boldly going where none (or exceedingly few) have gone before.

Now what would a subculture be without elitism within its ranks? Yes, even spelunkers find a way to look down on one another, so if you are an expert rock climber and you explore caves as an athletic challenge or for scientific research, you are a "Caver." And if you are a Caver, you consider the term "Spelunker" appropriate to describe The Hardy Boys in their quest to solve *The Mystery of the Haunted Mine*.

The motivation behind spelunking will determine where you find different varieties of spelunkers: either at a mountaineering club or supply store, or in affiliation with the National Speleological Society (U.S.) or the Cave Research Foundation.

## HOW TO RECOGNIZE:

Helmet with halogen flashlight, assorted rock-climbing equipment, slowly disappearing into hole in the earth, echo-laden voice.

## TO BE FOUND:

Carlsbad Caverns National Park (NM), Mammoth Cave National Park (KY), Sequoia National Park (CA).

## HEROES:

Cave cartographers: explorers of large, nationally known caves who map their interior for the purposes of study or subsequent cavers.

## THEIR IDEA OF FUN:

Some caves allow for beautiful photography, as stunning as any landscape.

## MOST DISTINCTIVE TRAIT:

Willingness to lower themselves into a hazardous environment that cannot help but resemble entering one's own grave.

## BIGGEST CONTROVERSY:

Federal and state governments have no authority to close or even regulate caves that are located on private property, so if there is a health hazard to spelunking (e.g., a virus breaks out among bats, seismic activity), they can do little beyond saying, "Be careful down there."

## BIGGEST MISCONCEPTION ABOUT:

That advanced caving is a form of "extreme sport": that term can connote a willful flirtation with danger that no conscientious caver would subscribe to.

## WHAT YOU MAY HAVE IN COMMON:

A level of comfort in cold, damp, unlit spaces; affinity for bats; the ability to tell a stalagmite from a stalactite; advanced knowledge of knots.

## BUZZWORDS:

A "karst" is an area of exposed bedrock that may contain caves; an "active cave" has flowing water; a "dormant cave" has no water, flowing or dripping; a "show cave" is open for tours, including self-guided tours.

## SIGN OF FAN:

Goes on Carlsbad Cavern tour, proclaims its total awesomeness to friends, promises self to investigate caves in home state.

## SIGN OF GEEK:

Forms undergraduate spelunking club in affiliation with geology department, embarrasses date with spelunking joke.

## SIGN OF SUPERFREAK:

Caves faster than a Frenchman in front of a German flag.

# RODEOERS

**ALSO KNOWN AS:**
*Rodeo Lovers*

**JUST DON'T CALL THEM:**
*Spectators of Animal Cruelty*

**CORE BELIEF:**
*Bronco and bull riding is the most exciting eight seconds in sports (eight seconds being the minimum time period one must spend on the animal).*

*"Rodeo makes a cowboy, and a cowboy makes the rodeo."*

—Anonymous

## WHO THEY ARE:

A multigenerational audience for an American entertainment as old as the Old West: a competition mainly involving the roping, tying, and riding of farm animals such as horses, bulls, and calves.

Timed Riding is the most popular, the most exciting, and the most potentially hazardous component of the rodeo, and while to the outsider it looks as if the bucking broncos are either wild or physically constrained to produce insanity, these horses have, over time, been bred and taught to buck and try to throw the rider.

Other rodeo events are entertainment and competitive versions of actual cowboy work, or "punching": roping, tying, racing, wrestling. Oh, and there are also clowns.

The Youth Rodeo Association (YRA) promotes the rodeo among children as young as eight, and professional contests nationwide are governed by the Professional Rodeo Cowboy Association (PRCA). Women have their own Professional Rodeo Association (WPRA), and even seniors can get into the act.

All told, coast to coast, there are more than 500 rodeo events per year, generating about $30 million in business. That ain't hay, pardner.

## HOW TO RECOGNIZE:

Dressed as cowboys and cowgirls, but without the leather gloves and numbers on their backs.

## TO BE FOUND:

Anywhere in America outside of New England, Alaska, Hawaii.

## HEROES:

Don Gay, eight-time world-champion bull rider; rodeo clowns; the Professional Rodeo Cowboys Association, based in Colorado.

## THEIR IDEA OF FUN:

The pageantry of rodeo is an all-family event, celebrating the iconic activities of the West as well as the bravery and physical prowess of the cowboy.

## MOST DISTINCTIVE TRAIT:

Respect: for the cowboy and the animal he or she is on.

## BIGGEST CONTROVERSY:

People and organizations who aren't satisfied with rodeo's insistence that "animal welfare" is the same or as good as "animal rights." Thanks to governing bodies, the rodeo makes sure animals are at least treated well and humanely.

## BIGGEST MISCONCEPTION ABOUT:

That they're stupid hicks who turn animal cruelty into a non-sport.

(There are at least four issues to debate in that sentence. We can, at least, agree that horses are animals.)

## WHAT YOU MAY HAVE IN COMMON:

Cowboy nostalgia, boots and hat, Coors in hand, smokeless between cheek and gum, tendency to say "Yee-hah."

## BUZZWORDS:

"Bareback" is riding *sans* saddle, a "bronco" is a horse that's never been taught to wear a saddle, and "bailing out" is to get off the animal by whatever means necessary.

## SIGN OF FAN:

Attends rodeo on visit to Midwest or West, discovers it's more exciting seen in person.

## SIGN OF GEEK:

Organizes rodeo team in high school, joins rodeo team in college.

## SIGN OF SUPERFREAK:

Writes a letter to that thar O-lympic committee? Askin' how come thar ain't no Rodeo Olympics, huh? Y'think this is easy? Kid stuff? I tell you what . . .

# THRU-HIKERS

**ALSO KNOWN AS:**
*End-to-End Hikers, Itinerant Campers*

**JUST DON'T CALL THEM:**
*Future Unidentified Bodies of the American Wild*

**CORE BELIEF:**
*Finish what you hike.*

*"I have two doctors: my left, and my right."*

—British historian G.M.Trevelyan (1876–1962), referring to his legs

## WHO THEY ARE:

People who hike a major designated trail end-to-end.

While a few intrepid outdoorsy types say "I'm Thru-Hiking," the rest of us walk more than two miles and say, "I'm through hiking." Thru-Hikers are "completists": when they say they walked the Appalachian Trail, they really walked the Appalachian Trail—all 2,165 miles of it, in one go.

Hiking an entire trail is beyond the physical abilities and vacation time of most people, so we're talking about an elite group who make marathoners look like they eat in baby bites. Of the roughly 2,000 people who attempt to thru-hike the Appalachian Trail every year, only about 10 percent succeed to join the 5,000 Thru-Hikers who can claim to have done so.

Thru-Hikers are expert hikers, campers, and naturalists, educated on survival techniques and usually taking on the challenge with a partner—a friend they can trust but whom they wouldn't feel bad about eating.

Seriously: hiking a long trail doesn't mean you must always stay on it, so Thru-Hikers will plan to depart the trail at towns along the way for the purposes of eating, bathing, and rejuvenating.

If you were to thru-hike the Appalachian Trail, a realistic goal would be to cover about eight miles a day, making the whole trip about nine months long—enough time to give birth to a new you.

## HOW TO RECOGNIZE:

If you are at either end of a trail, they are the bedraggled, bearded persons who beg you to take their picture giving the thumbs-up in front of the trail sign. Then they ask you for spare change, to purchase a bus ticket home.

## TO BE FOUND:

On the Appalachian Trail, the Continental Divide Trail, Vermont's Long Trail, the Pacific Crest Trail.

### Gimme Shelter

The Appalachian Trail has more than 250 "shelters" along its formidable length, but don't expect room service: we're talking lean-tos. They're available on a first-come-first-serve basis and depend on volunteers to build and maintain them.

## HERO:

Russian immigrant Lillian Alling, who anecdotally was living in New York in 1927 and became so homesick, she walked to the Bering Strait and caught a boat back to her homeland. She is mentioned in a 1958 book called *The New Way of the Wilderness* by Calvin Rutstrum.

## THEIR IDEA OF FUN:

Let's say the journey is *as important as* the destination, because reaching the destination is what it's all about.

## MOST DISTINCTIVE TRAITS:

Planning, commitment, follow-through.

## BIGGEST CONTROVERSY:

You cannot call yourself a Thru-Hiker if you hiked the entire Appalachian Trail but in bits and pieces over a series of visits: this is what's called "Section Hiking." To Thru-Hikers, this is like boasting you ate that restaurant's 72-ounce steak, except you had to take half of it home and finish it over the next three weeks.

## BIGGEST MISCONCEPTION ABOUT:

They're either drifters, hermits, or lost.

## WHAT YOU MAY HAVE IN COMMON:

Love of outdoors, physical challenges, inspirational stories.

## BUZZWORDS:

A "Nobo" is a hiker headed north, while a "Sobo" heads south; "yellow blazing" is hitchhiking (and cheating); and "cowboy camping" is to sleep outside without a tent.

## SIGN OF FAN:

Thru-hikes a city's "History Trail."

## SIGN OF GEEK:

Thru-hikes local Audubon "nature trail" (with help from Girl Scouts).

## SIGN OF SUPERFREAK:

Upon successful completion of Appalachian and Pacific Coast Trail, first words are, "Next stop: Asia!"

# NASCAR FANS

**ALSO KNOWN AS:**

Fan of the National Association for Stock Car Auto Racing, Inc.

**JUST DON'T CALL THEM:**

Goober, Jethro, Bubba, Ricky Bobby

**CORE BELIEF:**

Well, it ain't "Slow and steady wins the race," that's for damn sure.

*"You win some, lose some, and wreck some."*

—NASCAR driver Dale Earnhardt (1951–2001), who died in a racing crash

## WHO THEY ARE:

People who watch, support, work for, live, and/or breathe American stock car racing—whose largest governing body is the National Association for Stock Car Auto Racing, Inc. and whose annual Sprint Cup Series is the Carbureted Kentucky Derby (except that it lasts almost all year long: thirty-six races over ten months).

The entire reason the inventor of the first automobile built a second one was to have something against which the first one could race—and if that's not true, it should be. Racing cars for entertainment or competitive sport has been around for generations, but stock car racing is its own thing. Back in the day, a "stock car" was an ordinary car retooled specifically for speed and endurance: its counterpart, the "race car," was built from the start for the racetrack and not the open road. Today, of course, stock cars are built as such on an assembly line, for racing around an oval track at high speeds.

The NASCAR fan may be the most misunderstood sports fan on the planet, outside of people who show up to watch Curling. For starters, the NASCAR naysayer questions that stock car racing is a sport at all. To the outsider, NASCAR fans look like rednecks who watch a bunch of crashes-waiting-to-happen go round and round for hours.

But while basketball fans watch two teams duke it out, NASCAR fans watch more than forty teams compete at once. While baseball fans have to wait for spring so training may begin, stock car racing is year-round enjoyment. And while football fans watch their favorite team incrementally work their way toward a #1 ranking, NASCAR fans watch fortunes and rankings literally change overnight.

And contrary to popular prejudice, no one goes there to see a crash.

## HOW TO RECOGNIZE:

By their swag and wall posters, you shall know them.

## TO BE FOUND:

Assiduously keeping track of a very sophisticated scoring and ranking system that governs the sport; attending regional races; buying more sport-related merchandise than fans for any other sport.

## HEROES:

While other professional sports idolize and coronate a handful of superstars, NASCAR has scores of drivers and their expert teams.

## THEIR IDEA OF FUN:

Same as you: supporting local teams and favorite players, tracking stats, and expressing armchair (or in this case, backseat driver) opinions.

## MOST DISTINCTIVE TRAIT:

Loyal cross-generational family fanship.

## BIGGEST CONTROVERSY:

NASCAR's as-yet refusal to institute "green mandates," to reduce the environmental impact of cars running on lead-additive gasoline racing around a track all day long.

## BIGGEST MISCONCEPTION ABOUT:

That they're hicks, rednecks, and hillbilly morons.

## WHAT YOU MAY HAVE IN COMMON:

Need for speed.

## BUZZWORDS:

Grease monkey lingo, DNQ ("Did Not Qualify"), DNF ("Did Not Finish"), DOA ("Dead On Arrival").

## SIGN OF FAN:

Tells child that upcoming NASCAR race is just like Pixar's *Cars*.

## SIGN OF GEEK:

Thinks engaging state trooper in friendly debate about NASCAR will let him slip out of a speeding ticket.

## SIGN OF SUPERFREAK:

Has at least three generations of family simultaneously at racetrack.

# MARATHONERS

**ALSO KNOWN AS:**
*Long Distance Runners, Road Warriors, Fleet-of-Feet*

**JUST DON'T CALL THEM:**
*Future Knee Surgery Candidates of America*

**CORE BELIEF:**
*Running is about more than good health or helping a charity: it's about building self-confidence, pushing personal limits, and instilling discipline. (Oh, and that's all fun, too.)*

> *"If you want to win something, run 100 meters. If you want to experience something, run a marathon."*
>
> —Olympic gold medalist and marathoner Emil Zápotek,
> aka the "Czech Locomotive" (1922–2000)

## WHO THEY ARE:

People aged 16 to 103 who participate in official marathons: i.e., foot races of 42.195 kilometers in length.

Note the word "participate": marathons don't specify that you need to *run* them, or even complete them. Most people do marathons for recreational exercise or to achieve their "best time," not to win the cash prize or qualify for the Olympics or show up that guy from Kenya.

True-blue Marathoners are limit-pushers, adrenalin junkies, pursuers of the "runner's high," in which the body releases chemicals to keep itself chugging along, in spite of every muscle screaming out for relief. If it sounds masochistic, you won't find an argument among Marathoners.

Cities big and small across America host marathons, but the biggies are in New York, Chicago, and of course, Boston. The Boston Marathon is the world's oldest annual marathon: established in 1897, the race is held the third Monday of every April, or Patriots' Day.

## HOW TO RECOGNIZE:

They are the healthiest skeleton-like specimens you've ever seen.

## TO BE FOUND:

Carbo-loading the night before a marathon; lying down on the grass after the marathon wrapped in a shiny "mylar blanket" and looking like a baked potato. (The blanket is meant to prevent hypothermia in heat exhaustion.)

## HEROES:

Finishers.

## THEIR IDEA OF FUN:

Crossing a threshold of burning pain, even if for a mere 100 yards, to continually inch the body's endurance and abilities further.

## MOST DISTINCTIVE TRAIT:

They are the only creatures in the animal kingdom who run for reasons other than being chased or trying to catch something.

## BIGGEST CONTROVERSY:

In 2009, NBC-TV reality show *The Biggest Loser* gave contestants three weeks to prepare to run a full marathon, which experienced marathoners know is nowhere near enough time. Marathon training is a long, methodical, and careful process, and any suggestion that it's just a long jog potentially puts lots of amateurs in harm's way.

## BIGGEST MISCONCEPTION ABOUT:

That they could run faster than you anywhere, anytime, for any distance.

## How Do You Get to Marathon?

In 490 B.C., the Persians landed in Marathon in the interest of kicking ass. The Athenians sent a messenger (Pheidippides) to get help from the neighboring Spartans. Pheidippides ran 150 miles in two days, then ran the 25 miles from Marathon to Athens to announce the Grecian victory. He ran, he arrived, and he died on the spot. And so we call the 25-mile foot race a marathon.

## WHAT YOU MAY HAVE IN COMMON:

A love of marathons, except you're on the sidelines, drunk and cheering on people you don't know.

## BUZZWORDS:

"Hitting the wall" is when glycogen levels in a runner's muscles hit a low, necessitating a slowdown or shutdown.

## SIGN OF FAN:

Runs; tackles 5K, 10K; builds up to first marathon; finishing time automatically becomes "best time"; makes announcement on Facebook.

## SIGN OF GEEK:

Coordinates vacation to travel across the country to run marathon.

## SIGN OF SUPERFREAK:

Finds job 42.195 kilometers from home in order to run to and from work.

# PASTIMES AND CAREERS

- Grammaticasters
- Tavern Trivia Players
- Ghost Hunters
- Birders
- Scrabblers
- Fisch Heads
- Clowns
- Disney Cast Members
- Conspiracy Theorists
- Cryptozoologists

# GRAMMATICASTERS

**ALSO KNOWN AS:**
English majors, Librarians, Copy Desk Editors, Grammarians, Buzzkills

**JUST DON'T CALL THEM:**
Word Nazis

**CORE BELIEF:**
If language elects to be governed by laws, then someone must enforce the law.

> *"One arrives at style with atrocious effort, with fanatical and devoted stubbornness."*
>
> —French author Gustave Flaubert (1821–1880)

## WHO THEY ARE:

The Grammaticaster lives by the credo that if it is worth writing or saying, it's worth writing or saying in accordance with governing principles of grammar.

A "grammarian" may be simply concerned with grammar and usage; the Grammaticaster swears by them.

We all learn basic grammar and usage in elementary and middle school, but by the time we need to write in the professional world, we've forgotten everything. Worse, some of us don't care and just charge ahead, contributing to a world of misspellings, misplaced punctuation, and plain bad grammar. This sad state of affairs drives (and employs) Grammaticasters nationwide.

Grammaticasters work on the copy desk of newspapers, in the editorial and production departments of book and magazine publishers, on corporate communication teams, and wherever language must be letter-perfect.

Grammaticasters usually start out as English majors. According to the National Center for Education Statistics, in the academic year 2001–2002, English majors accounted for about 8 percent of the 1.3 million BA degrees conferred in America. For all the people needing to have their writing checked, that's not a lot of field experts: hence, perhaps, the Grammaticasters' feelings of being in a lonely minority.

## HOW TO RECOGNIZE:

Look for the red editor's pencil in their desk caddy, the furrow in their brow, the bug up their ass.

## TO BE FOUND:

With copies of *The Chicago Manual of Style, The AP Style Handbook,* and *Fowler's Modern English Usage* close at hand.

## HEROES:

Barbara Wallraff, language maven for the *Atlantic*; William Safire (1929–2009), columnist for the *New York Times Magazine*; Edwin Newman, venerated TV news anchor and language stickler.

## THEIR IDEA OF FUN:

Correcting, particularly finding, the error someone else missed (known among Grammaticasters as a "good catch").

## MOST DISTINCTIVE TRAIT:

Attention to detail.

## BIGGEST CONTROVERSIES:

*Who, whom*; ending sentences with a preposition; starting sentences with a conjunction; the "serial comma"; *lie, lay*—the list goes on. (Oops, sorry! Preposition-ending sentence!)

## BIGGEST MISCONCEPTION ABOUT:

That they're so uptight, you couldn't pull a needle out of their butt cheeks with a tractor. Think of the Grammaticaster as a lawyer of words: someone who has been trained and educated to pay attention to the devil in the details and who considers it a mark of professionalism to point them out.

## WHAT YOU MAY HAVE IN COMMON:

A desire to speak and write well.

## BUZZWORDS:

Misplaced modifiers, dangling participles, subject-verb agreement.

### Super Grammarians

At the bottom of the grammarian food chain is the person who has read a book like *Eats, Shoots & Leaves* and constantly corrects minor mistakes in punctuation. Higher up is the professional: the copy editor, the proofreader, the book editor. Above them are those who have graduate degrees in linguistics. These folks are elbow-deep in how the brain and societies develop grammar and language, in speech therapies, and in editing dictionaries.

## SIGN OF FAN:

Gets into a tizzy when billboard or sign spells a word incorrectly.

## SIGN OF GEEK:

Writes letters and e-mails to members of mass media who have gotten it wrong.

## SIGN OF SUPERFREAK:

Returns your e-mail with red all-cap corrections to every single grammar and usage error you've made.

# TAVERN TRIVIA PLAYERS

**ALSO KNOWN AS:**
Trivialists, Competitive Trivia Hounds, Trivia Teamplayers

**JUST DON'T CALL THEM:**
Drunks who for some reason won't play Trivial Pursuit at home

**CORE BELIEF:**
It's fun to challenge your brain while you're pickling it in beer.

> *"What mighty contests arise from trivial things!"*
>
> —Alexander Pope (1688–1744), *The Rape of the Lock*

## WHO THEY ARE:

With the rise of home entertainment centers, "men dens," and giant TVs (to say nothing of the recession), it's become harder for bars and taverns to put people in seats. Hence, bars and taverns will resort to gimmicks: karaoke, ladies' night, low-cost chicken wings, sports parties, and, lately, competitive trivia contests.

Here's how it works: Teams of trivia lovers compete for a variety of prizes, and the steady intake of alcohol ensures that regardless of winning or losing, hilarity will ensue. It's Irish *Jeopardy*.

Other trivia contests are more benign and family-friendly. Consider the Massachusetts-based Stump Trivia company, a division of Trailside Entertainment, which hosts trivia events in bars and restaurants in nineteen U.S. states. The company advertises itself as a fun event not only for the bar crowd but also for private functions and corporate events.

The public interest in trivia is sustained by continued iterations of Trivial Pursuit, the continuing success of TV shows *Cash Cab* and *Who Wants to Be a Millionaire?* and college-organized "Trivia Bowls."

## HOW TO RECOGNIZE:

On a regular night during the week, they take over your favorite local watering hole and may ask you how many strike-outs Sandy Koufax had.

## TO BE FOUND:

Taking up all the tables for four, huddling together and filling out answer sheets, laughing and shouting in angst at odd intervals.

## HEROES:

Cecil Adams, author of trivia column "The Straight Dope"; Noel Botham, author of *The Book of Useless Information* and other related titles.

## THEIR IDEA OF FUN:

Stumping opponents.

## MOST DISTINCTIVE TRAITS:

Big brains, big tabs.

## BIGGEST CONTROVERSY:

Diehard barflies and professional drinkers don't think watering holes should be places where yuppies engage in fun and games (other than darts). People over forty-five would prefer that their bar be less gimmicky.

## BIGGEST MISCONCEPTION ABOUT:

That successful trivia players are by definition people whose knowledge is broad but extremely shallow.

## WHAT YOU MAY HAVE IN COMMON:

You both were on your high school's Academic Decathlon team, and you both know that Captain James T. Kirk was born in Riverside, Iowa (YES! Score!).

## BUZZWORDS:

After a few rounds of trivia in a bar, every word is a buzzword.

## SIGN OF FAN:

Responds to Facebook Tavern Trivia invite, shows up for a goof, wins T-shirt.

## SIGN OF GEEK:

Forms Trivia Team, attends event religiously, always has fun.

## SIGN OF SUPERFREAK:

Holds regular pre-event team studying session on nights when not attending AA or TA meeting.

# GHOST HUNTERS

**ALSO KNOWN AS:**
*Paranormal Investigators, Supernatural Thrillseekers, Spiritualists*

**JUST DON'T CALL THEM:**
*Ghostbusters*

**CORE BELIEF:**
*"There are more things in heaven and earth, Horatio, than are dreamt of in your philosophy."*—Hamlet *(Act 1, Scene 5)*

*"Whoa . . . did you hear that?"*

## WHO THEY ARE:

Individuals, groups, or organizations dedicated to investigating ghosts: note that what they investigate is not the supposed existence of ghosts, but the presence of ghosts. Using a variety of audiovisual and electromagnetic equipment either to invite spirits or register their presence—ambient thermometers, EMF meters, motion detectors, infrared cameras—Ghost Hunters run the gamut from curious volunteers to businesses who take people's money in exchange for a report of "findings."

In other words, Ghost Hunters could simply be out for fun, or out to separate frightened people from their money.

In either event, one could argue that Ghost Hunters are a harmless manifestation of our interest in things larger or more mysterious than ourselves.

According to an Associated Press poll, roughly 34 percent of Americans believe in ghosts: some of those surely are among the 11,500 members of the International Ghost Hunters Society (*www.ghostweb.com*). The online site for Paranormal Societies lists more than 1,100 official societies nationwide, so there's bound to be a bump in the night near you.

## HOW TO RECOGNIZE:

Eyeballs and faces take on an eerie green glow when the lights are turned off.

## TO BE FOUND:

In abandoned mental institutions, asylums, and prisons; in nineteenth-century Victorian houses, formerly inhabited by someone who went totally bat-loco; in any structure unknowingly built on a former Native American burial site; on the SyFy network.

## HEROES:

Famous parapsychologists Venkeman, Stantz, and Spengler (aka The Ghostbusters); psychic researcher Harry Price (1881–1948), responsible for the formation of the University of London Council for Psychical Investigation, in 1934; paranormal researcher Hans Holzer (1920–2009).

## THEIR IDEA OF FUN:

Staying up all night looking at remote camera feeds, listening intently to audio recordings, reading electromagnetic meters and digital thermometers.

## MOST DISTINCTIVE TRAIT:

What some would call gullibility, they would call an open mind.

## BIGGEST CONTROVERSY:

Ironically, the biggest disputes involve the recent spate of ghost hunting TV programs, which were supposed to usher the field into the mainstream. Questionable methods of attracting ghosts (e.g., blood rituals on A&E's *Extreme Paranormal*) and allegedly staged paranormal activity impairs the credibility of the entire field.

## BIGGEST MISCONCEPTION ABOUT:

That whatever they find is what they think it is.

## WHAT YOU MAY HAVE IN COMMON:

Fear of the dark, belief in an afterlife, willingness to bore someone with the story of that one time when your uncle came to you in a dream and said goodbye to you and then you woke up and got a phone call that he had died the night before—for real!

## BUZZWORDS:

The ones to know here are to clarify what Ghost Hunters are *not*. A "paranormalist" is someone who studies broadly in the occult or "occult sciences," only part of which may include ghosts. A "parapsychologist" is concerned with telepathy, ESP, telekinetics, and the like; they are also interested in phenomena related to life after death, which creates some overlap with Ghost Hunters. An "anomalist" is someone who investigates any kind of weird stuff going on.

### SIGN OF FAN:

Is willing to spend the night, on a dare, in that creepy abandoned house.

### SIGN OF GEEK:

Owns ouija board, dozens of paperbacks on the paranormal, and this personal photo where if you look right there in the background you can totally see this weird overexposure and, see, that's a ghost.

### SIGN OF SUPERFREAK:

Finds himself lugging around a ton of audio and camera equipment at midnight on Halloween in a geriatric psych ward, wondering where his life went.

# BIRDERS

**ALSO KNOWN AS:**
Ornithologists, Bird Lovers, Bird Spotters

**JUST DON'T CALL THEM:**
Birdbrains, Feathered Freaks

**CORE BELIEF:**
Be kind to your fine-feathered friends.

> *"A bird doesn't sing because it has an answer;*
> *a bird sings because it has a song."*
>
> —Maya Angelou, author of *I Know Why the Caged Bird Sings*

## WHO THEY ARE:

People of all ages who delight in the observation, preservation, and protection of birds. They are not to be confused with the "Bird Lover," who is wont to keep specimens in a cage: to the Birder, this is like keeping a dog or a cat permanently under lock and key. The Birder may be more forgiving of the zoo or sanctuary that keeps endangered birds in protective cages or environments, but typically, Birders believe our feathered friends should enjoy the same freedoms of movement that we humans do.

The Birder is an outdoorsy type, fascinated by the sight of winged wonders in a natural habitat. And there is much to see: thousands of species of birds in a wide variety of settings, such as the beach, the woods, even the big city.

The National Audobon Society, founded by ornithologist and artist John James Audobon, has 500 chapters nationwide, with a presence in each of the fifty states. Other groups, such as the American Bird Conservancy, take a love of birds into the political and ecological sphere. According to a 2009 study, *Birding in the United States*, the combined number of American people who fish and hunt (approximately 50 million) is outnumbered by people who watch wildlife (approximately 66 million). The U.S. Fish and Wildlife Service estimated in 2006 that Birders contributed no less than $36 billion to the national economy. Pad your nest with that one!

## HOW TO RECOGNIZE:
Birders are the only people besides peeping Toms, assassins, and opera lovers still purchasing binoculars.

## TO BE FOUND:
Nature preserves, sanctuaries, bird-calling contests.

## HERO:
Amateur ornithologist Phoebe Snetsinger, who—pursuant to a cancer diagnosis—saw more than 8,400 species of birds in her life (more than anyone in history) and chronicled her adventures in *Birding on Borrowed Time.*

## THEIR IDEA OF FUN:
Being outdoors and witnessing the poetry in motion that are birds in their habitats. Like all pursuits, birding has pleasures both silently solitary and vociferously group oriented.

## MOST DISTINCTIVE TRAITS:
Good eyes, good ears, good note-taking ability.

## BIGGEST CONTROVERSY:
Wind farms on land and in the ocean can sometimes threaten the daytime and nocturnal migratory patterns of certain birds, which unfortunately pits two commendable conservation efforts against one another.

## BIGGEST MISCONCEPTION ABOUT:
That they're all grannies, and any men in the crowd are effete, retired, or gay.

## WHAT YOU MAY HAVE IN COMMON:
Their favorite bird may be the mascot of your favorite sports team (e.g., ravens, skyhawks, falcons, eagles, orioles, etc.).

## BUZZWORDS:
"Plumage" (feathers), "crown" (head), "fledge" or "fledgling" (bird with first feathers who has left the nest), "colony" (birds of a feather, nesting together).

## SIGN OF FAN:
Buys special seed for backyard feeders in order to attract certain species.

## SIGN OF GEEK:
Has one of those wall clocks with birds instead of numerals and chirping sounds instead of bells.

## SIGN OF SUPERFREAK:
Schedules vacation according to migratory patterns and times.

# SCRABBLERS

**ALSO KNOWN AS:**
*Scrabbleheads*

**JUST DON'T CALL THEM:**
*Scrabbies (it just sounds gross)*

**CORE BELIEF:**
*Vocabulary, not knowledge, is power.*

*"It's one thing to know how to play like an expert and quite another to do it all the time."*

—Cecilia Le, National SCRABBLE Championship (NSC) player

## WHO THEY ARE:

In the most general terms: men and women of all ages who play either Hasbro's SCRABBLE or similar games such as Lexulous (formerly Scrabulous). Both games challenge players to construct words in a crossword-like grid, scoring points for letters used and position played.

More specifically, Scrabblers are diehard, competitive, and occasionally cutthroat players who treat the game like it's chess or baseball: i.e., they belong to clubs and leagues and compete in tournaments.

SCRABBLE played tournament-style involves use of a game-clock (like chess) and points determined by time of play (if you go over your allotted time to make a word, you earn penalty points). Players are also compelled to use "Protiles," whose letters are not engraved: that way, you cannot reach into the bag of tiles and feel which letter to pull out, to your advantage. Impressed yet?

For details about tournaments and rankings, visit the website *www.cross-tables.com*. Tournament play in the United States and Canada is restricted to members of the North American SCRABBLE Players Association (NASPA).

## HOW TO RECOGNIZE:

When not playing their favorite game, they are scouring the dictionary and online resources to teach themselves two- and three-letter words.

## TO BE FOUND:

In SCRABBLE clubs, participating in the annual National SCRABBLE Championship (operated by the National SCRABBLE Association).

## HERO:

Architect Alfred Mosher Butts (no lie), who invented SCRABBLE in 1938.

## THEIR IDEA OF FUN:

Being able to make nine-letter words on the board by using all seven tiles on a rack, and linking to two other existing words.

## MOST DISTINCTIVE TRAIT:

Their love of a word-based game often extends to love of wordplay, such as anagrams, palindromes, and cryptics.

## BIGGEST CONTROVERSY:

Minor kerfuffles are fought over whether or not electronic versions of the game should accept words inappropriate for children (e.g., "tit") and whether future game iterations should have numbered tiles so that "texting terms" (e.g., "2mrw") could be accepted. But the bigger fish to fry have to do with the evolving rules of what words are acceptable for play and the relative merits of SCRABBLE and Lexulous.

## BIGGEST MISCONCEPTION ABOUT:

That their game is easy, governed largely by luck, and does nothing to enhance one's vocabulary or appreciation of language.

## WHAT YOU MAY HAVE IN COMMON:

Love of crosswords, esoteric vocabulary, and games in which you may do a tribal victory dance for beating your opponent by one point.

## BUZZWORDS:

An "Old McDonald" is any rack containing the letters E-I-E-I-O.

## SIGN OF FAN:

Plays game routinely with partner or spouse, cops to being "obsessed," always extends invitations to play (though you never accept).

## SIGN OF GEEK:

Plays both SCRABBLE and Scrabulous, practices with Boggle, Word Twist (Facebook), and Scramboni (Apple).

## SIGN OF SUPERFREAK:

Proudly tells you his or her division ranking in NSC.

# FISCH HEADS

**ALSO KNOWN AS:**
Chess Players, Fisch Fans

**JUST DON'T CALL THEM:**
The Mentally Ill

**CORE BELIEF:**
"There was never a genius without a tincture of madness."—Aristotle
(384–322 B.C.)

> "Chess is life."
>
> —Bobby Fischer (1943–2008)

## WHO THEY ARE:

Devotees of chess who idolize Robert "Bobby" James Fischer, renowned World Chess Champion, notorious wunderkind and recluse, lightning rod of controversy, and (willingly or not) poster child for the Chess Genius Gone Batty.

While clinical findings have never emerged confirming that Bobby Fischer was mentally ill, people close to him and at an objective remove wondered if—late in his life—he had lost some hold of reality. He reportedly idolized Hitler and accused America of being run by "Jewish bastards."

The fact that Fischer had a genius for a highly cerebral game couldn't help but encourage a connection between chess and lunacy. The 1997 movie *Searching for Bobby Fischer* (not about Fischer, but a New York prodigy proclaimed as his heir) features a scene which supports the stereotype that chess obsession will turn you into a deranged, muttering nerd.

The controversy enshrouding Fischer distracts the casual observer from his unprecedented and still-legendary achievements: at fourteen, he won eight U.S. chess championships; at fifteen, he became the youngest chess Grandmaster to date; and by his thirties, he was generally acknowledged as the leading chess player in the world, a Mozart of the chessboard.

Idolizing Fischer in spite of his political views is like idolizing Thomas Jefferson in spite of his alleged infidelities: neither makes one an anti-Semite or a racist.

The United States Chess Federation comprises approximately 80,000 members and more than 2,000 chess clubs and organizations nationwide.

## HOW TO RECOGNIZE:
They own their own timing clock.

## TO BE FOUND:
Chess clubs, chess tournaments, conventions of CCI (Chess Collectors International), city parks.

## HERO:
Just the one.

## THEIR IDEA OF FUN:
Revisiting and studying Fischer's games, particularly his famous championship games against Russia's Boris Spassky, whom Fischer played (and beat) twice, in 1972 and in 1992.

## MOST DISTINCTIVE TRAIT:
Strong opening game.

## BIGGEST CONTROVERSY:
In 1992, Fischer played a chess match in Yugoslavia: a no-no because that country was under a United Nations embargo at the time, and rather than engage in a dispute with the U.S. government, Fischer never went home again. He subsequently lived in various countries, avoiding publicity but taking the opportunity to make anti-American and anti-Semitic remarks. Fans and followers were left with the challenge of separating the man from the myth, and Bobby Fischer's chess genius from his less-than-enlightened views.

## BIGGEST MISCONCEPTION ABOUT:
That idolization of Fischer means sanction of every aspect of his life and personality. In the end, it's all about what takes place on the board.

## WHAT YOU MAY HAVE IN COMMON:
Love of the game; prodigy fetish; the belief that great people are necessarily crazy, difficult to understand, or jerks.

## BUZZWORDS:
The opening moves in a chess game are called, "opening theory," and Fischer was renowned for a strong opening game. Variations on opening strategies take on names that sound either like battleground maneuvers or Mafia executions: the "Ruy Lopez," the "Najdorf Silician," and the ever-popular "Neo-Grünfeld Defense."

## SIGN OF FAN:
Inevitable portrait of Fischer in game room.

## SIGN OF GEEK:
Openly frames attack strategy by asking WWFD?

## SIGN OF SUPERFREAK:
Simultaneously wins chess championship and loses respect of the Anti-Defamation League.

# CLOWNS

*"Be a clown, be a clown! / All the world loves a clown."*

—from "Be a Clown," music and lyrics by Cole Porter (1891–1964)

## WHO THEY ARE:

Men and women who participate in a performance tradition that is ancient, cross-cultural, historical, and even mythological in its dimensions. The clown—aka The Fool, the Comic Relief, the Trickster—plays a vital role not just in circuses but also in Native American dance ceremonies, the plays of Shakespeare, modern movies and TV shows, and the archetypes through which humankind understands itself.

If that sounds too highfalutin for someone who wears oversize shoes and a red ball nose, it's because the popular definition of the clown is often limited to the jaded clown Krusty from *The Simpsons* or to anonymous, acrobatic boobs who pile into a little car in between circus acts.

"Clowning" as a general term refers to physical comedy: ergo, Jim Carrey and Buster Keaton are clowns, while Chris Rock and Jerry Seinfeld are comedians.

In thirty years of its existence, the Ringling Brothers and Barnum & Bailey Clown College trained approximately 1,400 clowns, which means alumni could travel to reunions all in one car.

## HOW TO RECOGNIZE:

Common to all clowns is physical expressiveness and an exaggerated appearance.

## TO BE FOUND:

Studying at the Ohio College of the Clowning Arts, The Clown Conservatory (San Francisco, CA), the Institute of Canadian Clowning, or any number of workshops, classes, or seminars.

## HEROES:

NBC-TV weatherman Willard Scott, who was the first Ronald McDonald; actor Hugh Jackman, who used to be a party clown; Emmett Kelly, famous "tramp clown"; Alan Livingston, creator of Bozo the Clown; Bob Keeshan, who was the original Clarabell the Clown on *The Howdy Doody Show* and who went on to be "Captain Kangaroo."

## THEIR IDEA OF FUN:

Making people of all ages laugh—which sounds simple until you try it.

## MOST DISTINCTIVE TRAITS:

The willingness to be a clown requires a certain egoless disposition, a willingness to use the entire body (sometimes to the point of pain) for the sake of laughs, and an expansive generosity of heart.

## BIGGEST CONTROVERSY:

The enjoyment of the clown—to say nothing of an appreciation for their craft and history—is tainted by a popular reversal of thinking that suggests that clowns are evil: e.g., the Insane Clown Posse, Stephen King's *It*.

## BIGGEST MISCONCEPTION ABOUT:

That the only jobs available to Clowns involve making animal balloons at children's birthday parties.

## WHAT YOU MAY HAVE IN COMMON:

Love of performance, sense of humor, facility for physical comedy.

## BUZZWORDS:

Bozo the Clown is a "Whiteface": that is, a clown in white facial makeup and a colorful costume; an "Auguste" is a helper or servant to the Whiteface, and his or her anarchic failures to perform tasks are a source of comedy; a "Contra-Auguste" mediates between Whiteface and Auguste, trying (and failing) to maintain order.

## SIGN OF FAN:

Dons whiteface for children's party.

## SIGN OF GEEK:

Takes classes in clowning, balloon sculpture, juggling.

## SIGN OF SUPERFREAK:

Threatens to run off and join the circus, makes good on threat.

# DISNEY CAST MEMBERS

**ALSO KNOWN AS:**
*Goofy, Donald, Mickey, Minnie, Pooh, Eeyore, Cinderella, Jasmine*

**JUST DON'T CALL THEM:**
*Failed Actors*

**CORE BELIEF:**
*The customer is always right (and better be always happy, or it's their ass).*

*"It's a small world, after all."*

—from "It's a Small World" by Richard and Robert Sherman

## WHO THEY ARE:

Technically, Disney Cast Members are any individuals who work at a Disney park: tour guides, janitors, you name it.

More commonly, DCMs are people whose job it is to be Mickey Mouse, Minnie Mouse, any of the Disney "princesses," and Disney subsidiary characters such as Winnie-the-Pooh or Eeyore. Note the use of the word "be" Mickey Mouse, as opposed to "dress up as Mickey Mouse." Disney Cast Members, in costume, are expected to represent their character with all the detail, professionalism, grace, and bearing that the harshest critic would expect from Mickey, Goofy, etc. There's no "down time" in costume, no falling out of character. Once you're dressed up as Belle, Jasmine, or Cinderella, you are *her*.

Disney is the number two media conglomerate in the world, employing approximately 138,000 people worldwide—that's a big cast.

## HOW TO RECOGNIZE:

Only to be seen within limits of Disney parks or resorts, where they are the cleanest, best-dressed, politest people in the entire park.

## TO BE FOUND:

Disneyland, Walt Disney World, Tokyo Disney, Hong Kong Disneyland, Disneyland Paris, Shanghai Disneyland, or on one of the Disney Cruise Lines.

## HERO:

Britt Deitz, a fellow whose idea of repaying Disney Cast Members for happiness and joy is the website *www.disneycastmagic.com*, where he posts galleries of his photos of cast members—by the thousands.

## THEIR IDEA OF FUN:

Chances are good to excellent that DCMs are people who grew up adoring all things Disney, so supporting the Disney brand and passing on Disney magic to millions of children and their families is, as they say, what it's all about.

## MOST DISTINCTIVE TRAIT:

A smile (unless, of course, their character is a pirate or tomb raider or evil villain and has to scowl).

## BIGGEST CONTROVERSY:

As tightly controlled an environment as Disney parks and resorts are, they can't control you once you quit: hence, people like Kevin Yee, a 15-year DCM veteran and author of *Mouse Trap: Memoir of a Disneyland Cast Member* (Ultimate Orlando, 2008).

## BIGGEST MISCONCEPTION ABOUT:

That they're scary. Some small children, accustomed to seeing their favorite Disney character in two dimensions and of relatively diminutive size, may encounter a six-foot Eeyore with squeals of terror. Fortunately, DCMs know how to deal with this common occurrence, and make the kids feel okay.

### What Not to Ask a DCM

For the sake of everyone's good time, refrain from asking Cinderella if it's true that Walt Disney had himself cryogenically frozen and is buried underneath the Pirates of the Caribbean. It's an urban myth, and no one wants to talk about the death of Disney in front of the kids.

## WHAT YOU MAY HAVE IN COMMON:

Four-fingered gloves, permanent smile, anthropomorphic features.

## BUZZWORDS:

"Cross-U" is to work at a park location for which you weren't originally hired; "Onstage" is any public guest area; "Protein spill" is guest puke which needs to be cleaned immediately.

## SIGN OF FAN:

Has Flickr or Facebook gallery with photos of self and every possible DCM, even ones they don't like.

## SIGN OF GEEK:

As frequent Disney guest, knows all DCMs by their real names (but doesn't address them as such).

## SIGN OF SUPERFREAK:

Starts and leads support group for recovering Disney Cast Members.

# CONSPIRACY THEORISTS

**ALSO KNOWN AS:**
*Conspiracy Nuts*

**JUST DON'T CALL THEM:**
*Looney Tunes, Bat-Shit Crazies, Mental Defectives*

**CORE BELIEF:**
*That information and experience is like an iceberg: a small amount visible to everyone, a huge amount hidden under the surface.*

*"The truth is out there."*

—*The X-Files* (TV show)

## WHO THEY ARE:

Conspiracy Theorists advance explanations for major historical events, usually involving an official cover-up of facts and testimony.

Popular conspiracy theories include:

**Lee Harvey Oswald** did not act independently to assassinate John Kennedy: potential co-conspirators include Fidel Castro, the Mafia, the CIA, and the KGB.

**The 1969 Apollo moon landing** was staged in a film studio. (See the 1978 film *Capricorn One*.)

**The New Mexico government complex known as Area 51** is concealing evidence of intelligent life from outer space, including a spaceship that crashed in the town of Roswell in 1947.

**Elvis Presley** faked his own death in 1977 to escape publicity.

More recent theories posit that: epidemic diseases such as polio or AIDS were engineered in government laboratories to decrease minority populations; the British Royal Family had Princess Diana assassinated; the 9/11 terrorist attacks were committed with either the prior knowledge or participation of the U.S. government, to create a pretext for the Iraq War and the takeover of Middle East oil reserves; President Obama is advancing agenda toward World Government.

## HOW TO RECOGNIZE:

A quick scan of their bookshelves and DVD rack usually gives 'em away: look for "actual footage" of alien autopsies, *Communion* (Whitley Strieber), *None Dare Call It Conspiracy* (Gary Allen).

## TO BE FOUND:

Attending conventions, lurking, blogging.

## HEROES:

William Mark Felt, Sr. (aka "Deep Throat"), who revealed details about the Watergate cover-up to the press; Daniel Ellsberg, who published *The Pentagon Papers*, revealing secret government bombing during the Vietnam War; President Lyndon B. Johnson, who signed the Freedom of Information Act in 1966.

## THEIR IDEAS OF FUN:

Stepping through the looking glass, finding the missing piece of the puzzle, exchanging knowing looks.

## MOST DISTINCTIVE TRAIT:

Perennially convinced that there are more facts to uncover, more testimony to hear, and that nothing is ever settled once and for all.

## BIGGEST CONTROVERSY:

Conspiracies gone wrong, from the politically incorrect ("Jews run the media") to the just plain uniformed

(Jesse Ventura claimed that the U.S. government helped plan 9/11).

## BIGGEST MISCONCEPTION ABOUT:

That they're crazy, stupid, or just so pathetic in their own lives that they need to invent wild stories.

## WHAT YOU MAY HAVE IN COMMON:

Intellectual curiosity; a healthy skepticism to accept the official story as truth; love of mysteries; civic engagement.

## BUZZWORDS:

Literal cognomens for characters in their theories: e.g., the man on the grassy knoll in Dallas holding the umbrella is christened "Umbrella Man."

## SIGN OF FAN:

Creates e-mail news alert for terms "newly released files," "Area 51," "Yeti," "Moon landing," "Philadelphia Experiment," "Bush."

## SIGN OF GEEK:

Self-publishes book *The Untold Manipulations of Freemason Aliens on the Secret World Government.*

## SIGN OF SUPERFREAK:

Renovates house not to increase resale value but to unearth suspected government wiretaps.

# CRYPTOZOOLOGISTS

**ALSO KNOWN AS:**
*Monster Hunters*

**JUST DON'T CALL THEM:**
*Chasers of Wild Geese, Jackalopers, Snipe Hunters*

**CORE BELIEF:**
*"You should never ever doubt what no one is sure about."—Willy Wonka*

> *"Cryptozoological research should be actuated by two major forces: patience and passion."*
>
> —Dr. Bernard Heuvelmans (1916–2001)

## WHO THEY ARE:

The Latin form of their name means "people who study hidden animals"—but how, you ask, can you study something that's hiding? Through eyewitness accounts, photographs and video, folklore and legend, and any physical evidence of when the animal came *out* of hiding.

Detractors of Cryptozoologists like to classify them (i.e., dismiss them) as people who look for evidence of Bigfoot, the Loch Ness Monster, Yetis, El Chupacabra, and other mythical creatures commonly assumed to be nonexistent or hoaxes.

The world, however, is a mammoth and rich ecosystem, and humankind has yet to identify, classify, or even photograph every single living organism or nonhuman creature. Charles Darwin himself, in his expeditions, discovered creatures theretofore unknown to Western man, so who's to say unknown creatures—aka "cryptids"—aren't also out there? After all, the book *Cryptology: A to Z* (Fireside, 1999) has more than 125 entries in it!

## HOW TO RECOGNIZE:

Bookcases and wall posters advertise mythical beasts and creatures, ranging from griffins and sea monsters to Nessie and Sasquatch.

## TO BE FOUND:

Often at meetings, conferences, or conventions for investigators into the paranormal.

## HERO:

Scotland-born author and adventurer Ivan Terence Sanderson (1911–1973), thought to have been coiner of term "cryptozoology."

## THEIR IDEA OF FUN:

Scrutinizing "The Patterson Film" (i.e., the 1967 footage of what Roger Patterson claimed to be Bigfoot).

## MOST DISTINCTIVE TRAIT:

An open mind.

## BIGGEST CONTROVERSY:

Since capturing the Loch Ness Monster, prehistoric sea creatures, Yeti, or Blue Tigers requires means and wherewithal beyond the capabilities of a humble Cryptozoologist, he or she may only have sketchy photographic or physical evidence, which could be easily faked or falsified.

## BIGGEST MISCONCEPTION ABOUT:

That their interest in and pursuit of these unusual or mythical creatures automatically qualifies them as quacks.

## WHAT YOU MAY HAVE IN COMMON:

The experience of seeing an animal, bird, or "thing" that you could not identify.

## BUZZWORDS:

"Megafauna" is another term for a very large animal, and may be applied to Yetis, Bigfoot, "Nessie" and other creatures; "ABC" stands for "Alien Big Cat," or an unnaturally large feline—usually a panther or tiger—rumored to inhabit an area of wilderness (also called "Phantom Cats").

## SIGN OF FAN:

Brings camcorder and plaster cast-making kit on camping trip in American Northwest, in case of Sasquatch sighting.

## SIGN OF GEEK:

Petitions university for minor in Cryptozoology, adducing personal research on Giant Forest Hogs.

## SIGN OF SUPERFREAK:

Gives up trout and bass fishing for exclusive pursuit of coelacanth, a large fish thought to have gone extinct 65 million years ago but which has surfaced in modern times: see www.dinofish.com.

# POLITICS

- Tea Partiers
- Utopians
- Libertarians
- Tree Huggers
- ACT UP Members
- Conscientious Objectors
- Tax Protesters

# TEA PARTIERS

**ALSO KNOWN AS:**
*Fringe Republicans, Conservatives*

**JUST DON'T CALL THEM:**
*Right-Wing Lunatics, Third-Party Extremists, Teabaggers*

**CORE BELIEFS:**
*It's fiscally unwise to try to spend one's way out of a recession; the government shouldn't bail out big business before taxpaying citizens; and that Obama continually thumbs his nose at real Americans and what they want, what with his dialogues with Republicans and answering questions at town hall meetings and his willingness to compromise on core issues and whatnot.*

> *"The tree of liberty must be refreshed from time to time with the blood of patriots and tyrants."*
>
> —Thomas Jefferson

## WHO THEY ARE:

If you recall the second grade U.S. history lesson you've forgotten, the Boston Tea Party was half political protest, half fraternity prank: In December 1773, anywhere between 30 and 130 colonists stormed a British ship moored in Boston Harbor and dumped chests of tea overboard. This gesture protested The Tea Act, through which the American colonists were being taxed without the benefit of representation in British Parliament.

The modern American Tea Party Movement holds similar anti-authoritarian views toward the domestic economic policies of U.S. federal government, particularly with respect to The American Recovery and Reinvestment Act of 2009.

While the Tea Party came into being during the Obama administration, Tea Partiers may tell you that they are no fans of his predecessor's economic policies and that the Tea Party movement is not organized solely to impede the agenda of President Obama. Or not.

Given the nebulousness of the still-nascent movement, statistics are a little sketchy, but 600 people did attend the 2010 Tea Party Convention in Nashville, TN: that number at least represents the Tea Partiers who were willing to pay the $600 entrance fee. Survey firm The Winston Group polled 3,000 Americans in 2010 and estimated that Tea Partiers are 57 percent Republican, 28 percent Democrat, and 13 percent Independent.

## HOW TO RECOGNIZE:

Mouth open, mind closed, fist raised.

## TO BE FOUND:

Rallies, conventions, town halls, protests, talk radio, cable news.

## HEROES:

You would think it would be Boston politician James Otis (1725–1783), who popularized the slogan "Taxation without representation is tyranny," but somehow he's yet to emerge as the poster boy.

## THEIR IDEA OF FUN:

Organizing, exercising freedom of assembly, shouting, elevating blood pressure.

## MOST DISTINCTIVE TRAITS:

It depends on what you think about them: either their rejection of apathy as an acceptable response to government action, or their confusion of outrage with a legitimate economic or political point of view.

## BIGGEST CONTROVERSY:

The open question of whether they are a legitimate movement to be reckoned with in the long term or a disorganized, flash-in-the-pan aggregate of people who just want to get together and let everyone know how pissed off they are.

## BIGGEST MISCONCEPTION ABOUT:

There are several, considering the diversity of views within the movement and its lack (so far, anyway) of a central platform relating to issues other than economic ones.

## WHAT YOU MAY HAVE IN COMMON:

Dislike of "big government," hard-on for Sarah Palin.

## BUZZWORDS:

"Astroturfing"(i.e., an organized event or protest that feigns the appearance of grass-roots spontaneity).

## SIGN OF FAN:

Nods at tavern TV featuring Tea Party coverage, saying, "They got a point."

## SIGN OF GEEK:

Attends Tea Party rally.

## SIGN OF SUPERFREAK:

Cultivates interest in actual tea-bagging.

# UTOPIANS

**ALSO KNOWN AS:**
*Idealists, Pantisocrats (an eighteenth-century utopian idea of "government by all")*

**JUST DON'T CALL THEM:**
*Pie-in-the-Skyers*

**CORE BELIEF:**
*Today's work can build a better tomorrow.*

> *"Our business here is to be Utopian, to make vivid and credible, if we can, first this facet and then that, of an imaginary whole and happy world."*
>
> —H. G. Wells (1866–1946), *A Modern Utopia*

## WHO THEY ARE:

People who advocate, work toward, or actively try to construct an ideal community, society, state, or world. Typically, the characteristics of the utopia involve: an absence of war; redistribution of wealth; equality among people of different ethnicities, ages, and genders; communal sharing of goods and responsibilities; and the creation of circumstances that encourage and allow for the full flowering of humankind's potential.

Utopians need not necessarily believe that their vision of an ideal future can be realized within their lifetime, or ever; what they do believe, however, is that the envisioning of that ideal future is a worthwhile and necessary pursuit, and that we must take steps toward that vision if humankind is to advance or even survive.

Video games, surprisingly, have opened up a new frontier in Utopianism, as gamers can create and inhabit ideal societies in virtual environments such as Second Life. The online world of avatars may provide a space in which Utopian ideas are tested, if not realized.

Alas, real-life utopias are best known by their failures: Brook Farm, MA, and New Harmony, IN, are among the best-known in the United States.

## HOW TO RECOGNIZE:
Repeated use of the words "should," "must," "ought to," "needs to," "has to."

## TO BE FOUND:
Among academics, philosophers, social activists, hippies, New Agers.

## HEROES:
Thomas More (author of *Utopia*, 1516), Henry David Thoreau (for embodying a utopian relationship to Nature), the Amish.

## THEIR IDEA OF FUN:
The positing of a Utopian future or society has always been a good launching point for a discussion about politics, culture, economics, and foreign policy. It also makes for good dinner conversation, as evidenced by Plato's *Republic*, which is nothing more than a transcript of dinner guests debating the details of a Utopia.

## MOST DISTINCTIVE TRAIT:
Progressive views, socially and politically.

## BIGGEST CONTROVERSY:
Cynics argue that because attempts at communal utopian societies invariably fail (Brook Farm, MA; New Harmony, IN), that means that working toward Utopia, or even envisioning one, is a fool's errand.

## BIGGEST MISCONCEPTION ABOUT:
That idealism and optimism is a hallmark of naiveté, and that their notions about communal living and sharing of resources is Communist.

## WHAT YOU MAY HAVE IN COMMON:
A rejection of the Panglossian axiom that "all is for the best in the best of all possible worlds"; optimism; hope.

## BUZZWORDS:
"Dystopia" is the opposite of a utopia and is often framed as a backhanded gesture of pointing the way toward Utopia (cf. *1984* by George Orwell).

## SIGN OF FAN:
Political and social views are guided by personal vision of ideal society.

## SIGN OF GEEK:
Pens utopian manifesto, uses avatar in video game to advance ideas.

## SIGN OF SUPERFREAK:
Founds actual utopian community, takes blame for its eventual failure.

# LIBERTARIANS

**ALSO KNOWN AS:**
(but not always justifiably as) Conservatives, Free Marketers, Liberals, Tea Partiers, Right Wingers, Socialists

**JUST DON'T CALL THEM:**
Libbies (which connotes supporters of Women's Lib)

**CORE BELIEFS:**
Government, for all its benefits, will overstep its bounds if unchecked to curb or eradicate the rights of the individual citizen. If what I'm doing harms no one (other than myself), then leave me alone and let me do it.

> *"They that can give up essential liberty to obtain a little temporary safety, deserve neither liberty nor safety."*
>
> —Benjamin Franklin (1706–1790)

## WHO THEY ARE:

Men and women who espouse a political philosophy that emphasizes the rights and freedoms of the individual over those of the state.

Now, that's describing Libertarianism in its absolute simplest terms, solely for the purposes of shorthand. Libertarianism is one of the more diverse and nebulous political philosophies, comprising a broad spectrum of ideas and approaches to government and citizenship. The most heated arguments about Libertarians are often within Libertarian ranks, as to what their philosophy should mean or stand for.

Republicans and Conservatives agree with Libertarians that the federal government should be small and stay out of people's personal lives; however, the Right disagrees with Libertarians that this philosophy should extend to gay marriage and smoking pot in the privacy of your home.

Democrats and Liberals agree with Libertarians that government should not overstep its bounds to infringe on personal rights; however, the Left disagrees with Libertarians that government does wrong by extending financial "bailouts" to banks or by creating welfare programs or a "war on drugs."

Just as there are "Lazy Liberals," there are "Lazy Libertarians"—i.e., people who are just sick of the government mucking things up, taking their money in the form of taxes, and basically sending this once-great country to hell. These Lazy Libertarians don't know about related theories such as Objectivism, Geolibertarianism, or Libertarian Socialism, and they don't want to know.

Roughly 15 percent of Americans describe themselves as Libertarian, whatever that terms means to them, and there is an official Libertarian Party, which nominates someone for President every four years. (Bob Barr ran in 2008.)

## HOW TO RECOGNIZE:

Usually requesting that the government stay out of their [fill in the blank]: e.g., bedroom, classroom, boardroom, hydroponic garden, tax return, mind.

## TO BE FOUND:

Calling into talk radio, calling themselves "undeclared" or "swing" voters in election, bragging that their Presidential candidates receive more votes than any other "third party" candidate.

## HEROES:

See *www.libertarianhalloffame.org*, and don't get freaked out that there are Chinese and French people there.

## THEIR IDEA OF FUN:

(To paraphrase William F. Buckley Jr.'s description of the job of Conservatism and his magazine *National Review*) To stand athwart government and say "Stop."

## MOST DISTINCTIVE TRAIT:

Assertion of and dedication to personal freedoms.

## BIGGEST CONTROVERSY:

Popular adoption of author Ayn Rand as hero, when Rand—who espoused Objectivism—rejected Libertarianism.

## BIGGEST MISCONCEPTION ABOUT:

That they are anti-government and hence anarchists; that their support of a free market makes them corporate shills or enemies of the working man; that their premium on individual liberty shows a self-centered disregard for the public welfare; and that they're just cynical, third-party outsiders.

## WHAT YOU MAY HAVE IN COMMON:

A distrust of government to solve the social, economic, and cultural problems that face a community or society at large.

## BUZZWORDS:

Liberty, freedom, rights, social contracts.

**SIGN OF FAN:**

Wraps self in flag.

**SIGN OF GEEK:**

Wraps self in flag, then burns flag just because it should be within citizen's right to do so.

**SIGN OF SUPERFREAK:**

Wraps self in flag, burns flag, objects to taxes on purchase of new flag.

# TREE HUGGERS

**ALSO KNOWN AS:**
*Preservationists, Hippies, Crunchy Types, Green Activists*

**JUST DON'T CALL THEM:**
*Nature Nazis*

**CORE BELIEF:**
*To paraphrase the religious leader Hillel: If we are not for Nature, who will be? And if not now, when?*

> *"Woodman, spare that tree! / Touch not a single bough! / In youth it sheltered me / And I'll protect it now."*
>
> —American poet George Pope Morris (1802–1864)

## WHO THEY ARE:

Environmentalists not content to buy "green" toilet paper or put an eco-friendly bumper sticker on their Prius, but rather men and women who take an active role in defending Nature and the interests of the ecosystem: in fighting this defense, the antagonist is usually industry or corporate America.

Of course, Tree Huggers are not concerned exclusively with trees, but with Nature as a whole and humankind's relationship with same.

Tree Huggers' opponents typically stereotype them to be flaky, dangerously liberal utopians armed with faulty science. Conversely, Tree Huggers may paint their opposition as knee-jerk capitalists who reject any environmental concerns that compromise the expansion of the U.S. economy or further regulate industry.

## HOW TO RECOGNIZE:

Usually chained to a Redwood.

## TO BE FOUND:

In full force on Earth Day, at rallies and festivals; in college and university towns; at health food supermarkets and farmers markets; urban homesteading.

## HEROES:

Al Gore, Rachel Carson, Shel Silverstein (*The Giving Tree*).

## THEIR IDEA OF FUN:

Disrupting, through means either legal or illegal, what corporate interests refer to as "progress," "the bottom line," and "capitalism."

## MOST DISTINCTIVE TRAIT:

Dedication to their cause sometimes results in their being lax with respect to personal grooming habits and to appreciating the connection between wardrobe and making a professional impression on others.

## BIGGEST CONTROVERSY:

Tree Huggers tend to come from a different socioeconomic and educational background than the loggermen with whom they put themselves at, um, loggerheads. From the loggers points of view, Tree Huggers should be taking their protest to corporate headquarters and not slowing up men who are just doing a job to feed their families.

## BIGGEST MISCONCEPTION ABOUT:

That they think three-inch fish and spotted owls are more important than human beings. Typically, Tree Huggers who challenge industrial interference in natural environments are looking more long-term and holistically with respect to potential impact on people and the economy, to say nothing of the environment.

## WHAT YOU MAY HAVE IN COMMON:

Environmentalist, "green" attitude or way of life; willingness to be chained to large objects.

## BUZZWORDS:

Mostly logger terms, studied under the "Know thy enemy" principle: "blow-down" are trees felled naturally by wind; "clear-cutting" is the total removal of trees from an area; "old-growth forests" contain very tall or old trees and a unique ecosystem.

## SIGN OF FAN:

Selfless dedication to the preservation of America's forests extends as far as the rear bumper of SUV.

## SIGN OF GEEK:

Visits website of nonprofit Tree Huggers of America, clicks on and reads every one of seemingly endless links.

## SIGN OF SUPERFREAK:

Engages in "Tree Sitting"—i.e., physically occupying a tree to prevent logging or at least stall loggers while lawyers do their work.

# ACT UP MEMBERS

**ALSO KNOWN AS:**
Members of the AIDS Coalition to Unleash Power, Gay Rights protestors, Gay Activists

**JUST DON'T CALL THEM:**
Act Out, Gays (i.e., you don't need to be homosexual to support gay rights)

**CORE BELIEFS:**
The federal government needs to form a coherent, aggressive, and national policy to fight AIDS instead of spending money on war and pork projects. Also, religious communities should live up to their self-professed values of inclusion and compassion and not marginalize homosexuals as "sinners."

*"SILENCE = DEATH"*

—ACT UP campaign slogan

## WHO THEY ARE:

Members or supporters of a political action group focused on fighting the AIDS epidemic—the key word being "action," meaning in-the-street protest, not armchair sympathy or writing polite letters.

By taking a vociferous role as agents of change, members of ACT UP risk being labeled "militant" (or worse) by the opposition. That label easily extends itself to others such as: angry, humorless, hateful, prone to violence—even if there is no evidence to support such labels.

What distinguishes ACT UP from other political action groups is its lack of a "leader," spokesperson, or president: the committee-based organization is intentionally loose and grounded in grassroots development to allow for flexibility, innovation, and empowerment of its membership.

Given this "looseness," some ACT UP chapters or groups have renamed themselves, merged with other social action groups, or simply disbanded.

## HOW TO RECOGNIZE:

Group symbol is a pink triangle (the Nazi equivalent of the yellow Star of David, for homosexuals) with the aforementioned favorite quote.

## TO BE FOUND:

On Wall Street, protesting for lower prices and improved access to AIDS vaccines and drugs; in or near Catholic churches, protesting the Church's official stance on homosexuality as a sin or unnatural behavior.

## HERO:

Founder Larry Kramer (1935– ), an author and public health advocate who formed ACT UP at the Lesbian and Gay Community Services Center (NY) in 1987.

## THEIR IDEA OF FUN:

Empowering its members in the methods and means of creating grass roots activism.

## MOST DISTINCTIVE TRAIT:

Initiative.

## BIGGEST CONTROVERSY:

Interrupting Catholic Mass and straying into peripheral issues such as abortion and sex education doesn't help defeat the stereotype of the group as a incoherent gang of anarchists.

## BIGGEST MISCONCEPTION ABOUT:

That they're "radicals," "militants," "Catholic bashers," "domestic terrorists" and part of the "gay agenda" to brainwash all of America into accepting their values.

### Still Acting

ACT UP, while arguably not as visible or member-strong as in the last decades of the twentieth century, is still a going concern and invites interested individuals either to join or form their own chapters or groups.

## WHAT YOU MAY HAVE IN COMMON:

An arrest record for civil disobedience; gay friends.

## BUZZWORDS:

"DIVA TV" ("Damned Interfering Video Activist Television") is a video unit within ACT UP, creating its own commercials, documentaries, and footage of protests and events.

## SIGN OF FAN:

SILENCE = DEATH pin one of dozens attached to backpack, military jacket, hat, or cubicle wall.

## SIGN OF GEEK:

Sends Facebook invite to civil disobedience protest, blogs experience.

## SIGN OF SUPERFREAK:

Volunteers to be arrested, attempts recruitment in holding cell, sends police Facebook invite to next protest.

# CONSCIENTIOUS OBJECTORS

**ALSO KNOWN AS:**

*COs*

**JUST DON'T CALL THEM:**

*Cowards, Traitors, Wussies*

**CORE BELIEF:**

*It cannot fall to a human being or a government to take another human being's life, or to occupy another country militarily, even for "peace-keeping" purposes.*

*"War will exist until the distant day when the conscientious objector enjoys the same reputation and prestige as the warrior does today."*

—U.S. President (and veteran) John F. Kennedy

## WHO THEY ARE:

The Conscientious Objector refuses either combat duty or military service entirely, on the grounds that his or her conscience objects.

Such objections are not always sustained. Laws have varied over time and from country to country concerning who qualifies to be a CO, and why, and what this means concerning their civic duty.

Men and women who declare themselves COs range from anti-militarists who oppose the whole concept of an army to devoutly religious people who do not answer the query "What would Jesus do" with the reply, "Go for the kill shot."

One may also object to killing in one's capacity as a Jew, Muslim, Hindu, or yes, even an atheist.

Despite the fact that we Americans live in a country that loves to celebrate freedoms (not just of thought, but of action), COs get a ton of grief—and if you think they get a lot from their family or their friends, you should see what they get in the military.

Acording to the Government Accounting Office, between 2002 and 2006, the U.S. Armed Forces processed 425 applications for CO status: 53 percent were approved, and 44 percent were denied.

Critics, however, question these statistics, as they fail to include military personnel who have expressed an interest in CO status, sought out organizations such as the Center for Conscience and War, or who submitted and then withdrew their application.

## HOW TO RECOGNIZE:

They're pursuing CO status during peacetime and not at the last minute during a draft.

## TO BE FOUND:

Anywhere you may find someone with a conscience and the will to make an objection.

## HEROES:

Proponents of nonviolence such as Jesus, Martin Luther King Jr., and Ghandi; Boxer Muhammad Ali, who applied for (and was denied) CO status during Vietnam; Olaf from e.e. cummings's poem "I Sing of Olaf Glad and Big"

## THEIR IDEA OF FUN:

Exercise—of what they see as an inalienable right to object.

## MOST DISTINCTIVE TRAIT:

As debatable as it may be to some, courage: No one goes through the trouble of filing for and securing CO status casually.

## BIGGEST CONTROVERSY:

The purpose or sincerity of their beliefs. Those who willingly join the armed forces may see the CO as someone using religion or personal philosophy to dodge his or her civic responsibility.

## BIGGEST MISCONCEPTIONS ABOUT:

That they're cowards who have no interest in serving their country; that they don't "support the troops"; that they advocate a foreign policy of "live and let live" toward dictators, fascists, and other bad guys.

## WHAT YOU MAY HAVE IN COMMON:

An aversion to being shot at or to killing someone you don't know.

## BUZZWORDS:

"Pacifist" is someone who objects to war; "nonresistant" is an advocate of nonviolence; and "anti-militarist" is someone who objects to the concept of a military.

## SIGN OF FAN:

Objects to serving in military in combat position.

## SIGN OF GEEK:

Objects to serving in military.

## SIGN OF SUPERFREAK:

Objects to playing "Call of Duty" or "Stratego."

# TAX PROTESTERS

**ALSO KNOWN AS:**
*Anti-Taxers*

**JUST DON'T CALL THEM:**
*Tax Evaders*

**CORE BELIEF:**
*Tax as little as possible for the maximum public benefit.*

> *"Taxation without representation is tyranny."*
> —James Otis (1725–1783)

## WHO THEY ARE:

People who, for a variety of personal or political reasons, renounce or refuse paying taxes. (Typically, the taxes in question are income taxes: good luck refusing to pay sales tax.)

Opposition to paying taxes may relate to a protest of how the government spends tax revenue: e.g., Tax Protestors during the Vietnam War equated paying taxes with a sanction of U.S. foreign policy in East Asia.

More commonly, Tax Protestors believe that their interests are not represented in government. The model for this philosophy is the Boston Tea Party, which, while inarguably an illegal act, is associated with the worthwhile patriotic cause of United States independence.

One of the fruits of that independence is that you're free to protest paying taxes. Where one gets in trouble is when protest takes the form of *not* paying taxes. Some Tax Protestors may refuse to file a return; others may set up an illegal tax shelter. For as many ways of avoiding paying taxes, there are penalties for being caught doing so.

It should be noted that the U.S. Tax Center estimated that in 2009, approximately 50 percent of U.S. households paid no income tax—because legally, they didn't have to, owing to exemptions and low income, among other factors.

## HOW TO RECOGNIZE:

Often found among Libertarians, Republicans, Tea Party Members.

## TO BE FOUND:

In a cranky mood, come April 15.

## HERO:

Henry David Thoreau (1817–1862), the author of *Walden*, who famously accepted imprisonment instead of paying back taxes, on the grounds that his taxes were supporting slavery and the Mexican-American War, which he opposed.

## THEIR IDEA OF FUN:

Finding loopholes and exemptions.

## MOST DISTINCTIVE TRAIT:

If taxes don't tax them, the protesting does.

## BIGGEST CONTROVERSY:

Alleged hokum in their arguments, which includes the charge that the 16th Amendment giving the federal government the right to impose income tax is either unconstitutional or was never ratified by the necessary number of states. A popular counter-argument to tax protests is that it's hypocritical to benefit from Social Security and Medicaid while protesting the paying of taxes.

## BIGGEST MISCONCEPTION ABOUT:

That a refusal to pay taxes—or as much taxes as one does—is unpatriotic.

## WHAT YOU MAY HAVE IN COMMON:

The belief that you already pay too much in taxes; you don't see enough of a return for the taxes you pay; your interests aren't represented in government.

## BUZZWORDS:

Flat tax, capital gains tax, inheritance tax—plus the ocean of arcane terms, initialisms, and acronyms that is the U.S. tax code. Consult your accountant.

## SIGN OF FAN:

Grouses openly about paying taxes to anyone who will listen.

## SIGN OF GEEK:

Applies expansive estimations when calculating deductions in order to pay less in taxes, assuming the I.R.S. will never bother to investigate.

## SIGN OF SUPERFREAK:

Attempts to have name legally changed to "Kiss My Ass," so that this is the first thing the I.R.S. sees on tax return.

SEX

- Furries
- Swingers
- Polyamorists
- Sadomasochists
- Cartoon Porndogs
- Adipophiles
- Bears

# FURRIES

**ALSO KNOWN AS:**

*FurFans*

**JUST DON'T CALL THEM:**

*Perverts, Freaks, Nut Jobs*

**CORE BELIEF:**

*Life is too short to be human.*

> *"I think I could turn and live with animals, they are / so placid and self-contain'd, / I stand and look at them long and long."*
>
> —Walt Whitman, *Leaves of Grass*

## WHO THEY ARE:

People who enjoy dressing up, in whole or in part, to resemble either a fur-covered animal or an imaginary furry creature of their own devising. The purpose of doing so is largely for role play or game play, or to express identification with an animal.

Sound odd? Think again. Children play games, pretending to be animals. Adults play video games in which their avatars may be animalistic. Celebrities provide the voices for animals in the movies. *Playboy* dresses women up with rabbit ears and a tail. The human fascination and identification with animals is endless. "Furries" express and explore this identification in a colorful fashion.

Furries tend to be tolerant and accepting concerning sexual orientation: some see the Furry interest, then, as a creative manifestation or dramatic expression of that tolerance. Regrettably, press coverage of Furries that has focused solely on their sex lives has colored the public perception of them to be just perverts with tails. Not so.

## HOW TO RECOGNIZE:

"Follow the fur."

## TO BE FOUND:

"FurFest" conventions; role play interactions; behind bedroom doors; inside closets.

## HERO:

Bugs Bunny, not only for his furry features and winning personality but also for his repeated film appearances in drag.

## THEIR IDEA OF FUN:

Pretty much anything that involves another Furry. Not unlike chess, being a Furry is something you could do alone, but it's not as stimulating.

## MOST DISTINCTIVE TRAIT:

You can't deny they feel nice.

## BIGGEST CONTROVERSY:

Public perception and acceptance. Being burned in the media makes you reluctant to talk to sociologists and researchers who wish to learn more about your group and publicize a positive image.

## BIGGEST MISCONCEPTION ABOUT:

That they're weirdos. Sexual foreplay and intercourse is a highly sensuous realm, often enhanced by fantasy and role play. It's a bit of a double standard for someone pretending, during sex, to be a cowboy or the head of the high school cheerleading squad to scoff at someone who pretends to be a bear or a lynx; similarly, the tactile pleasures of having sex with a naked woman wearing a fur coat or a man wearing a cowhide leather outfit are fundamentally similar to someone enjoying having sex while dressed up as a furry animal.

## WHAT YOU MAY HAVE IN COMMON:

Non-Furry Americans assign each other animal traits all the time. We call other humans "pigs" and "dogs." Animals are the basis of dozens of idioms explaining human behavior: "stubborn as a goat," "sly as a fox." "Furries" simply express and explore this identification in a dramatic and colorful fashion.

## BUZZWORDS:

"Fursona" is the persona of the animal creature the person inhabits.

## SIGN OF FAN:

Buys animal Halloween costume, doesn't go trick-or-treating.

## SIGN OF GEEK:

Whiskers on face are the kind you draw on, using eye pencil.

## SIGN OF SUPERFREAK:

Back of closet has extensive selection of strap-on tails.

# SWINGERS

**ALSO KNOWN AS:**
Couples in "open relationships," with "an arrangement" or "an understanding"

**JUST DON'T CALL THEM:**
Cheaters, Sex Addicts, Whores, Mansluts

**CORE BELIEF:**
That the remedy to boredom in the marital bed is to invite other people into it, just like how your boredom with what's on television will be magically fixed by adding one more channel.

> *"Take my wife—please!"*
>
> —comedian Henny Youngman (1906–1998)

## WHO THEY ARE:

Men and women who, by mutual agreement, engage in sexual relationships with other people as a couple. Note that the "broadening," if you will, of the marital bond is not something each individual pursues on his or her own: Swingers hook up with other couples and trade partners.

Like Polyamorists, Swingers believe that honesty, openness, and mutual consent take the sting out of adultery. Swinging can be a casual, one-time pursuit, or it can be an occasional indulgence over an extended period of time. Statistics about how many Americans "cheat" on their spouses often does not separate out those who have sex outside of the relationship with his or her partner's consent.

Swinging, of course, has been around for centuries but is most often associated with the 1970s in America. Movies such as *The Ice Storm* and the short-lived TV series *Swingtown* showed both the good and the bad of swinging (albeit with the scales tipped a little more toward the bad, perhaps to appease advertisers and conservative viewers).

According to The North American Swing Club Association, approximately 15 percent of American couples have experimented with swinging.

## HOW TO RECOGNIZE:

If a woman is giving you the eye at a party, you've found a flirt. If you look over at her boyfriend or husband and he's grinning and nodding at you, you've found some swingers.

## TO BE FOUND:

One click away, on the Internet; at parties; in clubs.

## HEROES:

For men: Jack Kennedy, Tiger Woods, Magic Johnson; For women: Emma Bovary, Anna Karenina; For both: Stifler's Mom in *American Pie*.

## THEIR IDEA OF FUN:

Going to key-swapping parties.

## MOST DISTINCTIVE TRAITS:

Flirtatious conversation, skillful maneuvering under tables, knowledge of local motel scene.

## BIGGEST CONTROVERSY:

Their belief that the swinging lifestyle can be sustained over a lifelong marriage. The swingers' reply would be that a lifestyle choice doesn't have to be a lifelong choice.

## BIGGEST MISCONCEPTION ABOUT:

Both husband and wife are gorgeous.

## WHAT YOU MAY HAVE IN COMMON:

Wandering eye, active fantasy life, disenchantment with partner, STDs.

---

### *Non-Swinging Swingers*

Consider this agreement: If one person in a committed couple crosses paths with someone they want to have sex with, the partner is told up front. The couple can then talk about it and figure out what to do with those feelings. Some people find this approach liberating, as it does away with jealousy and sneaking around. Of course, some couples with this arrangement *never* get to the point of taking it to the next level, but hey—it often brings them closer together and helps them be more honest with each other.

---

## BUZZWORDS:

"Soft swap" is limited to oral sex and kissing; "soft swinging" is two couples having sex in the same vicinity; and "group sex" involves a larger group of people.

## SIGN OF FAN:

Husband and wife get drunk, neck with neighbors, and awkwardly avoid neighbors for the rest of their lives.

## SIGN OF GEEK:

Husband and wife indulge in "cyber-cheating" or boning someone else's avatar: no harm, no foul (so they think), and they take the thrill to their own bed.

## SIGN OF SUPERFREAK:

Husband and wife swing with so many people, that after great sex they can't remember who to thank.

# POLYAMORISTS

**ALSO KNOWN AS:**
Non-monogamists

**JUST DON'T CALL THEM:**
Polygamists (who have multiple marriage partners), Polyannas

**CORE BELIEF:**
You can't call it "cheating" if there's honesty and mutual consent.

*"Poor, poor fool, why can't you see /*
*She can love others and still love thee."*

—"Just Me, Just Me," poem by Shel Silverstein

## WHO THEY ARE:

Couples (hetero-, homo-, or bisexual) who, with mutual consent, date or "see" other people. Unlike Swingers, who partake of occasional indulgences, Polyamorists have sustained relationships outside their primary one.

A key distinction here is that the "other people" in these polyamorous relationships also know and consent to the arrangement. Countless couples, married or no, abide by a principle of "See other people if you must, just don't tell me about it." And of course, the mistress (or "manstress") may not know about such a principle—or even that a wife or husband exists at all.

Polyamorists are all about honesty, openness, complete disclosure, and goodwill. To them, what's offensive to a relationship is not spending time with or opening one's self emotionally or sexually to another: it's the lying, deception, jealousy, and acrimony that usually accompanies the mismanagement of such actions.

## HOW TO RECOGNIZE:

Apart from the wink that *both* members of a couple give you at a party, polyamorists have adopted a variety of symbols to communicate their preference with discretion: a red heart with a blue infinity symbol, a red-blue-and-black ribbon with a "pi" symbol; and even a parrot ("Polly," get it?).

## TO BE FOUND:

Among unmarried, usually urban, twenty-somethings, or among the parents of twenty-somethings whose sexual or romantic needs aren't being met after decades of marriage; also among artists, celebrities, free-thinkers.

## HEROES:

Indie filmmakers Daryl Wein and Zoe Lister-Jones may be the first polyamorists to translate their lifestyle choice into a movie: 2009's *Breaking Upwards*, for which they were writers, actors, and directors.

## THEIR IDEA OF FUN:

Sharing the love.

## MOST DISTINCTIVE TRAITS:

That they're people braving exploration beyond the boundaries of convention and the status quo to find fulfillment, often (believe it or not) nonsexual. Polyamorists may be looking for a wider emotional community, a deeper understanding of their own feelings or capacity to love, or mutual empowerment within a relationship.

## BIGGEST CONTROVERSY:

Obviously, that polyamory is frowned upon by mainstream society and major religions. The thornier issue is that an absence of research data makes it difficult for polyamorists to convince skeptics that such arrangements not only can work but can be fruitful and beneficial to everyone involved.

## BIGGEST MISCONCEPTION ABOUT:

That they're sex addicts and commitment-phobes looking to excuse their aberrant behavior under the guise of a benign philosophy.

## WHAT YOU MAY HAVE IN COMMON:

Skepticism about the possibility of a lifelong monogamous love relationship; a loving dissatisfaction with some aspects of your partner's personality or behavior; a wandering eye; lots of love to give.

## BUZZWORDS:

Coded language of polyamory: "My wife and I have an *understanding*"; "I have an *arrangement* with my boyfriend"; "My husband and I are *discreet.*"

## SIGN OF FAN:

Encourages partner to read articles in polyamory magazine *Loving More*.

## SIGN OF GEEK:

Attends "Poly Con" (a polyamorist convention or conference).

## SIGN OF SUPERFREAK:

Requires extra table for six for the "meet the parents" weekend.

# SADOMASOCHISTS

**ALSO KNOWN AS:**
S&M fans, B&Ders (bondage and domination), BDSMers

**JUST DON'T CALL THEM:**
Bullies, Sickos

**CORE BELIEF:**
You can't have pleasure without pain, and vice versa.

*"Hurts so good!"*

—John Cougar

## WHO THEY ARE:

People who derive erotic pleasure from the infliction or reception of physical pain.

Donatien Alphonse Francois, aka the Marquis de Sade (1740–1814), didn't invent sadism, but insofar as the term is understood in a sexual context, his formal title christened the practice. Ditto, Leopold von Sacher-Masoch (1836–1895). Sexual sadists enjoy inflicting pain or discomfort; sexual masochists enjoy receiving it.

The various methods, scenarios, and role play under which such pain is either received or inflicted opens up the broad and ever-widening S&M spectrum.

Contrary to popular stereotypes, BDSM need not involve humiliation or degradation. Lovemaking of any kind involves some degree of domination and/or submission, and couples who wouldn't think to describe themselves as Sadomasochists may engage in "light S&M": e.g., holding your partner's hands down or tying them down, handcuffs, spanking, or rough physical play.

## HOW TO RECOGNIZE:

S&M doesn't require black leather dominatrix outfits, chains, collars, and bondage apparatus, but if by sheer accident you notice these items in a friend's closet, you've struck Sadomasochist (so to speak).

## TO BE FOUND:

In the private lives of people whom you think of as hopelessly normal; also, in the lives of people with issues related to passivity, aggression, or persecution.

## HERO:

When Jane Wiedlin, guitarist for the 1980s girl group The Go-Go's, appeared in the fourth season of VH1's reality show *The Surreal Life*, she revealed the "dirty little secret" that she was into BDSM. (Wiedlin has also made public comments denying she is really a dominatrix, and her website makes no mention of BDSM.)

## THEIR IDEA OF FUN:

Highly physical foreplay and intercourse, typically with role play.

## MOST DISTINCTIVE TRAITS:

They can dish it out *and* take it.

## BIGGEST CONTROVERSY:

The fact that rape is primarily a crime of violence, not sex, can make the boundaries between sadomasochism and criminal perversity blurry.

## BIGGEST MISCONCEPTION ABOUT:

As with most sexual subcultures, that they're sick. The prejudice against S&Mers is that their interest in passivity or aggression in the bedroom reflects an unhealthy equivalent in their public lives.

## WHAT YOU MAY HAVE IN COMMON:

Algophilia (sexual arousal from pain), an interest in hojojitsu (a Japanese martial art of bondage), a love of Pony Play (riding your partner like a horse), use of a Sybian (a motorized dildo on a saddle), knowledge of making knots.

## BUZZWORDS:

The "safeword": i.e., a coded word which the masochist speaks when he or she either has had enough or wants to indicate that the games have crossed a line and must end. Why not just say "No" or "Stop"? Because there may be pleasure in saying those words in the throes of sexual excitement. The safeword could be any word, but is mutually understood as Stop.

## SIGN OF FAN:

Uses bathrobe belt to tie partner to bed frame, but lightly.

## SIGN OF GEEK:

Engages in S&M play in bed, but doesn't call it S&M: e.g., spanking is "slapping," and requests to "punish me, dungeon master" come out as "be rough."

## SIGN OF SUPERFREAK:

Installs bondage apparatus in ceiling over bed and double lock on bedroom door.

# CARTOON PORNDOGS

**ALSO KNOWN AS:**
*Dudes*

**JUST DON'T CALL THEM:**
*Creeps, Nerds, Onanists, Pervs*

**CORE BELIEF:**
*Even cartoon characters need someone, every now and then.*

*"I'm not bad . . . I'm just drawn that way."*
—Jessica Rabbit, in the 1988 film, *Who Framed Roger Rabbit?*

## WHO THEY ARE:

People (usually men) who are sexually aroused by adult comics and/or erotic cartoons.

The sexualization of characters from comic strips or animated cartoons encompasses a broad spectrum: at one end are comics or cartoons such as *Family Guy* or *Futurama* that flirt with the occasional sex joke but are never (or rarely) obscene; and at the other end are explicitly pornographic cartoons or comics, featuring either established cartoon characters (anyone from Mickey Mouse to Peggy from *King of the Hill*) or characters original to the pornographic piece. The explicitness of the sexual content varies and, like other pornography or erotica, caters to a particular fetish or fantasy.

In Japan, comics and cartoons with explicit sexual content are called *hentai* (though the Japanese may insist on a difference between comics for an adult audience and comics that are flat out dirty).

Animated erotica or cartoons constitute a thin fraction of the $15+ billion porn industry, largely because most people prefer looking at people more than at drawings. Whether or not you call hyper-sexualized comic book heroines or adult-themed graphic novels (e.g., *Luba* by The Hernandez Brothers) "porn" is a matter of taste: as U.S. Justice Potter Stewart said of pornography, you know it when you see it.

## HOW TO RECOGNIZE:

Hairy palms, eyesight trouble, nervous tics.

## TO BE FOUND:

What comic book stores still exist usually segregate the adult section to the rear of the store, with or without a curtain partition. Cartoon porndogs (like all porn enthusiasts) are most likely to congregate online, exchanging files in chat rooms or sharing files on blogs, such as *www.cartoonpornblog.net*.

## HEROES:

Artists Milo Manera, the Italian illustrator of *Click* (1983) and *Butterscotch* (1986), Adam Hughes, especially for his work on *Wonder Woman* and *Catwoman*; and Robert Crumb, creator of *Fritz the Cat*.

## THEIR IDEAS OF FUN:

Jerking off; reading comics; reading comics while jerking off; sitting around with friends and playing elimination rounds of "Who Would You Do?."

## MOST DISTINCTIVE TRAIT:

Anxiety about being found out.

## BIGGEST CONTROVERSY:

Whether or not cartoons of naked women exploit actual women.

## BIGGEST MISCONCEPTION ABOUT:

That their fetish is any weirder than yours.

## Why Are These Comic Pages Stuck Together?

It's understandable that women (or even men) may ridicule the Cartoon Porndog at best and, at worst, be totally skeeved out by them, on the idea that cartoon porndoggery represents a creepy sexual perversion of childhood. Bear in mind that comics and cartoons combine a realm of unbridled imagination with sexual fantasy: i.e., cartoon characters can have sex in ways that the most limber porn stars couldn't even dream of.

## WHAT YOU MAY HAVE IN COMMON:

Love of boobs; knowledge of comics or cartoon trivia; an external hard drive wholly dedicated to "the files."

## BUZZWORDS:

"Tijuana Bibles" were early twentieth-century underground comics that cast popular cartoon characters of the day (Popeye, Mutt & Jeff) in sexual situations.

## SIGN OF FAN:

Wouldn't kick Leela from *Futurama* out of bed.

## SIGN OF GEEK:

Asks girlfriend or wife to dress up as Leela from *Futurama*, in bed.

## SIGN OF SUPERFREAK:

Sends naked photos of self to Leela from *Futurama*.

# ADIPOPHILES

**ALSO KNOWN AS:**
*Fat Admirer, Fat Lover*

**JUST DON'T CALL THEM:**
*Pervs by the Pound*

**CORE BELIEF:**
*"There's just more of you to love."*

*"Once you've had fat, you never go back!"*

—Fat Bastard, *Austin Powers: The Spy Who Shagged Me*

## WHO THEY ARE:

Men or women who are attracted to the overweight or make a fetish of human fat. The term "adipophile" derives from adipose tissue, in which the human body stores fat.

Every trend inspires a counter-trend, so when the predominant manufactured image of beauty and glamour gives us girls and boys who look like they haven't eaten in weeks, you will inevitably see people gravitate toward men and women who are built like planets.

Note that Adipophiles aren't exclusively interested in the morbidly obsese: they also take a shine to the curvy and the hefty. (In more specific terms, anyone with a body mass index higher than 30 is considered obese.)

What's their deal? It varies. A person who doesn't have a hang-up over his or her BMI can indicate someone with a self-possessed self-acceptance, which has a certain sex appeal. Some folks just like big bodies, in the way that other folks like big butts, big tits, big hands, or big . . . personalities.

And some Adipophiles (who may be thin themselves) see someone with a little body fat, they see someone who likes to eat and therefore enjoy life.

## HOW TO RECOGNIZE:

When they yell out, "Hey, Fatty!" it's a compliment.

## TO BE FOUND:

Picking up guys in buffet lines; reading *Dimensions Magazine*; protesting size discrimination with National Association to Advance Fat Acceptance.

## HEROES:

Gabourey Sidibe (actress), John Goodman (actor), U.S. President William Howard Taft, Jack Sprat.

## THEIR IDEA OF FUN:

Watching the first few episodes of TV's *The Biggest Loser*—after that, their interest starts to wane.

## MOST DISTINCTIVE TRAITS:

Extraordinary disdain for skinny models, male and female; for some, an interest in raising awareness about anorexia and bulimia.

## BIGGEST CONTROVERSY:

Where the line gets drawn. A simple fondness for love handles doesn't qualify as adipophilia. A "Fat Admirer" has a distinct preference for a heavy partner. The "Fat Fetishist" has a hard time or complete inability to enjoy a partner unless they are fat: now we get into territory of enablers ("feeders") and enabled people ("feedees" who let themselves be overfed, and "gainers" who do it themselves). "Stuffing" refers to overeating to distend the stomach and give the appearance of being overweight.

## BIGGEST MISCONCEPTION ABOUT:

That there's something wrong about their preference. Sure, obesity and unhealthy weight gain are America's number one health problem, but it also won't kill you to have a little body fat to keep you warm in the winter.

## WHAT YOU MAY HAVE IN COMMON:

Love of jiggling, the belief that bigger is better.

## BUZZWORDS:

"avoir du pois" (av-WAHR doo PWAH): French for "having a few pounds"; "Reubenesque": after the painter Paul Reubens and his predilection for, um, well-rounded nude models; "zaftig": Yiddish for pleasingly plump.

## SIGN OF FAN:

Instead of looking you in the eye when you're talking, stares at your love handles.

## SIGN OF GEEK:

When partner asks, "Do I look fat in this?" doesn't look up and replies, "Damn, I sure hope so!"

## SIGN OF SUPERFREAK:

Secretly sneaks fat content into partner's diet; derisively calls partner "skinny bitch" or "pencil chest"; gives lover big box of chocolates when it's not Valentine's Day.

# BEARS

**ALSO KNOWN AS:**
Hairy homos, gargantuan gays, Ursa Majors

**JUST DON'T CALL THEM:**
Fag, Queer, Mary—not unless you have your running shoes on

**CORE BELIEF:**
Big on inclusion (big on everything, in fact).

> *"He sized up me / I sized up him /*
> *That great big bear / Oh, way up there!"*
>
> —"The Bear Song" (traditional)

## WHO THEY ARE:

Despite what American TV and movies would have you believe, not all homosexual men are mincing, prancing, Chardonnay-sipping urbanite fairies whom a good breeze would blow away.

Bears are gay or bisexual men who are physically imposing (either in physique or girth) and who embody a hyper-masculine lifestyle. They tend to be men of the outdoors and the blistered hand, with unruly facial and body hair.

The gay community—to the extent that such a thing exists as a cohesive whole—does not have a settled definition of a "bear." Some gay men identify bears in terms of physical size (in *The Simpsons* episode "Three Gays of the Condo," Homer Simpson is called a bear), while other gay men associate bears with also being hyper-masculine.

How many bears are currently on the loose in America? Well, given 120 million adult males in America, and the guesstimate that one in 10 people are homosexual, and the fact that two-thirds of Americans are obese or overweight, that comes out to about eight million Bears. And they say there are no good men left out there . . .

## HOW TO RECOGNIZE:

beards (not the female kind); slightly less body hair than El Chupacabra; sometimes dressed like the lumberjack on Brawny paper towels or wearing a black leather vest that doesn't come close to buttoning over their naked abdomen.

## TO BE FOUND:

Rainbow Motorcycle Club (San Francisco, CA); reading *Bear Magazine*; and (this is just a rumor, mind you) among forest rangers, lumber crews, blue-collar bars and taverns, biker rallies, and fishing boats.

## HEROES:

Bevis, the lumberjack in Monty Python's "Lumberjack Song"; Wolverine from *X-Men*; Mr. Slave from *South Park*; Glenn Hughes, the original biker in The Village People; Robin Williams; Burt from Burt's Bees; Santa.

## THEIR IDEA OF FUN:

Any outdoorsy man's idea of fun (just gay).

## MOST DISTINCTIVE TRAITS:

Hung like Redwoods, and the biggest love handles you'll ever squeeze.

## BIGGEST CONTROVERSY:

Some "muscle-bears" show animosity toward "chubs" (overweight bears) and "twinks" (hairless, effeminate gay men).

## BIGGEST MISCONCEPTIONS ABOUT:

Well, that they're straight, first of all; second, that their favorite football team is from Chicago; and third, that the lumberjack or biker outfits are just a pose ('cause honey, nobody dresses like that unless it's for real).

## WHAT YOU MAY HAVE IN COMMON:

An interest in motorcycles, log rolling (by which I mean burling, not the . . . oh, never mind), truck and tractor pulls, axe throwing, two-man crosscut sawing, chainsaw carving, speed chopping.

## BUZZWORDS:

Elderly bears are "Gummy Bears"; doctor and male nurse bears are "Care Bears"; Alaskan bears are "Polar Bears"; and cowboy boot–wearing bears in a line at a hoe-down are "Dancing Bears."

## SIGN OF FAN:

Smiles and nods approvingly at sight of man sporting chest carpet.

## SIGN OF GEEK:

Has photo of '70s-era bare-chested Burt Reynolds as screen saver.

## SIGN OF SUPERFREAK:

Organizes protest outside body-waxing salon, begging male customers to rethink their decision, for the love of God!

# SOCIETY

- Gawkers
- Slummers
- Shriners
- Townies
- Hipsters
- Beauty Queens
- Hot Rodders
- MENSA Members
- Bennies
- Greeks
- HOGs
- Junior Leaguers
- Genealogists

# GAWKERS

> *"We are all in the gutter, but some of us are looking at the stars."*
> —Oscar Wilde (1854–1900)

## WHO THEY ARE:

American consumer culture is designed to give us way, way too many choices. If you go into the supermarket not knowing what type of orange juice you want, you'll be holding up the line. So it is with celebrities: There used to be a manageable, finite number of stars in the firmament of fame; now the Hubble lens of mass media has shown us that everyone is, was, or can be famous.

So can you blame the Gawker? Even if you went off the grid to get away from it all, you'd run into the cast of a reality show about deep woods survival.

Gawkers prefer their soap operas and romance novels to be live action, carried out day to day in the lives of the rich, famous, infamous, and train wrecks waiting to happen. They consume celebrity news like sperm whales inhaling plankton, helping a magazine such as *People* top AdWeek Media's "Hot List" in 2010 for advertising revenue and page growth. (*People*'s revenue for 2006 reportedly topped $1.5 billion.)

## HOW TO RECOGNIZE:

When you approach their cubicle, they jump in their seats and hurriedly click out of websites like Gawker.com, TMZ, and Perez Hilton, saying, "What? What? I'm really busy right now!"

**TO BE FOUND:**

Glued to a TV or computer screen, nose deep in *US, People, InStyle* or some other bastion of journalism.

**HERO:**

Photographer Annie Leibowitz has made a career out of turning celebrity journalism into an art form.

**THEIR IDEA OF FUN:**

Posting comments online about red carpet messes, love children, implant disasters, hook-ups, break-ups, pre-nups, post-nups.

**MOST DISTINCTIVE TRAIT:**

Schadenfreude (look it up).

**BIGGEST CONTROVERSY:**

Where "the line" is: the thin one that separates harmless fandom from intrusive felony. Few are the Gawkers who have enough of an objective perspective on their own behavior to realize that meeting your heroes is always a bad idea, that fame doesn't "rub off" on you, and that celebrities only love you from a safe distance.

**BIGGEST MISCONCEPTION ABOUT:**

That a morbid or obsessive interest in the lives of celebrities means that they have no lives themselves. It could be that Gawkers have too much of a life, for which celebrity gossip is a distracting anodyne.

## The Balance of (Human) Nature

If you can settle the argument of which came first, the chicken or the egg, you should be able to tackle the issue of celebrities and Gawkers: i.e., you can't have one without the other, and each feeds the other in a syngergistic *pas de deux.*

**WHAT YOU MAY HAVE IN COMMON:**

An interest in which 1970s TV or movie star is currently "fighting for their life"; a love of drama; a comfort level in calling someone else's wardrobe choices a "hot mess."

**BUZZWORDS:**

Brangelina, TomKat, Bennifer.

**SIGN OF FAN:**

Subscribes to the *National Enquirer,* but only "ironically"; belongs to Angelina Jolie Fan Club.

**SIGN OF GEEK:**

Home coffee table looks like magazine rack at gynecologist's office; always talking about how much her life is like Angelina's.

**SIGN OF SUPERFREAK:**

Has own celeb gossip blog or writes for trashy magazine, still considers himself/herself a "journalist"; currently stalking A-Jo.

# SLUMMERS

**ALSO KNOWN AS:**
*Class Tourists*

**JUST DON'T CALL THEM:**
*Trawlers, Reverse Elitists, Yuppie Scum*

**CORE BELIEF:**
*Poverty, non-Caucasian ethnicity, and blue-collar backgrounds all add up to an enviable decency and attunement to what is truly important in life.*

> *"From the meanest creature one departs wiser, richer,*
> *more conscious of one's blessings."*
>
> —Pozzo, *Waiting for Godot* by Samuel Beckett

## WHO THEY ARE:

People of middle- to upper-class background who seek authenticity or adventure among the "lower orders," usually by visiting bars or other establishments seen as places where "real" people meet.

Common to all slumming is a patronizing misperception of people and places of a different economic or cultural background.

For example, a middle-class couple out on the town may find upscale restaurants to be superficial and contrived: therefore, they venture into a less economically developed part of the city and have dinner at a small Indian food eatery. They emerge feeling gratified at finding "a jewel in the rough" and, once safely home, are thankful for all the blessings life has bestowed on them.

In another scenario, a student at an expensive university hooks up with a young woman who is his waitress. She has no plans to attend college, and the boy finds her hardscrabble, no-nonsense approach to life refreshing. He thinks he will show her "the good life," while she will teach him how to love.

Thus the Slummer romanticizes the less privileged, believing that they live a simpler, more wholesome, or more authentic life.

## HOW TO RECOGNIZE:

Depending on what demographic they're slumming in, Slummers may dress as a means of identification: e.g., baggy jeans, peasant skirts, Che T-shirts.

## TO BE FOUND:

Among people born into privilege and stupidity.

## HERO:

Jesus, for consorting with the poor, the sick, the working classes.

## THEIR IDEA OF FUN:

Renting in "ethnic" neighborhoods, trilling "R's" in Spanish words and place names, accusing everyone but themselves of being racist or classist, buying foreign beer, listening to "world" or folk music.

## MOST DISTINCTIVE TRAITS:

Romantic outlook, patronizing attitude, self-hatred.

## BIGGEST CONTROVERSY:

Slummers will hightail it back to their soft, comfortable homes at the soonest sign of inconvenience or trouble with the lower orders.

## BIGGEST MISCONCEPTION ABOUT:

That Slummers are no different than people of privilege who genuinely wish to work with and learn about the less fortunate, and who truly see the positive aspects of their lives.

## WHAT YOU MAY HAVE IN COMMON:

White guilt.

## BUZZWORDS:

"Noble savage," "hooker with a heart of gold," "the backbone of America," "salt of the earth."

### Lights! Camera! Slum!

Hollywood adores Slumming. Look no farther than *Pretty Woman* and *Maid in Manhattan*, in which working gals are "rescued" by a wealthy Prince Charming. The slum runs both ways: the rich girl can take up with the rough-hewn boy (*Good Will Hunting*, and *Howards End*). Rich parents can "adopt" wayward youths (*Six Degrees of Separation*), while rich youths are thrown in with "common" families (TV's *The Simple Life*).

## SIGN OF FAN:

Spends spring break at high-end Mexican resort, insists on traveling alone in sections of "the real Mexico."

## SIGN OF GEEK:

Adopts cause related to the poor of America or some other country, spends less time volunteering than hectoring middle-class friends with guilt trips.

## SIGN OF SUPERFREAK:

Rebels against privileged family by marrying down and staying down.

# SHRINERS

*"Old Shriners never die, but you'll have to join to find out why."*

—Anonymous

## WHO THEY ARE:

Thanks to Hollywood, we all know that Freemasons are a fraternal organization founded by aliens whose secret messages imprinted in money lead freelance adventurers to buried treasure. Well, clandestinely running the universe can be taxing, so in 1870, some New York Freemasons decided to establish a branch of their organization that would be solely dedicated to fun and fellowship.

One of the founders attended a party thrown by an Arabian diplomat, the entertainment for which was a kind of floor show theater with Oriental trappings. Cool idea, the New Yorker thought: I'll steal it. Hence, the Arabic theme of the Shriners.

Today, the Shriners are best known for their hospitals for children (which charge nothing for treatment), as well as for the annual college-level all-star football game, The East-West Shrine Game. They also sponsor an annual Shrine Circus to raise funds for children.

The Shrine Circuses certainly rake in the peanuts: the *Orlando Sentinel* reported that in 1984, the 175 Shriner Circuses held over the previous year generated $17.5 million in proceeds. (The paper also reported that in 1984, the Shriners donated a grand total of $182,000 to charity: See Controversy section.)

## HOW TO RECOGNIZE:

At your next Fourth of July parade, look for the guys driving tiny cars and performing pseudo-Middle-Eastern music on a float while wearing red fezzes.

### Shriners: The Next Generation

Your grandfather's generation filled what available free time it had by joining service organizations: The Shriners, The Lions Club, or The Elks. Adult men—especially G.I.s returning from war, needing purpose and camaraderie—gravitated to these fraternal groups that had a strong charitable component. Today, their ranks are thin and are thinning further. If you're looking to volunteer your time and energy, boys, follow in your grandad's footsteps—a worn path, sure to satisfy.

## TO BE FOUND:

In Shrine Auditoriums and Shrine Centers, which used to be called "mosques"; at their annual Imperial Council meeting, held in a big city and near an open bar.

## HEROES:

Besides the children‽ Founders Walter M. Fleming (1838–1913 ) and William Florence (1831–1891); Jack H. Jones, current "Imperial Potentate" and "First Lady" Charlene McGuire.

## THEIR IDEA OF FUN:

The entire point of the Shriners is fraternity, fun, fellowship and service.

## MOST DISTINCTIVE TRAIT:

They are the only non-Muslim Americans who dress like Muslims.

## BIGGEST CONTROVERSY:

Financial accountability. While the Shriners are virtually unanimously seen as The Good Guys, there have been inquiries into exactly how much collected money goes to benefit children in Shriners Hospitals. The larger issue is organizational control of fundraising and transparency thereof. While some complaints may be legitimate and worth investigation, you might as well ask Santa what kind of benefits package he gives his elves.

If you're feeling really cynical, you could call the Shriners a bunch of old drunks who don't really work all that hard to benefit their causes—the accusation might stick, but you'll likely come across as a hater who picks easy targets.

It's conceivable that a Muslim or Arab could interpret the trappings of the Shriners as a mockery of Arab culture. A legitimate rebuttal to this complaint is that one cannot maneuver tiny cars in the desert.

## BIGGEST MISCONCEPTION ABOUT:

That their affiliation with the Freemasons makes them party to history's secrets, bizarre rituals, and that they drink a lot.

## WHAT YOU MAY HAVE IN COMMON:

Fezophilia.

## BUZZWORDS:

Administrative higher-ups are called "deacons," but they're as much deacons in the religious sense as the fezzes are hats in the high-fashion sense.

## SIGN OF FAN:

Cheers at sight of Shriners in Fourth of July parade, donates money or volunteer time to Shriners Hospital.

## SIGN OF GEEK:

Petitions to become member of the Shriners.

## SIGN OF SUPERFREAK:

Attempts to drive tiny car on major interstate.

# TOWNIES

*"If you lived here, you'd be home by now."*

—Anonymous

## WHO THEY ARE:

Townies are any native inhabitants of a town or city, but the term is seldom applied to babies, the infirm or elderly, shut-ins, or pets. More commonly in its usage, Townie describes a vocal and conspicuously visible segment of the local population who express civic pride in ways both lawful and loutish. According to the U.S. Census, there are 18,443 places in America designated as "towns"; assuming that more than one Townie lives in each township and that even more Townies live in municipalities of other classifications, the odds are good that the American Townie population would be best housed in a larger metropolis than you'd think.

While Townies have been known to reclaim this label for themselves, applying it to themselves with pride (cf. "queer"), the term is most often derogatory, directed at a local's attitude, fashion sense, speech patterns, accent, vernacular or wanting intelligence.

The stereotypical Townie is between 18 and 44, no slave to fashion, loud, boorish, and drunk. Male Townies are derided as morons; female Townies, as sluts. In this cartoonish light, Townies are also targeted for being paragons of bad taste, faux "gangstas," racists, misogynists . . . gosh, what am I missing here?

The fact is, not everybody on Earth is dying to escape his or her hometown. Either by choice or the demands of work and family, some people simply "never leave," and if the town in question is nice, there's no reason that being a Townie should carry any kind of opprobrium.

## HOW TO RECOGNIZE:

The person who is giving grief to someone who is not a Townie is the Townie.

## TO BE FOUND:

Spilling out of pubs and taverns in closest proximity to college or national-level sporting events; sending over to a table of college kids an order of shots that turn out to be glasses filled with urine; attending Town Council meetings, specifically regarding the local university's expansion plan.

## HEROES:

Local pols, community activists, third-generation merchants.

## THEIR IDEA OF FUN:

Rolling these frickin' college kids who think they're so frickin' smart.

## MOST DISTINCTIVE TRAITS:

Pride, defiance, outrage, stubbornness.

## BIGGEST CONTROVERSY:

Without an influx of new families, tourists, college kids, or national retailers, the town that Townies love so much would decline and die.

## BIGGEST MISCONCEPTION ABOUT:

That provincialism is an indicator of lack of intelligence, ambition, tolerance, or common sense.

## WHAT YOU MAY HAVE IN COMMON:

Civic pride, xenophobia, a funny local accent.

## BUZZWORDS:

A "carpetbagger" is an individual who moves into a town and identifies themselves as a resident, only for selfish purposes. See The Clintons moving to a tony suburb of New York so that Hillary could legally run for Senate of that state.

## SIGN OF FAN:

Child has same high school chemistry teacher as parents did.

## SIGN OF GEEK:

Parents live in same house as their parents did, have kept color and décor.

## SIGN OF SUPERFREAK:

Ancestors settled town, built town, and still own the town.

# HIPSTERS

**ALSO KNOWN AS:**
Hepcats, Hepsters

**JUST DON'T CALL THEM:**
Hippies, Bohemians

**CORE BELIEFS:**
The only place to be is where it's at, and the only way to be is with it; and if you don't know what it is or where it's at, they don't want to know you.

*"What makes 'hip' a special language is that it cannot really be taught."*
—American author Norman Mailer (1923–2007)

## WHO THEY ARE:

In post-war America of the 1940s, a segment of the rising white urban middle class selectively co-opted African-American culture—jazz, bebop (i.e., jazz you can't dance to), marijuana, social consciousness—to form a kind of artistic, intelligentsia chic. People who were "hip" (or "hep") were in the know, clued in, savvy, and smooth. The Bomb and the Cold War introduced into the mix an element of existential angst and paranoia, and the Abstract Expressionist movement and the Beat Generation broadened the horizons of what people were "hip" to.

The difference between the Hipsters and the Bohemians was that Hipsters needn't be artists themselves: they just read the right books (*The Man in the Grey Flannel Suit*, *The White Negro*), listened to the right records (Charlie Parker, Theolonius Monk), dug the right scene and denounced "squares."

Today, "hipsterism" has evolved into something nebulous: it's become as much an insult as a badge of pride. Hipsters are still identified as young, non-affluent, culturally engaged, and "hip" to trends and fads, but which fads and what cultural products is open to debate, perhaps because the Internet has flooded the marketplace with things to be hip to. At the bottom line, the Hipster shuns anything too mainstream, too popular, too bourgeois. Instead of denouncing the Square, the modern Hipster denounces the Sell-Out.

## HOW TO RECOGNIZE:

Hipters aim for a nonchalant conspicuousness, so watch and listen for the casually loud young man or woman talking about bands, clothing, trends, ethnic restaurants, gadgets, or websites you've never heard of.

## TO BE FOUND:

Ordering wheat grass smoothies, wearing custom-made "ironic" T-shirts, growing facial hair, striking up a debate about ambient musicians, pursuing retro trends.

## HEROES:

Living examples include author Dave Eggers, filmmaker Wes Anderson, actress Ellen Page, bands who play at the annual Coachella Music Festival.

## THEIR IDEA OF FUN:

Finding out that you have no idea who or what they're talking about, for this confirms their hipster cred and superiority.

## MOST DISTINCTIVE TRAIT:

The fact that you can't tell them anything about what you've seen or read or found or are into, because they will only say either that they knew about it first or that what you're saying is painfully unhip.

## BIGGEST CONTROVERSY:

Hipsters not only look unfavorably on those whom they deem unhip: they often look unfavorably on other Hipsters. Aging Hipsters tend to hold onto what they consider hip instead of evolving with the times, and this creates a "Hip Gap" between generations.

## BIGGEST MISCONCEPTION ABOUT:

That they're not willing to let you in on what's hip.

## WHAT YOU MAY HAVE IN COMMON:

Intellectual curiosity, active social life, broad base of friends and contacts, high level of media consumption.

## BUZZWORDS:

No subculture changes slang as quickly and comprehensively as the Hipster, who is also most likely to use as much slang as possible. Today's Hipster is a close monitor of and contributor to Urbandictionary.com.

## SIGN OF FAN:

Hangs with Hipsters, mimics their every move.

## SIGN OF GEEK:

Proactively frames own yardarms of Hipsterism, attracts converts.

## SIGN OF SUPERFREAK:

Has no settled wardrobe, speech pattern, preferences, or personality: whatever is hip that day, they are.

# BEAUTY QUEENS

**ALSO KNOWN AS:**
Women of Pageantry

**JUST DON'T CALL THEM:**
Pros

**CORE BELIEF:**
Smile and wave.

*"Smilers wear a crown, losers wear a frown."*

—Victor Melling (Michael Caine), in *Miss Congeniality* (movie, 2000)

## WHO THEY ARE:

Young women who see beauty contests as a stepping stone to bigger things: a scholarship, a national beauty title, a record deal, a job in journalism or meteorology, nude modeling, or a career in acting (possibly directing).

Parades of female pulchritude are as old as the oldest profession, although the Miss America Pageant began only in 1921, the year after the 19th Amendment to the U.S. Constitution gave women the right to vote.

Today, it's frowned upon to call these pageants "beauty contests," since it's not just about beauty: there's also the talent portion, as well as the answering of questions about world peace. In addition to Miss America, there is Miss World (the oldest international pageant), Miss Universe (the most publicized international pageant), Miss Earth (a "green" pageant), and even Mrs. America, in which 2004's Mrs. Rhode Island competed while six months pregnant with twins. Add to these top-tier pageants a host of state, regional, and theme-related contests, and you have a land of opportunity for girls of all races, colors, and creeds to trade on their looks.

And depending on the contestant's birthplace and circumstances, the beauty pageant may be the quickest way to a college scholarship, media attention, or even job opportunities. The Miss America Pageant continues to be America's largest provider of scholarship money for women: approximately $50 million to 12,000 women every year.

## HOW TO RECOGNIZE:
Petroleum jelly on professionally whitened teeth, adhesive tape strategically placed in swimsuit portion, "royal wave" (fingers together, hand cupped, rotating wave on axis of wrist).

## TO BE FOUND:
Waving from convertibles in parades, wearing high heels with a bikini.

## HEROES:
1963 America's Junior Miss (Diane Sawyer), 1971 Miss Black Tennessee (Oprah Winfrey), 1983 Miss America (Vanessa Williams), 1984 Miss Wasilla, Alaska (Sarah Palin), 1986 Miss Ohio (Halle Berry), 1998 Miss Corpus Christi, Texas (Eva Longoria).

## THEIR IDEA OF FUN:
Embodying what they believe is a positive role model for young girls.

## MOST DISTINCTIVE TRAIT:
Poised and preening perfection.

## BIGGEST CONTROVERSY:
Several topics compete for the title of Most Controversial: breast implants; plastic surgery; nude photos of a contestant that magically emerge *after* she's won a title; and parents who prep their little girls for Miss America by entering them in toddler beauty contests. Oh, and something about pageants objectifying women and stuff.

## BIGGEST MISCONCEPTION ABOUT:
That walking on a stage, smiling, and waving is easy. Beauty Queens make a major investment in time, energy, and especially money for entry fees, clothing, travel, makeup, and dozens of other expenses unseen by and unknown to the viewing audience. The support of family in the pursuit of that crown is a must.

## WHAT YOU MAY HAVE IN COMMON:
Undergraduate degree in Communications, Cosmetology, or Political Science.

## BUZZWORDS:
"Glitz events" emphasize looks, while "Natural events" emphasize talent, interview, and non-beauty portion.

## SIGN OF FAN:
Wins title of "Miss Maple Syrup Festival."

## SIGN OF GEEK:
Writes college admission essay on winning "Miss Teen, Worcester, Massachusetts."

## SIGN OF SUPERFREAK:
Daily work outfit consists of sash and tiara.

# HOT RODDERS

**ALSO KNOWN AS:**
Road Warriors, Gearheads, Motorheads, "Classic Car" enthusiasts

**JUST DON'T CALL THEM:**
Golden Oldies

**CORE BELIEF:**
She doesn't drive it.

*"I feel the need . . . the need for speed!"*

—*Top Gun* (movie, 1986)

## WHO THEY ARE:

Collectors or racers of a particular kind of retro automobile, engineered for speed and flashy looks.

Some G.I.s came back to America from World War II feeling restless and confined by the new trend toward upward mobility into the middle class. On the West Coast and in the Southwest, you had unused military airports with long landing strips. Applying their technical know-how to the new American status symbol (the automobile), Hot Rodders stripped cars to make them lighter, flashier, and most of all, faster. Baby Boomers, excited by rock and surf culture, soon took the wheel and celebrated the Hot Rod in songs like The Beach Boys' "Little Deuce Coupe" and Charlie Ryan's "Hot Rod Lincoln."

Hot Rod culture continues to this day, fueled by 1950s, 1960s, and even 1970s nostalgia and the fact that today's cars look painfully boring in contrast.

Some Hot Rodders' cars are just for show and are not "street-legal," except in parades or en route to local showcase events, but all are focused on flash, dash, and colorful splash.

## HOW TO RECOGNIZE:

By their cars: as polished as a new apple, exposed engine (or car hood up to reveal engine), fuzzy dice and other 1950s regalia, antique car license plate, big tires.

## TO BE FOUND:

In the parking lot of a supermarket on a Friday or Saturday evening, for a free exhibition and social time; in Fourth of July parade; hot rod festivals, swap meets, and 1950s-themed events at drive-ins, malt shoppes, diners, etc.

## HEROES:

John Milner (Harrison Ford), the drag racer in *American Graffiti* (movie, 1973); artist Ed "Big Daddy" Roth (1932–2001), creator of the hot rod character "Rat Fink."

## THEIR IDEA OF FUN:

Revving engine, turning heads, peeling out; trading stories and information with fellow enthusiasts.

## MOST DISTINCTIVE TRAIT:

The only thing more closely attached to the car than they are is the paint job.

## BIGGEST CONTROVERSY:

Debate between Hot Rodders whose cars date from the 1950s and 1960s and which are outfitted with original or time-specific parts and Hot Rodders whose cars are old but are "pimped" with new parts and modern technology.

## BIGGEST MISCONCEPTION ABOUT:

That they're stuck in the past, arrested in adolescence, and that they're idiots for investing so much time and energy in a car that's too valuable or good-looking to park anywhere unattended.

## WHAT YOU MAY HAVE IN COMMON:

Nostalgia for bygone aesthetic of automobiles.

## BUZZWORDS:

Grease Monkey-Speak, plus "cherry" means "mint new," "A-bone" is a Model A coupe, and "genie" is "genuine."

## SIGN OF FAN:

Reads Tom Wolfe's hot rod chronicle *The Kandy-Kolored Tangerine-Flake Streamline Baby*, subscribes to lowbrow hot rod art mag *Juxtapoz*, tells self "one of these days" he'll own a hot rod.

## SIGN OF GEEK:

Buys basic Rod and gets tattoo, only to suffer from Engine Envy at local Custom Car festival.

## SIGN OF SUPERFREAK:

Becomes mechanic just to specialize in pimping rides, hottening rods.

# MENSA MEMBERS

**ALSO KNOWN AS:**
*Eggheads, Brainiacs, Teachers' Pets*

**JUST DON'T CALL THEM:**
*People Who Test Well*

**CORE BELIEF:**
*The mind is a muscle requiring constant exercise, and as a bonus, this exercise doesn't require sharing a shower room with sweaty people who can see how fat you are.*

> *"Knowledge is power."*
>
> —Sir Francis Bacon (1561–1626)

## WHO THEY ARE:

Members of the world's largest, oldest organization for people with high IQs.

Taking its name from the Latin words for "mind" and "table" (Round Table of smart people, get it? Of course you do.), MENSA has about 100,000 members around the world, a little more than half in the United States. Approximately 40 percent of those U.S. members are baby boomers, between the ages of forty-seven and sixty-four. Provided you score highly enough on the standardized tests approved by the organization, you could become a member of MENSA before you finish elementary school.

Roland Berrill and Lancelot Ware, who founded MENSA in England after World War II, envisioned a "high-IQ society" based on intelligence and blind to social distinctions. MENSA would bring smart people together, facilitate the sharing of ideas and experience, and who knows: from a simple tea party where eggheads could be among their own kind could emerge a gathering of forces that could rid the world of all known diseases or something.

Today, as more American schools, beset with budget difficulties, cut funding for the gifted, MENSA plays an active role in the development of programs and scholarships for the future Einsteins of the world.

## HOW TO RECOGNIZE:

If they're in MENSA, they'll probably let you know without your having to ask.

## TO BE FOUND:

Playing games that don't involve balls or wearing equipment (crosswords, acrostics, cribbage, chess, Go); single-handedly anchoring your Tavern Trivia Team; attending annual MENSA gathering (location varies) with roughly 2,000 other people.

## HEROES:

Celebrities who admit to belonging to MENSA, including Lisa Simpson and actors James Woods and Geena Davis.

## THEIR IDEA OF FUN:

Playing word games; wordplay; reading; the fine arts.

## MOST DISTINCTIVE TRAIT:

The whole point of MENSA is that the only common trait among all its members is IQ.

## BIGGEST CONTROVERSY:

Membership is predicated on your score on MENSA-approved standardized tests, the yardarm being that you must fall in the 98th percentile of intelligence (that is, your IQ is higher than 98 percent of the general tested population). Detractors—some with a very high IQ—argue that intelligence is far more sophisticated than what can be measured on a single test, and that such tests do not so much measure IQ as predict future academic performance.

## BIGGEST MISCONCEPTION ABOUT:

That they're geeks, elitists, and social defectives.

## WHAT YOU MAY HAVE IN COMMON:

Membership in your high school's National Honors Society; a college degree; consistently solid performance on *Jeopardy*; inner conflict about being "different."

## BUZZWORDS:

Some MENSA members form "SIGs," special interest groups that convene smart people of a shared interest, pastime, scholarship, or field.

## SIGN OF FAN:

Takes MENSA test just to see if he'll pass; and once passed, doesn't join group but tells everyone that he could get in if he wanted to, 'cause he passed.

## SIGN OF GEEK:

Actually joins MENSA, refers to self as "Mensan" with straight face.

## SIGN OF SUPERFREAK:

Argues that female Mensans have more intelligent menses.

# BENNIES

*"Life's a Beach."*

—Anonymous

## WHO THEY ARE:

Individuals and families who patronize New Jersey beaches in the summer, having come from northern areas such as: Bayonne, Elizabeth, Newark, and New York—hence, the acronym BENNY.

Any tourist destination has a love-hate relationship with its seasonal interlopers. Bennies support the area's restaurant base, but try getting a good table in the summer. Bennies help make the area a desirable vacation spot, but their word of mouth can bring in more visitors than the area can handle. What makes the Benny situation unique is that it's a lot of New Yorkers visiting New Jersey, bringing with them their attitude of superiority.

Shore residents will probably put the Benny "Mason-Dixon line" somewhere around Driscoll Bridge: anyone north qualifies as a Benny.

Statistically, New Jersey brings in about $38 *billion* annually from tourism, so love Bennies or hate 'em, they come bearing coin of the realm.

## HOW TO RECOGNIZE:

Usually in pairs, often accompanied by screaming children or sullen tweens; overly concerned with sunscreen application; wearing sneakers instead of flip-flops; making vain attempts to haggle with vendors and argue with seaters at restaurants; asking for directions or change for parking meters.

## TO BE FOUND:
Turning Route 37 East in Toms River, NJ, into a parking lot.

## HEROES:
Turnabout being fair play, the cast of MTV's *Jersey Shore.*

## THEIR IDEA OF FUN:
Supporting the Jersey Shore economy with their tourist dollars while at the same time taking advantage of every bargain, discount, and freebie imaginable.

## MOST DISTINCTIVE TRAIT:
As tourists, they tend to act like they own the place and yet don't treat the place as if they did.

## BIGGEST CONTROVERSY:
As above, the "Benny" acronym based on geography, but it can easily slip into a stereotype of gender and ethnicity. To some, Bennies are not so much tourist families but Italian-American youths in wife-beater shirts, designer sunglasses, gold chains, and, let us say, limited intellect. The fact is, these represent only a corner of the total Benny picture.

## BIGGEST MISCONCEPTION ABOUT:
That without them, the seaside retail district and summer economies of New Jersey would get along just fine.

### Anti-Benny Campaign
The website *www.bennygohome.com*, a "Jersey pride" campaign against Bennies and all they stand for, reportedly understands the value that tourism plays in the life of a community, but site organizers claim that tourist revenues end up largely in the hands of corrupt politicians who then fail to represent the cultural integrity of the area or the interests of residents. Naturally, the site itself seeks to profit from Bennies: just from distaste of them. Shirts extolling Jersey pride and Benny animosity are available for purchase.

## WHAT YOU MAY HAVE IN COMMON:
The conviction that Cape Cod and Rhode Island beaches are too far away.

## BUZZWORDS:
Bennies say they're going to the "beach," while true New Jerseyites call it the "shore."

## SIGN OF FAN:
Dines at Benihana, thinking it's food for New Jersey tourists.

## SIGN OF GEEK:
Totally plans to start, like, a Benny Anti-Defamation League or somethin'.

## SIGN OF SUPERFREAK:
Buys land on Jersey Shore to build mega-mansion beach house and gentrify the locals out of town.

# GREEKS

**ALSO KNOWN AS:**
Frat Boys, Sorority Sisters

**JUST DON'T CALL THEM:**
Delta House (the rambunctious fraternity in Animal House), Practitioners of the Greek Arts (aka homosexuality), Drunks

**CORE BELIEF:**
The fraternity or sorority may have an official motto, but standard bedrock values are solidarity and community service.

*"Fat, drunk, and stupid is no way to go through life, son."*

—Dean Wormer, *Animal House* (movie)

## WHO THEY ARE:

Members of unisex social organizations for college students: fraternities for males, sororities for females.

Popular depictions of "Greek life"—in the movies, on *Saturday Night Live*—portray "frat boys" as slow-witted, abusive drunks and "sorority sisters" as vacuous, chirpy, and elitist. More common examples from reality would make for less interesting TV: fraternities can have as few as six members and comprise engineering students, and a sorority's main activities may be study groups and volunteering in the community.

Arguably, anti-Greek sentiment and stereotypes create an environment in which Greeks are less likely to cause mayhem and risk having their charter revoked, and you certainly don't need to pledge to a fraternity in order to get into trouble at college.

College students who become Greeks are most likely looking for structure, support, friendship, and purpose in what may be their first time living away from home.

And before you knock Greeks as louts and beer hounds, note that according to The North-American Interfraternity Conference, 48 percent of all U.S. presidents, 42 percent of U.S. senators, 30 percent of U.S. congressmen, and 40 percent of U.S. Supreme Court justices belonged to fraternities.

## HOW TO RECOGNIZE:

Often by a pin or a sweater bearing Greek letters, but potentially also by any other form of attire or colors.

## TO BE FOUND:

At colleges and universities that allow them—not all of them do.

## HEROES:

Otis Allan Glazebrook, founder of the first national fraternity Alpha Tau Omega (1865), and the twelve female Monmouth College students who founded the first international sorority, I.C. Sorosis, in 1867.

## THEIR IDEA OF FUN:

"Rush Week," a period of fun activities and social events at which prospective Greeks may shop around for where to pledge.

## MOST DISTINCTIVE TRAIT:

Loyalty (not to you, to their own).

## BIGGEST CONTROVERSY:

Incidents of hazing that result in injury, alcohol poisoning, or death; uneasy relationship between off-campus frat houses and local residents.

### Semper Phi

Don't tell the boys at Delta House, but the first Greek-lettered student society was not "I Tappa Kegga," but Phi Beta Kappa, founded in 1776 at the College of William Mary by a kid who had been blackballed by the campus's two other student groups. PBK was the first to adopt Greek letters and the first to develop national as well as local chapters. Today, PBK is an academic honor society with more than a half million living members, including Condoleezza Rice and Ashley Judd. Smart folks, Phi Beta Kappas: I bet you they could even tap a keg (if you showed them).

## BIGGEST MISCONCEPTION ABOUT:

That they're organizations set up exclusively for the ritualized humiliation of "pledges," sanctioned elitism and exclusion, and the abuse of alcohol.

## WHAT YOU MAY HAVE IN COMMON:

School spirit, friends on the football team, approval of the sentiment "Gaudeamus igitur." (Ask a Phi Beta Kappa.)

## BUZZWORDS:

A prospective Greek is a "pledge" to a local division of a fraternity or sorority, or a "house." Because of concerns over safety (or good press), not a few frats and sororities have eliminated the physical challenges or rituals associated with membership known as "hazing."

## SIGN OF FAN:
Attends Greek parties, chips in for keg.

## SIGN OF GEEK:
Participates in "Rush Week," pledges, joins fraternity, volunteers for a titled office like Treasurer.

## SIGN OF SUPERFREAK:
After graduation, conspicuously displays frat "paddle" in office to tip off interviewees, creates "separate pile" of CVs from fellow frat brothers or sorority sisters.

# HOGS

**ALSO KNOWN AS:**
Members of the Harley Owners Group (HOG), a company-sponsored organization promoting solidarity among Harley owners

**JUST DON'T CALL THEM:**
Better off riding Hondas or Yamahas

**CORE BELIEF:**
Fuck it, let's ride (a street paraphrase of an official Harley slogan, "Screw it, let's ride").

*"You don't buy a Harley with your mind;
you buy it with your heart and your balls."*

—actor Robert Patrick (1958– ), who played the T-1000 in
*Terminator 2: Judgment Day* (movie, 1991)

## WHO THEY ARE:

Owners of an American motorcycle that, since its inception in 1903, has come to represent open-road freedom and bad-boy cool.

That, at least, is the brand image. Some motorcycle enthusiasts (and not a few mechanics) will tell you that Harley is more hype than heat, and that most of what you're paying for is the name. The downside, too, of owning such a universally recognized emblem of cool is that someone else may want it more than you do. Harleys are, anecdotally, expensive to insure because they're high on the theft list.

Harley Davidson dealerships may sponsor local HOG chapters, comprising Harley owners who may organize ride-related or charity events (such as for Harley's official charity, the Muscular Dystrophy Association).

The Harley Owners Group counts its membership at over one million riders.

## HOW TO RECOGNIZE:

If you are riding a foreign-made motorcycle and bikers traveling in the opposite direction do NOT wave at you, those bikers are the Harley owners.

Harley owners are also bigger purchasers of brand merchandise (ties, jackets, mugs, you name it) than other motorcycle owners.

## TO BE FOUND:

At America's most famous motorcycle rallies: Sturgis, South Dakota; Laconia, New Hampshire; Daytona, Florida.

### Harleys on Film

The twenty-first century saw the median age of Harley owners pass forty-five years old—inevitable, perhaps, given the brand loyalty and the inevitable aging process, but undeniably there are plenty of suburban Boomer males and pre-retirees looking to speed through their midlife crisis on the backs of a Harley. The backlash among the genuine biker crowd is dramatized in the 2007 movie *Wild Hogs*.

Chances are, if a movie is American-made, the hero is on a Harley. Other famous HD film appearances are the bikes you saw in the movies *Easy Rider* and *Terminator 2*, as well as the chopper Bruce Willis rode in *Pulp Fiction* and Cyclops's ride in the *X-Men* movies.

## HEROES:

Company founders William Harley and Arthur Davidson, CEO Keith Wandell, the children and families of the Muscular Dystrophy Association, fellow riders, trustworthy mechanics.

## THEIR IDEA OF FUN:

Sharing the road, sharing the ride, sharing the fun.

## MOST DISTINCTIVE TRAIT:

Loyalty to the brand and to fellow riders earns them the privilege of complaining about the product once in a while.

## BIGGEST CONTROVERSY:

Buying a motorcycle is (or should be) more complicated than a knee-jerk brand choice or thinking it's just a bicycle with an engine. For better or worse, the Harley mystique can shut down that part of a consumer's brain that makes informed, careful, considered decisions, and that potentially can lead to increased safety risks on the road.

## BIGGEST MISCONCEPTION ABOUT:

That they're either authentically members of some thuggish gang or suburban white guys pretending to be members of some thuggish gang.

## WHAT YOU MAY HAVE IN COMMON:

Mid-life crisis; a wife or girlfriend (aka your "woman" or "old lady") who likes opening her leather vest to show off her fake boobs.

## BUZZWORDS:

Any motorcycle made in China or Japan is a "rice burner."

## SIGN OF FAN:

Buys Harley coffee mug; "just lookin'" at dealership.

## SIGN OF GEEK:

Buys Harley, makes pilgrimage to Harley headquarters, despite its being in Milwaukee, Wisconsin.

## SIGN OF SUPERFREAK:

Dies with (Harley logo) boots on.

# JUNIOR LEAGUERS

**ALSO KNOWN AS:**
Members of the Association of Junior Leagues International Inc. (AJLI)

**JUST DON'T CALL THEM:**
Girl Scout Dropouts

**CORE BELIEF:**
The mutual enrichment of volunteerism.

*"WOMEN BUILDING BETTER COMMUNITIES"*

—Official Junior League slogan

## WHO THEY ARE:

Female members of a volunteer organization dedicated to improving the mental, physical, educational, and environmental health of communities.

The AJLI originated in early twentieth-century New York as an opportunity for well-heeled women to dedicate time and energy to the poor by means of "settlement houses": what we might call today "neighborhood centers." The settlement house allowed volunteers to live and work among the poor, to better understand and service their needs.

Evolving into a broader volunteer organization, the AJLI made a name for itself as a way for young women to create and improve opportunities for the less privileged.

Depending on your Junior League chapter, you need to be at least eighteen or twenty-one to join, and membership requires paying dues and a year of sponsorship in which you attend functions, learn the ropes, work hard, and lay the foundation for what is hoped to be a lifetime of service.

The AJLI is not for the casual volunteer or the bored, wealthy housewife who just wants to write a check and put in an appearance at some glamorous fundraisers. In the past decade, the AJLI has made strides to diversify its leadership and membership, so as to shed a stereotype of white liberal ladies who need something noble to do to occupy their time.

At present, the AJLI comprises more than 160,000 members.

## HOW TO RECOGNIZE:

Female; average age, twenty-five to thirty-four; mostly college graduates, married, with children, and working either full- or part-time.

## TO BE FOUND:

In any one of 293 chapters in the United States, Canada, Mexico, and the United Kingdom.

## HERO:

Founder Mary Harriman (1881–1934), the daughter of a railroad magnate, who decided to do something socially beneficial with her wealth and position in society.

## Just Call Her Junior

To paraphrase an old commercial for the Boys Scouts of America: When your daughter joins the Junior League, there's no guarantee that she'll become a Supreme Court Justice (Sandra Day O'Connor), a Pulitzer Prize-winning author (Eudora Welty), or even First Lady of the United States (Eleanor Roosevelt, Betty Ford, Nancy Reagan, Barbara Bush) . . . but you never know!

## THEIR IDEA OF FUN:

Creative ideas to improve the lives of families and children. Years before chef Jaime Oliver came to American TV with his "Food Revolution," the AJLI was sponsoring its "Kids in the Kitchen" program to fight obesity and help kids make smart dietary choices.

## MOST DISTINCTIVE TRAITS:

Civic duty, community ties.

## BIGGEST CONTROVERSY:

Not that this will make the front page of the *National Enquirer*, but the ALJI presents many notable women as alumnae of the organization when in fact the those women's greatest accomplishments were realized long after they left ALJI. Happy now, party pooper?

## BIGGEST MISCONCEPTION ABOUT:

That they're all about white gloves and doilies.

## WHAT YOU MAY HAVE IN COMMON:

Concern not only for the development and advancement of the underprivileged, but also for the volunteers who serve them.

## BUZZWORDS:

In their first year of involvement, Junior Leaguers are called "Provisional," meaning that they are in training;

subsequent, higher levels are "Active" and "Sustainer," and requirements for these upper two levels vary by League chapter.

## SIGN OF FAN:

Annual donation to Junior League is paid in lip service.

## SIGN OF GEEK:

Monthly donation to Junior League is paid via wire service.

## SIGN OF SUPERFREAK:

Daily donation to Junior League is paid by putting money (and time) where mouth is.

# GENEALOGISTS

**ALSO KNOWN AS:**
*Your Cousin Who Keeps Track of These Things*

**JUST DON'T CALL THEM:**
*Necrophiliacs*

**CORE BELIEF:**
*Know thyself.*

*"We Are Family"*

—song by 1970s disco group Sister Sledge

## WHO THEY ARE:

Individuals interested in the recording of family history, both statistical (names, dates) and anecdotal, in the interests of preservation or personal discovery. Some genealogists are amateurs, content to trace their family tree back to great-great-grandparents and no farther, others more interested in going as far back as records and research will allow. A rarefied few not only do their own research but also (for a fee) help other people do theirs.

With the emergence in 2010 of TV programs such as PBS's *Faces of America* and NBC's *Who Do You Think You Are?* genealogy has gained mainstream momentum as a way to address the perennial American challenge of defining one's identity.

The Internet has been a godsend to genealogists, not only with large research sites such as Ancestry.com (host of 8 billion records), Geni.com, and Familysearch.org (the latter belonging to the Church of Jesus Christ of Latter-Day Saints, possessors of countless family records), but also individual websites of researchers publishing their own family trees and trading information with newly found family.

Also relatively new are companies offering DNA testing, which, while offering the surety of science, can draw only on its existing databanks of genetic samples and point you generally to geographical family origins.

One thing on which all genealogists agree: once you start, the research quickly becomes addicting, revealing, surprising, and fun.

## HOW TO RECOGNIZE:

Wandering around cemeteries, looking for headstones, and taking photographs of ones they find; committing stories from relatives to audio or video; self-publishing family histories.

## TO BE FOUND:

Cranking a microfilm machine; poring through records of marriage, birth, and death; touching up old photos with computer software; making popcorn while awaiting 2012 and the release of records from the 1940 U.S. Census.

## HEROES:

Those who work to preserve the past: archivists, librarians, historians; author and historian John Farmer (1789–1838), founder of systematic genealogy research in America; Alex Haley, author of *Roots*.

## THEIR IDEA OF FUN:

Spending all afternoon in the state archives to uncover that one crucial bit of information.

## MOST DISTINCTIVE TRAIT:

Never lacking for stories.

## BIGGEST CONTROVERSIES:

The careless and totally unsafe way relatives store or keep irreplaceable family photos, documents, and artifacts; the occasional unreliability of U.S. Census information.

## BIGGEST MISCONCEPTION ABOUT:

That their field of interest is dull and irrelevant.

## WHAT YOU MAY HAVE IN COMMON:

Besides genetic material? A love of mysteries and detective work; a premium on the value of family; love of personal stories (and secrets).

### Family Duty

No matter who you are or where you come from, it's a safe bet that your ancestors sacrificed and suffered a lot more than you ever have or will, and in many cases, those sacrifices were made so that future generations of the family would have it better. You needn't be guilt ridden by that, but it might motivate you to honor your ancestors by knowing or assembling their stories—for your eyes, and someone else's.

## BUZZWORDS:

"Removed," meaning a gap of a generation: e.g., your mother's cousin is your first cousin, once removed.

## SIGN OF FAN:

Builds one-page family tree, collects family photos, shares results at reunion.

## SIGN OF GEEK:

Builds multipage family tree; discovers cousins in the last state in America you thought you'd have relatives in.

## SIGN OF SUPERFREAK:

Builds online family tree running to thousands of names; discovers relationship to Mayflower captain, President James Garfield, and Madonna.

**TECHNOLOGY**

- Hackers
- HTPCers
- Early Adopters

# HACKERS

**ALSO KNOWN AS:**
*Hacks, Cyber-Criminals, Identity Thieves*

**JUST DON'T CALL THEM:**
*Code Monkeys*

**CORE BELIEF:**
*If it can be done, let it be done, to show it may be done or to prevent another from doing the same.*

*"Should we fear hackers? Intention is at the heart of this discussion."*
—American author and computer security consultant Kevin Mitnick (1963– )

## WHO THEY ARE:

In the fields of computers and technology, a Hacker manipulates a system to achieve ends not originally intended by the programmer, engineer, or creator. In this sense, "hacking" may have both a positive and negative connotation. A Hacker may be someone who comes up with an innovative or impromptu solution to a computational problem or crisis, or the Hacker may be someone who creates the crisis.

Our attitude toward Hackers surely relates to our ambivalence about the machine: should the machine malfunction or work in ways contrary to our interests (oh, say, by trying to take over the world and eliminate humankind), then we need the Hacker; but if the Hacker is the one breaking into the bank's database or the corporate entity's computer to steal Social Security numbers and Personal Identification Numbers (PINs), well, obviously, that's not a good thing.

Consider, for example, the five-man gang operating out of Atlanta, GA, who in 2008 hacked into electronic payment service company RBS WorldPay to rip off $9 million from ATMs. (Don't worry, folks: they were caught.)

The truly dumbass Hacker—who occasionally appears on the news—is the college kid who hacks into the U.S. Department of Defense as a way of presenting his qualifications to work computer security.

Other Hackers may technically perform illegal acts, but do so for the purposes of pranks and tomfoolery. One person's joke, however, is another person's lawsuit.

Example: In 2008, the Massachusetts Bay Transportation Authority (MBTA) filed suit against three students of the Massachusetts Institute of Technology (MIT), who gave a presentation at the annual DEF CON Hacking Conference about how to hack your way to free rides on Boston's subway system. The suit was later dropped when the naughty boys agreed to work with the MBTA to improve their security system.

Sounds funny, but violating the Computer Fraud and Abuse Act is nothing to sneeze at.

## HOW TO RECOGNIZE:

In front of a computer, diligently at work, may jerk or jump in chair with paranoia at an unexpected sound.

## TO BE FOUND:

Where computer know-how is high, and often where human morality is in flux.

## HEROES:

The good Hackers who use their superior Hacking skills to combat evil: e.g., Jeff Goldblum's character in

*Independence Day,* who saves the earth by hacking into an alien mother ship.

## THEIR IDEA OF FUN:

Making things happen while remaining invisible, anonymous, and not subject to retribution or discovery (kind of like being God).

### Easy Hack, Easy Capture

The simplest (not to say the easiest) hack is to guess someone's security password and gain access to their ATM account or e-mail. The latter is exactly what twenty-two-year-old college student David Kernell did in 2008, when he gained access to Sarah Palin's Yahoo! account. Kernell got headlines, laughs from many, and a felony and misdemeanor charge. The felony charge alone is potentially worth twenty years behind bars.

## MOST DISTINCTIVE TRAIT:

Loves, and lives for, a challenge.

## BIGGEST CONTROVERSY:

The open question as to whether Hackers will be the soldiers of the future, inflicting more damage to an enemy with the click of a mouse than the pulling of a trigger. Should Hacking be taught? Should Hackers be hired by law enforcement or the military, and should Hacking be a weapon in warfare?

## BIGGEST MISCONCEPTION ABOUT:

That they're super nerds whose prolonged exposure to computers has arrested their moral maturity.

## WHAT YOU MAY HAVE IN COMMON:

Frustration and dissatisfaction with computer software and hardware: it's just Hackers are able to do something about it.

## BUZZWORDS:

"Pen Testing" is shorthand for "Penetration Testing" or Hackers employed to test a company's security system or firewall; the moral spectrum of Hackers is described by "White Hat," "Gray Hat," and "Black Hat" Hackers.

## SIGN OF FAN:

Hacks into friend's blog, replaces every word with "blah" as April Fool's Day joke.

## SIGN OF GEEK:

Majors in computer science at MIT or Caltech, engages in hack rivalry between two schools.

## SIGN OF SUPERFREAK:

Works for federal government, can't tell you doing what.

# HTPCERS

**ALSO KNOWN AS:**
Media Center Moguls

**JUST DON'T CALL THEM:**
Coach Potatoes, Dorks in Debt

**CORE BELIEF:**
Screw cineplexes.

*"Television! Teacher, mother, secret lover!"*
—Homer Simpson, "The Shinning" (Season 6, Episode 6)

## WHO THEY ARE:

People who invest in Home Theater Personal Computers (HTPCs): that is, a multimedia integration between a computer and usually High-Definition Television, creating an ultimate experience in home theater and personal computing (that is, ultimate until next year, when most of the components require upgrades).

HTPC history and development follows the vector of a simple question: What is the best way—i.e., the most affordable, most efficient, most convenient way—to get the optimal viewing, listening, and interactive experience from the two screens that occupy most of our time: the TV screen and the computer screen? For example:

**Which will give you a better picture**—your computer screen or your TV screen? Do you even know the resolution numbers for either?

**Would you rather rent DVDs or watch them "on demand" online,** via a service such as Netflix?

**Are you content to play your Wii on your TV,** or do you want to enhance the experience by getting a wireless hookup to the Internet?

These are but a few of dozens of questions HTPCers ask, and the answers can get both technical and expensive.

## HOW TO RECOGNIZE:

Seldom out of the house.

## TO BE FOUND:

Explaining intricacies of system to fathers-in-law; anxiously insisting on helping nephews and neighborhood kids set up gaming because—don't touch that, it's very expensive; losing patience, trying to explain to wife how to program show on Lifetime Channel.

## Technology Fast, Law Slow

The longheld HTPC dream is that one day, you'll be able to sit comfortably at home, and for nominal or no fees, be able to access every movie and TV show ever made, whenever you want. It seems like a futuristic fantasy, but the fact is, we have the technology now to make that happen: what's gumming up the works is an invention older than computers or TV or even technology itself—the law. Financial and copyright law continues to impose a drag on the realization of HTPC dreams. Get with it, lawyers!

## HEROES:

For HTPCers of a certain age, it's people like Hugh Hefner, who were able to luxuriate in their "private home screening rooms"; for younger HTPCers, it's celebrities on MTV

"Cribs," for whom a home theater is standard.

## THEIR IDEA OF FUN:

Jacking up the bass for *Transformers 2: Revenge of the Fallen* so that it rattles the wedding china in the cabinet two rooms over.

## MOST DISTINCTIVE TRAIT:

Frighteningly tech-savvy.

## BIGGEST CONTROVERSY:

If you're not an informed and careful consumer, your HTPC could be drawing a sizeable amount of energy. Given the state of the economy and environment, it behooves the HTPCer to investigate myriad ways in which his or her "energy draw" can be reduced.

## BIGGEST MISCONCEPTION ABOUT:

That the application of their extreme computer knowledge to a home entertainment system makes them less geeky and more manly.

## WHAT YOU MAY HAVE IN COMMON:

Equal amount of life spent in front of either TV or PC, except HTPCer kills two birds with one stone.

## BUZZWORDS:

A "DMR" or Digital Media Receiver allows you to access audio or video computer files and play them on TV; the HTPCer is aiming for the easiest and user-friendliest "GUI" or Graphical User Interface; and a "PVR" (Personal Video Recorder) or "DVR" (Digital Video Recorder) records and stores video from the TV to a suitably large hard drive.

### SIGN OF FAN:

Successfully hooks up DVR to record *Lost* while out shopping for more sophisticated equipment.

### SIGN OF GEEK:

Thinks Hulu.com is a TV network, and since everything is available for viewing all the time, has no concept of what a "rerun" is.

### SIGN OF SUPERFREAK:

Dozens of DVDs on shelf replaced with dozens of external hard drives of stored data.

# EARLY ADOPTERS

**ALSO KNOWN AS:**
Gadget Geeks, First in Line, EAs

**JUST DON'T CALL THEM:**
Beta Boobs, People with an IQ of 1.0

**CORE BELIEF:**
Early adoption can shape the future.

*"He who comes first, eats first."*

—Eike Von Repkow (1180–1235)

## WHO THEY ARE:

People who place the highest premium on being the first to own a new consumer item, especially one related to personal technology such as computers, cell phones, and media devices.

Most EAs obtain products the traditional way: by waiting in line at the store, on the first day of the product's release. A smaller segment of EAs receive new products before anyone else because they're tech reviewers for a major newspaper or magazine. These days, with the ascension of blogs and the competition given to "word of mouth" by "word of web," one can be sure that more non-professional, non-press-related EAs will be tapped by companies to receive new products before their official release, either to identify bugs or to generate buzz.

Although EAs are most commonly identified with computers and related gadgets, there are EAs for computer games, automobiles, toys, candy—really, any consumer product that is wholly new or receives an upgrade or a new twist.

EAs enjoy fame that is local. For example, if you've never heard of Eddie McCurty of Fort Worth, TX, you might know him better as The Person Who Bought the First iPad.

## HOW TO RECOGNIZE:

Excitedly talking and blogging about some new gadget or technology you've never heard of before.

## TO BE FOUND:

Cozying up to contacts in retail stores, at tech fairs, in press rooms, and online to squeeze out any bit of information they can to leverage their own EA status.

## HEROES:

EAs who not only purchase the first line of a product but who do other consumers a favor by rooting out bugs and flaws, posting comments and reviews online: see online Forums on sites for Microsoft and Apple.

## THEIR IDEA OF FUN:

Scanning the web (e.g., *www.gizmodo. com*) for industry news, "leaks" of upcoming releases (whether the leaks are authorized or not), other EA reviews.

## MOST DISTINCTIVE TRAIT:

Knee-jerk instincts that may bypass the frontal lobe of the brain.

## BIGGEST CONTROVERSY:

The initial launches of a totally new device (e.g., the iPad or the next generation of cell phone) notoriously contain flaws and bugs that the manufacturer has yet either to identify or resolve. The EA doesn't mind this, necessarily, because flaws and bugs give him or her something to talk and blog about.

## BIGGEST MISCONCEPTION ABOUT:

That they suffer from a neurotic need to be "first" which supersedes an actual need or desire to own the product.

## WHAT YOU MAY HAVE IN COMMON:

An interest in discussing: personal technology and how to improve it; marketing strategies; the ways in which companies listen (or don't listen) to consumer feedback.

## Defusing Diffusion

If, like an EA, you really want to know everything there is to know about early adoption, read Everett M. Rogers's book *Diffusion of Innovations*, which contains theories of how technology spreads through a culture. Rogers, a sociologist and scholar, examines types of adoption, stages of adoption, and the financial and social implications of the adoption process.

Don't look for this key technology text in the "New Arrivals" section of the bookstore, however: it was published in 1962.

## BUZZWORDS:

People who buy early but don't camp out are the "early majority"; people who take a "wait and see" approach but still buy are the "late majority"; and people who are married with kids and still have a VCR and, at long last, finally join the twenty-first century by buying a DVR are, appropriately, "laggards." See the sidebar for the author of these terms.

## SIGN OF FAN:

Goes to store the week a new Apple product is released, buys it.

## SIGN OF GEEK:

Camps out in front of the store, is the first in line to buy new Apple product.

## SIGN OF SUPERFREAK:

Camps out at the back of the line, so he can be the first to buy the next generation of the Apple product.

# ABOUT THE AUTHOR

Kate Stevens is herself a freak: a Beatlemaniac, a Trekkie, and an occasional Nudist. She is the author of *Instant Gratification* (Adams Media, 2010). A former newspaper editor and reporter, Stevens lives in Rhode Island with her freaky family.

# DAILY BENDER

# Want Some More?

Hit up our humor blog, The Daily Bender, to get your fill of all things funny—be it subversive, odd, offbeat, or just plain mean. The Bender editors are there to get you through the day and on your way to happy hour. Whether we're linking to the latest video that made us laugh or calling out (or bullshit on) whatever's happening, we've got what you need for a good laugh.

If you like our book, you'll love our blog. (And if you hated it, "man up" and tell us why.) Visit The Daily Bender for a shot of humor that'll serve you until the bartender can.

Sign up for our newsletter at

## *www.adamsmedia.com/blog/humor*

and download our Top Ten Maxims No Man Should Live Without.